Adult Literacy Now

edited by Maurice C. Taylor

CULTURE CONCEPTS INC.

Toronto, Canada

IRWIN PUBLISHING

Toronto/Vancouver, Canada

Canadian Cataloguing in Publication Data

Main entry under title:

Adult literacy now

ISBN 0-7725-2863-2

1. Literacy. 2. Adult education. I. Taylor, Maurice Charles, 1952- .

LC5254.A383 2000   374',012   C00-932537-9

Development editing by Thelma Barer-Stein, Ph.D., Culture Concepts Inc.
Inputting and copy editing by Karen Philips
Copy editing by Kate Revington
Text design by Leanne O'Brien/ArtPlus Ltd.
Page layout by ArtPlus Ltd.
Cover design by Sarah Coviello/ArtPlus Ltd.

Published by
Irwin Publishing Ltd.
325 Humber College Blvd.
Toronto, ON M9W 7C3

Printed and bound in Canada

1 2 3 4 5   04 03 02 01 00

Acknowledgements

The publisher and William Fagan would like to thank Jeanette Windsor for permission to reproduce her poem in William T. Fagan's chapter "The Dominant Literacy: Subdued Lives" (page 63).

The publisher and Sharon Skage would like to thank the US Department of Education, Planning and Evaluation Service, for permission to use excerpts from *Even Start: Evidence from the Past and a Look to the Future*, appearing on page 229 in "Evaluation in Family Literacy: Consequence, Challenge and Choice" by Sharon Skage.

The publisher and Jan Greer would like to acknowledge the following individuals who generously allowed Ms Greer to include their comments in her chapter "The Influence of Significant Males on Boys' Literacy Levels": Ron Buck, Neil Griffiths, Bob Stranach, and the Honourable Marilyn Trenholme Counsell, Lieutenant Governor of New Brunswick.

The publisher and Isa Helfield would like to thank the publisher for permission to reproduce excerpts in Isa Helfied's chapter "A Critical Reflection on the Rights of Passage: From Student to Teacher" from *The End of Education* by Neil Postman, © 1995, reprinted by permission of Alfred A. Knopf, A Division of Random House Inc.

TABLE OF CONTENTS

F O R E W O R D

With this book, *Adult Literacy Now,* the reader is given a careful look at one of society's hidden challenges. This is not an issue that is attended with loud debate — adults who struggle with reading and writing are normally quiet about their plight. Their silence should not cloak the extent and importance of this issue. Creating a culture of literacy is vital to our success as a nation and to the individual's sense of worth.

In an interview with Peter Calamai, John Ralston Saul noted that 150 years ago Ontario's landowning farmers, many of whom were illiterate, championed the laws that created the basis of public education. "They fought for education," Saul said, "because they knew that literacy was central to democracy."

It is impossible to imagine a robust economy without an informed electorate. A population that reads, questions, and exercises its rights with confidence safeguards the balance of powers that regulates government, promotes a diversified and strong economy, and oversees the integrity of social programs.

Our collective well-being, however, ultimately springs from the advancement of each citizen. The everyday skills of writing shopping lists, reading bank statements, and helping children with homework are small acts that confirm individual membership in a social network that joins those who read and write.

While literacy confers full participation in the public arena, it also bestows unlimited possibilities for personal growth. Every individual who loves reading must recall the wonder and exhilaration of that first spellbinding book. It is the individual equivalent of civilization's discovery of fire. This second fire kindles the inner life of the mind and gives warmth and light to the spirit. As Michael Ignatieff writes, "We have needs of the spirit because we are the only species whose fate is not simply a mute fact of our existence but a problem whose meaning we attempt to understand."

With *Adult Literacy Now,* due attention is paid to the range of human needs that adult literacy addresses. In issues where social policy and individual necessity intersect, there are large areas that are complex and sensitive. These require the anxious deliberation of people with will and vision — many of whom, I am sure, will be readers of this book.

Adrienne Clarkson
Governor General of Canada

Adult Literacy Now is a book that signals the recognition of a field of practice that is a central activity in adult education and training. It is a testimony to the unprecedented expansion of programs and services involving large numbers of literacy workers who have now arrived at professional maturity. The contents of the book define both the new conditions of responsibility as well as the areas of growth. With the breaking of the millennium, people working in the field need to feel connected with the different domains of practice in order to shoulder new obligations and challenges in adult learning. *Adult Literacy Now* attempts to do this.

One of the distinguishing features of the book is that it brings together four faces of the adult literacy picture — community-based literacy, workplace literacy, family literacy and school-based literacy. These four specialities represent the most important converging themes in adult literacy and learning. By reading about these interrelated areas under one cover, it is easier to nurture the cross-linkages and to build connections among the major domains of practice. The overall design of the book allows practitioners in various capacities and in a multitude of settings to see how the four parts of the literacy picture intersect and complement one another.

Over the years, great strides have been made in our field. Public awareness has increased, information sharing has occurred, access to literacy services has improved, and the quality of programs has been enhanced through innovative learning materials. But amid these many accomplishments, there has been little time for serious reflection. To help fill this void, all chapters in this book feature critical reflection on literacy developments in Canada. As Brookfield (1991, 1995) points out, critical reflection involves the identification of a problem or incident that represents some aspect of practice requiring examination and possible change. He believes that by identifying our own assumptions that underlie the beliefs and actions connected to this problem, we can better analyze the nature of our practice. This process results in the capacity to imagine and explore alternatives to existing ways of thinking.

Within this critical framework, authors discuss their assumptions, values and experiences, as well as their critical reflections on the topic, and conclude with their visions for the future. Throughout the book, attention to the belief that professionalization in adult literacy depends on traditional scholarly knowledge and on the construction of new knowledge borne from practice is evident. Both of these epistemological stances are crucial to understanding the complexities and tensions of literacy, and serve as guideposts for the reader.

As an organizing structure for the book, each of the four themes is comprised of six chapters. The first chapter is referred to as the framing chapter. It maps out the terrain of the specific area and acted as the vehicle for critical reflection as writers from the field worked together to identify their topics. The next four chapters represent some problem, incident or aspect of practice requiring examination, while the final chapter provides a synopsis for the theme. The book is introduced with a foundational chapter tracing the development of the literacy field in Canada, and the epilogue considers the new responsibilities of a field that has come of age. Acknowledgments and thanks go out to a very distinguished team of writers and to the National Literacy Secretariat, in particular Brigid Hayes, who believed that all of this could be done.

Maurice C. Taylor
Ottawa, Ontario

REFERENCES

Brookfield, S. (1991). *Developing critical thinkers: Challenging adults to explore alternative ways of thinking and acting.* San Francisco, CA: Jossey-Bass.

Brookfield, S. (1995). *Becoming a critically reflective teacher.* San Francisco, CA: Jossey-Bass.

THE EDITOR

Maurice C. Taylor is professor in the Faculty of Education at the University of Ottawa where he teaches and supervises graduate students in adult education. Author of more than 60 publications and books, he has served on many international and national associations and committees to promote adult literacy and learning. Over the years he has worked with literacy educators to help bridge the gap between theory and practice in adult education.

THE CHAPTER AUTHORS

Adrian Blunt is an associate professor in the College of Education at the University of Saskatchewan. Adult literacy, interwoven with development, equity and social justice issues, is the focus of his academic and community work. In Canada, he has worked in literacy as an instructor, instructor trainer, program planner, evaluator and researcher. Overseas, he has worked in Tanzania to link literacy learning with local economic development; in the Philippines, on urban street education and integrated rural development projects; and in Indonesia, to train post-secondary instructors and curriculum developers.

Marilyn Chapman is an associate professor in the Department of Language and Literacy Education at the University of British Columbia, where she integrates her research interests in early literacy and writing with her teaching at both undergraduate and graduate levels. She is an instructor, coordinator, and researcher in a collaborative university/school district Literacy Teacher Education/Professional Development program. She has maintained active involvement in British Columbia's Language Arts and Primary Program development since 1988.

Hilary Craig was born and grew up in Zimbabwe where she and her Canadian family lived from 1981 to 1984. She has an honours degree and postgraduate teaching certificate from the University of Western Ontario and a Bachelor of Social Work from the University of Regina.

She taught English as a Second Language in elementary schools, and at community colleges, at university, and started a workplace program in London, Ontario. In Zimbabwe, she worked as a writer and researcher on literacy topics and also worked with a small neighbourhood sewing cooperative. A founding member of Saskatchewan Literacy and a former editor of that organization's *Literacy Works,* she is now working as the Saskatchewan Provincial Family Literacy Coordinator.

David Dillon teaches in the Faculty of Education at McGill University in Montreal where he works with pre-service and in-service teachers in the areas of literacy and social justice education.

William T. Fagan is a recognized leader in literacy at local, national and international levels. He is involved in many facets of literacy as a university instructor and director of the Reading and Language Centre at the University of Alberta, as a writer of literacy materials, as a researcher, and as an instructor/facilitator of literacy in many settings. Currently, he is a community literacy worker, a visiting professor at Memorial University of Newfoundland, and chairperson of the Literacy Development Council of Newfoundland and Labrador.

Victor Froese is a professor emeritus, University of British Columbia, where for about ten years he served as the head of the Department of Language Education. He has spent the last decade on large-scale literacy assessment research projects at the provincial, federal and international levels. He has edited and authored a number of methods textbooks and published numerous articles and book chapters on the teaching and assessment of literacy.

Jan Greer is the executive director of the New Brunswick Committee on Literacy (NBCL). The NBCL is a volunteer group of community and government representatives, delivering projects in New Brunswick and working on special projects with other groups. Greer is working on an honours degree in English at St. Thomas University in Fredericton. She also writes a monthly column for a daily newspaper and prior to NBCL, she worked as a print and broadcast journalist.

Ruth Hayden is a professor in the Department of Elementary Education at the University of Alberta. Her research focuses on cross-cultural aspects of family literacy and to further that interest, she has liaised with colleagues in Ireland, France, and Israel. She collaborates with Prospects Literacy Association in Edmonton, researching and evaluating the range of family literacy programs offered. Her work is published in a variety of national and international educational journals.

Yvonne Hébert is a professor in the Faculty of Education, University of Calgary, where she teaches courses on bilingualism, literacy, immigration and integration. Recipient of the Killam Doctoral Bursary and a post-doctoral SSHRC fellowship, she has also participated in the National Core French Study as research developer of the *General Language Syllabus* (1985–1990). Leader of the education domain of the Prairies Centre of Excellence for Research on Immigration and Integration, she is currently doing research on identity formation of adolescent immigrants and citizenship education.

Isa Helfield has served in the field of education for over 25 years. Her experience includes teaching in Quebec and Ontario in both youth and adult education sectors. For several years, Helfield has been actively involved in the field of literacy. Presently she is a board member of Literacy Partners of Quebec and of the Movement for Canadian Literacy in Ottawa. In addition, she is a freelance writer who has contributed several articles on education to various publications.

Ellen Long spent six years teaching adult basic education and was an English as a Second Language teacher for the Metro Toronto Labour Education Centre before becoming director of research for ABC Canada. She has designed and conducted numerous primary research studies in the field of literacy and is the author of *Conquering Test Writing Anxiety: Helping Students Develop Confidence and Skills* (Irwin Publishing, 2000.)

Sande Minke has been working in the literacy field for 15 years in school board and community-based adult ESL, literacy and workplace programs and has served on regional, provincial and national boards, advisory councils and committees. Currently she is a field consultant for the Literacy and Basic Skills (LBS) program of the Ontario Ministry of Training, Colleges and Universities, and is a provincial leader in workplace literacy.

Mary Norton has been engaged in the adult literacy field in various capacities since the 1970s. Currently, she is a coordinator/facilitator at the Learning Centre in Edmonton and an adjunct assistant professor at the University of Alberta, Faculty of Education. Her interests include participatory education, women's learning, and research in practice. She is also exploring the uses of singing and movement in literacy education.

Anthony Paré is chairman of the Department of Educational Studies at McGill University and former director of the University's Centre for the Study of Teaching and of Writing. His teaching and research interests include language across the curriculum, academic, professional, and workplace literacy, and field education.

B. Allan Quigley is an associate professor of Adult Education at St. Francis Xavier University in Antigonish, Nova Scotia. His career began with CUSO and he taught his first adult literacy program in northern Saskatchewan in 1972. He has since worked as a community programmer, teacher, researcher and policy advisor on adult education in both Canada and the US. He was awarded the Kenneth J. Mattran Award for Literacy Leadership in 1997, and the Houle Award for his book, *Rethinking Literacy Education,* in 1998.

Christine Racicot is an M.A. student at the University of Calgary in the Department of Educational Research. Her fieldwork experience has been in community and educational settings with immigrant youth in Calgary, Alberta. Racicot's written work for which she is frequently teamed with Professor Yvonne Hébert, focuses on minority francophone curriculum in Canada and on literacy issues, one project being *Report on a Literacy Dialogue* (1999). She is now researching identity formation of adolescent immigrant students in Calgary within the Prairies Centre of Excellence for Research in Immigration and Integration.

Heather J. Richmond is an assistant professor in the Faculty of Education at St. Thomas University, in Fredericton, New Brunswick. Here she teaches reading and literacy and special education to pre-service teachers. Her Ph.D. is in literacy education, and her research interests include studying community-based literacy programs, investigating definitions and models of literacy as well as the learning and teaching styles of the participants.

Rhonda Rubin works as a speech and language pathologist for the Extra Mural program in southeastern New Brunswick. She is currently completing doctoral studies in Education (Psychopedagogy) at the University of Ottawa. Her dissertation is in the area of family literacy practices in low-income homes.

Maureen Sanders has worked as a teacher and reading specialist in school systems and has taught at the university level. She began working in the adult literacy field in 1989, and is executive director of Prospects Literacy Association in Edmonton. She oversees a wide range of adult and family literacy programs delivered in cooperation with many community agencies. She currently directs a collaborative project to develop a centre for family literacy in Edmonton.

Marilyn T. Samuels is a professor in the Department of Educational Psychology and the learning disability specialist in the Disability Resource Centre at the University of Calgary. Her research and practice have focused on assessment and treatment for persons with learning and literacy difficulties. She has a particular interest in using interactive cognitive approaches with adults having low literacy skills. She has worked with schools, post-secondary institutions and business, implementing dynamic assessment and cognitive education programs.

Sharon Skage has worked in literacy since 1989. She worked for the Family Literacy Action Group from 1994 to 1997 and coordinated the development of volunteer tutor program standards and evaluation methods for the Association of Literacy Coordinators of Alberta and co-edited a national directory of family literacy projects in 1998. Present work involves adapting an intensive model of family literacy from the United Kingdom for use in Alberta and working to establish a provincial centre for family literacy.

Nancy Steel has practiced workplace essential skills education for 13 years. She has worked in a variety of industries across Canada to promote programs among business and labour, assess needs, develop programs, evaluate programs, train trainers, and undertake research. Currently she is living and working in Calgary as an independent workforce education consultant, enjoying the challenge and diversity that the workplace education field offers.

Susan Sussman has been the executive director of the Ontario Literacy Coalition since January 1993. She served as president and past president of the Movement for Canadian Literacy from 1995 to 1998. Sussman holds an M.A. in Communications and Education from Columbia University's Teachers College and has nearly three decades of experience in teaching, educational research, strategic planning, social planning, human resources management and non-profit management.

Adele Thomas, Ph.D., is an associate professor, Faculty of Education, Brock University, Ontario, where she teaches undergraduate and pre-service education courses and supervises graduate student research. In addition to research interests in family literacy and early childhood education, she has co-authored curriculum materials for family literacy practitioners and parents, and has collaborated with local school and community organizations in developing the Family Learning program, an intergenerational family literacy program.

Audrey M. Thomas has worked since 1994 with the BC government and has responsibility for adult basic education and literacy. She has been a literacy researcher, author, editor, trainer, organizer, university instructor and volunteer in Ontario, Saskatchewan and BC over a 25-year period. She also helped to found the Movement for Canadian Literacy, Project Literacy Victoria, and Literacy BC, becoming president of the latter. She was chair of the Board of Frontier College from 1995 to 1997.

Ian Thorn has been a national representative with the Communications Energy and Paperworkers Union for 17 years. He first became active in literacy work in 1993 with the Alberta Workplace Literacy Advisory Committee. In addition to activities in his union, he has worked with the following literacy organizations: Western Canada Workplace Education Skills Training Network (WWESTNET), Western Labour Learning Network (WLLN), Testing of Workplace Essential Skills (TOWES), the Alberta Federation of Labour Literacy and Union Education project, the Atlantic Region Workplace Education Institute (1998), Workplace Education and Development (WED) and the Canadian Labour Congress Training Strategy Committee.

Wendell C. Wiebe obtained a B.A. in 1982 and an M.Ed. in 1987. He helped establish the Winnipeg Transition Centre (1988) which continues to assist adults in finding employment. Wiebe is presently the manager of Staff Development at Bristol Aerospace Limited. In addition to his responsibilities, Wiebe has played an active role in the executive of the Manitoba Aerospace Human Resource Coordinating Committee, which is a sector council whose mandate is to develop the workforce. Presently, he holds the position of vice president on the Board of Directors for the Manitoba Prior Learning Assessment Centre.

How Adult Literacy Became of Age in Canada

Audrey M. Thomas

This introductory chapter traces some antecedents to the present adult literacy tapestry in Canada and deals with developments that many authors of this volume have lived through and helped to shape. For these long-time literacy practitioners, as well as those new to the literacy field, a brief revisiting of the past reinforces the progress made up to the present and leads to some prediction of where the field may be heading.

While there are commonalities of philosophy and approach to be found in adult literacy work today, the evolution of the underlying infrastructures manifests in different delivery and support mechanisms across Canada. The history of adult literacy in Canada is the history of many adult literacies, through which the federal government presence can be found in different ways in different periods. However, its presence is always shaped by the constitutional fact that education in Canada is under the control of the provinces and there is no strong central federal power in education per se.

This short introductory chapter cannot do justice to the rich history that has evolved and is developing in Canada on adult literacy. Nevertheless, there is considerable evidence that adult literacy has come of age. First, there is the chronological factor. Many practitioners across the country have now worked in the adult literacy field for over 20 years — the time it takes to be deemed mature in life! Second, there has been an abundant and growing literature on adult literacy practice in Canada, particularly in the last decade, and this is showing promise as the bridge to school literacy.

Third, the field is characterized by great diversity within and across political jurisdictions. All provinces and territories have government personnel with responsibility for literacy programming. The definitions of literacy for funding purposes and the number of personnel and actual resources devoted to literacy differ, but there is a government presence. This is often taken for granted by those working for non-governmental organizations (NGOs) and is one of the ongoing tensions in the field. The literacy issue, as defined by Statistics Canada (1995), is so all-encompassing with varied solutions that there are simply not enough resources to do the job. Yet the amount of funds put into adult literacy and basic education program delivery by provincial/territorial governments greatly exceeds the $30-million annual budget of the National Literacy Secretariat (NLS). The latter, however, through its literacy activity enhancement grants has enabled many innovative developments to take place and these usually have higher profiles than the ongoing delivery work.

What NLS has helped make happen is the trend towards the development of sub-fields within adult literacy. Once, literacy was the main domain of the formal public educational institutions. Now, community-based literacy has become a field with its own distinguishing characteristics. The ubiquity of literacy issues and proposed solutions have also led to an increase in the field of workplace literacy. The importance of early literacy development and of providing parents and caregivers with some tools to facilitate this development has led to the emergence of family literacy. These three distinct specialty areas collaborate with the formal education system and other existing structures. The synergy between them and the new learning that is emerging has served to inform practice in the very formal structures initially established to provide the basic skills — the regular school system. Thus, this present book, with its four sections, reflects a field which has matured considerably since the mid-1970s and represents developments undreamed of in the 1950s. The challenge for the field is to maintain its maturity and continue to discover the points of convergence. This book is a first attempt in this direction and all stakeholders will need to be involved in the enterprise.

This introduction highlights some key events, policies and reports that impinged on adult literacy development in Canada. For more detailed chronologies of adult education developments within which the literacy movement in Canada is situated, the reader is referred to Draper (1989) and Thomas, Taylor & Gaskin (1989). Darville (1992) looks at policy issues and Godin (1996) describes government efforts in the mid-1990s.

ANTECEDENT DEVELOPMENTS: 1948 TO 1967

The establishment of the United Nations (UN) and its specialized agencies, especially the United Nations Educational, Scientific and Cultural Organization (UNESCO), in the 1940s was crucial for developments in adult literacy world-wide. Article 26 of the 1948 *Universal Declaration of Human Rights* deals with the right to education and is cited in relation to literacy work. UNESCO held the First International Conference on Adult Education in Elsinore, Denmark, in 1949 and followed this event with a world survey on illiteracy in 1953. The Second UNESCO Conference on Adult Education was held in 1960 in Montreal and literacy was placed on the international development agenda. In 1965, Iran hosted the First World Conference of Ministers of Education to discuss adult illiteracy. The starting day of this event was September 8, which afterwards became designated as International Literacy Day.

The 1950s and 1960s saw the creation of several North American organizations that were ultimately to play various roles on the Canadian scene and whose initial inspiration had been the literacy work of Dr. Frank Laubach. Laubach Literacy Inc. (LLI), World Education, Inc., and World Literacy of Canada (WLC) were all formed in 1955. LLI eventually established a domestic division, the National Affiliation for Literacy Advance, which held its first national conference in the United States in 1968. In the meantime, Literacy Volunteers of America, Inc. (LVA), had incorporated in 1967. Although LVA offered several differences in their approach and training than Laubach, it had sprung from the same source.

In Canada, an analysis of the 1961 Census results showed the extent of the need for adult basic education (ABE). In 1967, the federal government replaced the *Technical and Vocational Training Act* of 1960 with the *Adult Occupational Training Act* and implemented the *Canada Manpower Training program,* thus becoming even more involved in the training of Canadians. Also in 1967, the *Canada New Start program* was established and eventually led to new curricula and programs with an ABE and literacy focus. The foundation was laid for the next decade.

THE YEARS OF FEDERAL TRAINING AND SPORADIC GRASS-ROOTS RESPONSES: 1968 TO 1978

Basic Training for Skill Development (BTSD) was the dominant ABE program of the 1960s and early 1970s. It was joined by a shorter more job-focused program — *Basic Job Readiness Training* (BJRT) in 1973. The intention of these programs was to get adults trained and into work. However, a policy review in 1977 by the newly formed Canada Employment and Immigration Commission found that many of the BTSD trainees were preparing themselves for post-secondary education. This led to a tightening up of the federal regulations, a decline of federal trainees in these programs, and increased pressure on the provincial education systems and the community to address ABE and literacy needs.

At the grass-roots level, several community outreach efforts began to appear across Canada: the first Laubach Literacy training workshop and council were established in Nova Scotia in 1970; a voluntary ABE program was started in London, Ontario, in the early 1970s; the Regina Public Library first dealt with literacy needs in 1971; popular education work based on Paulo Freire's ideas had been going on in some of the poorest neighbourhoods in Quebec.

In 1975, WLC initiated the Canada Project. The results of this one-year project were a report by Thomas (1976) and the first national conference of its kind held in Toronto in May 1976. Thomas was kept on at WLC to do follow-up work and organize another conference. The latter took place in Ottawa in 1977, and became the founding conference of the Movement for Canadian Literacy (MCL). At this event, the long history and contribution to literacy of Canada's Frontier College were recognized by the announcement of an Honourable Mention and medal from UNESCO — the first time such an award had been made to a Canadian organization. A francophone contingent from Quebec participated in the conference. These developments served to define the adult literacy field in Canada and provided the beginnings of new organizations, initiatives and networks.

THE YEARS OF STRUGGLE – GRASS-ROOTS AWARENESS, ADVOCACY AND ORGANIZATION: 1978 TO 1987

As MCL suffered from lack of resources, the organizations best able to take advantage of the situation to move ahead were Frontier College and the Laubach groups. The former became an advocate for the literacy cause. The latter coalesced into a stronger Canadian regional organization, and then incorporated as Laubach Literacy of Canada in 1981. Other groups that emerged included networks of librarians, the Metro Toronto Movement for Literacy, and the Movement for Alberta Literacy (MAL), both in 1978. These groups initially worked with MCL but eventually became independent organizations. For example, MAL became the Alberta Association for Adult Literacy (AAAL) in 1981. In BC, practitioners held the first annual meeting of the Adult Basic Education Association of British Columbia (ABEABC) in 1979.

Despite the enormity of the challenges, people were fired with enthusiasm and hope. The first Canadian television program on the issue was broadcast by the Canadian Broadcasting Corporation on its *Fifth Estate* program in January 1978. If anyone had doubted the statistics, the aftermath of this program cast those doubts away. The statistics became real people with requests for help. This stimulus prompted the formation of more community organizations and efforts to meet the need. Several post-secondary institutions also responded with community outreach programs in 1978: Douglas College in BC; Alberta Vocational Centre in Calgary; and Parkland Community College, Saskatchewan.

In the early 1980s, the federal government continued to decrease its share of ABE institutional training and this also helped fuel the grass-roots advocacy movement. The state of literacy in the nation was captured by Thomas (1983). This report found a new audience and was used for advocacy purposes even though Statistics Canada challenged the Census statistics as a proxy measure of literacy. Subsequent surveys by the Creative Research Group (1987) and Statistics Canada (1991), although using more sophisticated methodologies, also pointed to the same conclusion: Canada had a sizeable population with literacy difficulties.

MCL remained a flickering flame in the 1980s and staged a think tank in 1983, where leading practitioners gathered to talk about literacy and issued a statement for discussion purposes. Internationally, the *Udaipur Declaration* of 1982 and the UNESCO *Right to Learn*

Declaration of 1985 provided new ammunition to help make the case for literacy. Provincial ministries were approached to issue proclamations for International Literacy Day in their jurisdictions.

Ontario, Canada's most populous province, had the most difficulty in bringing its various elements together around literacy. However, the first Ontario provincial literacy conference took place in the spring of 1984, and by 1986, the Ontario government was organizing to give literacy work more prominence and support. The Ministry of Citizenship and Culture was made the lead ministry, and an Ontario Community Literacy grants program was established. By 1990, Ontario had developed a cohesive model of four cultural streams across a multi-sector delivery system that included colleges, school boards, community agencies and labour organizations.

At the national NGO level, Frontier College had undertaken much advocacy and development work with the corporate sector. The Business Task Force on Literacy emerged in the mid-1980s and eventually became the core of ABC Canada. At this time also, Peter Gzowski initiated his Golf Tournaments for Literacy which expanded across the country and helped raise millions of dollars for literacy groups. Along the way, Senator Joyce Fairbairn of Alberta became interested in the literacy issue and a staunch supporter of the cause.

By 1985, consultations were being held between the NGOs, literacy practitioners, and representatives of the federal government, and the Council of Ministers of Education, Canada. The Canadian Association for Adult Education was politically active on behalf of literacy at this time and there was the beginning of a wider coalition-building movement among national NGOs with a literacy interest. Ten national NGOs met at Cedar Glen in Ontario and developed the *Cedar Glen Declaration*. The Declaration was a call for action and was used as a basis for discussion with federal government representatives. MCL found itself the lead literacy advocate.

There had been cause for optimism as the 1986 *Speech from the Throne* announced federal intentions to become involved in literacy. Southam News had sponsored a survey on literacy skills and the results provided fodder for a series of articles by Calamai (1987) in the Southam press. In October 1987, in Toronto, at an international and national seminar on literacy in industrialized countries, the then Secretary of State announced the federal government's intervention of $1-million to be disbursed to various organizations that year and the development of the National Literacy Secretariat (NLS). In 1988, the federal government announced $110-million for literacy over the next five years. For many it seemed the years of struggle were over.

THE YEARS OF PROMISE: 1988 TO 2000

The NLS has two major streams of funding. In the federal-provincial or cost-shared stream, the NLS works with its provincial and territorial counterparts on a variety of literacy projects proposed annually within those jurisdictions. Grants are awarded in the categories of public awareness, access and outreach, coordination and information-sharing, development of learning materials, and research. The NLS will only fund program delivery in the context of a demonstration or pilot project. The national stream of funding respects the same general categories and is also project-based. It is available to the provincial and territorial literacy coalitions, the six national literacy organizations, and other national or provincial organizations or groups whose main focus may not be literacy per se, but whose clientele may have literacy needs. Examples of these include the John Howard and Elizabeth Fry societies, the Canadian National Institute for the Blind, the Salvation Army, the Canadian Public Health Association, aboriginal organizations and so on.

The excitement generated by the formation of the NLS was compounded as literacy practitioners, learners and others began to develop plans for International Literacy Year (ILY) — 1990. This was to be the start of a decade of literacy action leading to the millennium. ILY turned out to be a frenetic year of literacy activity: new groups formed; new literacy partners were added to the roster of the faithful few; media attention was at an all-time high; there were conferences and seminars galore, as well as travelling books of learners' writings, a travelling musical, plays, pins, posters, postage stamps, T-shirts and mugs! Provincial governments had struck committees and task forces to develop plans for the year and literacy strategies for the future. Reports were made on developments and progress to the Canadian Commission for UNESCO.

After the hype of ILY, people settled down and started to reflect on literacy practice. Of concern was the ongoing status of the NLS and literacy funding after the initial five years and in the wake of budget cuts. However, with political changes at the federal level, the first ever minister with special responsibility for literacy — Senator Joyce Fairbairn — was appointed in 1993; funding was restored in 1994; and, in the 1997 federal budget, funds were increased for the NLS to $30-million annually. The areas earmarked for increases were family and workplace literacy. The continued development of infrastructure was to be encouraged by putting more resources into literacy research, resource centres and electronic communication.

The International Adult Literacy Survey (IALS), whose first results were published in 1995 by Statistics Canada, has helped change the nature of the discourse on literacy in the 1990s. Plans are being made for an International Life Skills Survey (including literacy) in 2002. Presently, the IALS has provided a standard definition of literacy and some common language for talking about the issue. It has also shown that literacy is complex, that it is embedded in community, family and workplace contexts, and that these, in turn, influence literacy outcomes.

Literacy activity is now happening everywhere to a greater extent than ever in Canada. It is no longer the domain of the formal education systems alone, and therein lie the strengths and the challenges that many of the chapters in this book address further.

REFERENCES

Calamai, P. (1987). *Broken words: Why five million Canadians are illiterate.* Toronto, ON: Southam Newspaper Group.

Creative Research Group. (1987). *Literacy in Canada: A research report.* Prepared for Southam News, Ottawa, ON.

Darville, R. (1992). *Adult literacy work in Canada.* Toronto, ON: Canadian Association for Adult Education and the Centre for Policy Studies in Education, University of British Columbia.

Draper, J. A. (1989). A selected chronology of literacy events. In M. Taylor & J. Draper (Eds.), *Adult literacy perspectives.* Toronto, ON: Culture Concepts Inc.

Godin, J. (Ed.). (1996). *Working in concert: Federal, provincial and territorial actions in support of literacy in Canada.* Ottawa, ON: National Literacy Secretariat.

Statistics Canada. (1991). *Adult literacy in Canada: Results of a national study.* Ottawa, ON: Minister of Industry, Science and Technology, Canada.

Statistics Canada and Organization for Economic Co-operation and Development. (1995). *Literacy, economy and society: Results of the first International Adult Literacy Survey.* Ottawa, ON: Minister of Industry, Canada.

Thomas, A., Taylor, M., & Gaskin, C. (1989). Federal legislation and adult basic education in Canada. In M. Taylor & J. Draper (Eds.), *Adult literacy perspectives.* Toronto, ON: Culture Concepts Inc.

Thomas, A. (1976). *Adult basic education and literacy activities in Canada, 1975–76.* Toronto, ON: World Literacy of Canada.

Thomas, A. (1983). *Adult illiteracy in Canada: A challenge* (Occasional paper No. 42). Ottawa, ON: Canadian Commission for UNESCO.

SECTION 1

Community- Based Literacy

FRAMING CHAPTER

Learning in the Borderlands
Perspectives and Possibilities in Community-Based Learning

Mary Norton

The Learning Centre, where I work, is an adult literacy and education agency on the north border of downtown Edmonton. A community worker started the Centre in 1981 to provide tutoring and learning support for women in Edmonton's inner-city neighbourhoods. Today, both women and men come to the Centre from nearby neighbourhoods and from farther afield to learn and to teach, to engage in meaningful activity, and to be with others.

I have been involved with the Centre for similar reasons since 1981: as a government consultant, as a volunteer tutor, and since 1992, as a paid coordinator. To anchor this chapter, and to invite you in, I start with a lens on the Centre.

A LENS ON THE CENTRE

The phone rings and Tammy answers: "The Learning Centre. May I help you?" She writes down the caller's name and number and puts the note in a message slot. Then, binder in hand, she drops by each learning group to record attendance, asking whomever is handy for help reading unfamiliar names. She's already read my response to her journal entry, rather pleased that she can now read my cursive writing. Tammy is becoming an active reader, taking risks with words that would have stymied her before.

I'm reminded of how the year before, Tammy introduced an ice-breaker at the Students Meeting Students Conference, reading from the script she'd composed and practiced. Her peers on the conference committee had similarly prepared and carried out key roles in the two-day conference: they'd chaired the event, managed registration, facilitated groups, and introduced speakers and workshop leaders.

As Tammy answers phone calls, a group summarizes interviews they have conducted with volunteer coordinators at local agencies. Their research is for a booklet about volunteer occupations. Another group is reading and writing on their own or in pairs, with peer or community tutors. While most of the tutors are volunteers, Mary is paid. A student herself, Mary tutors about five hours each week, when not engaged in other learning.

Barb and Yolande are reading together from I remember (n.d.), a collection of stories from the Northwest Territories. The cover illustration prompts Yolande to regale us with a story about childhood tree climbing. Yolande has written many stories about life in the bush, about caring for younger siblings, and about her transition to town life (Herman, 2000).

Both Yolande and Barb have had stories published in the English Express. This easier-to-read newspaper also featured an article by Holly Williams (1997), describing her adventures traveling via the paper. Each month, Holly and other students volunteer alongside members of the Heritage Club, an organization of retired Canada Post employees, to package 35,000 copies of the paper for mailing worldwide. As well as raising funds for the Centre, this work invites people from varying backgrounds to meet and to learn about each other.

Before leaving, a woman talks to me about setting aside the book she's reading in order to start If you could see me now (Battell and Nonsuch, 1996). The book is a collection of stories of survival and hope by women who've lived with abuse. One of the stories is by a woman from the Centre. Reading, talking and writing about abuse has been one way for women to address this issue.

These snapshots provide local context for discussion of some key themes in community-based learning: literacy, critical pedagogy, participatory education, voice, and sharing power. To situate the discussion in broader contexts, I briefly review the evolution of community-based literacy in anglophone Canada.

EVOLUTION OF COMMUNITY-BASED PROGRAMS

Many literacy programs that are now called community-based were initiated in the 1970s and 1980s to address perceived needs for literacy programming. As one response, volunteers began to organize and provide instruction, mainly through one-to-one tutoring. Starting in the 1970s, Laubach Literacy councils were formed throughout the Atlantic provinces, in anglophone Quebec and Ontario, and in parts of Western Canada (Collins, 1996). Other volunteer tutor programs were also initiated across anglophone Canada and provincial and territorial governments developed policies to support them. Some of these programs called themselves community-based, described as "a relatively new approach, carried on mostly by small independent organizations in close connection to the communities in which they are located" (Gaber-Katz & Watson, 1991, p. xv).

The 1980s and 1990s saw further development of volunteer-based programs and a shift towards describing them as *community-based* by the programs themselves, by literacy organizations and by provincial and territorial governments. In some jurisdictions, the term *community-based* is also applied to learning centres and classes with paid instructors. Yet, despite this common use of the term, I found few definitions either in program descriptions or in profiles of government program support (Godin, 1996). Apart from comments about responding to community or learner needs, there seems to be an assumed understanding of what community-based literacy means.

While accepting the tacit meanings, I also understand community-based approaches as rooted in and shaped around critical awareness, reflection and action about power and power relations, inside and outside programs. There are similarities between this understanding of community-based approaches and what others name as "literacy from a critical perspective" (Gaber-Katz & Watson, 1991) or as "participatory" or "popular education" (Auerbach, 1993; Beder, 1996). Isley (1985) used the term *community-oriented* to explain similar stances. Although historically such stances were a hallmark of "community-based literacy programs" (Hamilton & Cunningham, 1989), community-oriented approaches can be a compass and touchstone for literacy work in a range of settings.

POWER

Starhawk (1987) writes about three kinds of power: *power-over, power-from-within, and power-with*. Recalling that power means to be able, she describes power-from-within as growing from the experiences, skills and stances that enable people to say, "I can." In contemporary literacy programs, concepts of power-from-within are often framed in terms of personal or individual empowerment. In community-oriented approaches, building power-with, while addressing power-over, is also a guiding perspective.

Power-over is often thought of in terms of persons, groups or institutions having power over others. Such power is sustained by social, political and economic systems and by the policies and assumptions that certain groups have a right to power. These assumptions are often reflected in prevailing discourses, which help sustain existing power relations.

Horsman (1990) describes discourse as the complex set of language, meanings and assumptions that shape our understanding and influence our actions. For example, discourses of illiteracy have been constructed around assumptions about causal links between low literacy and workplace accidents, unemployment, poor health, poverty and crime.

Community-oriented approaches operate within an alternate discourse. While issues such as low literacy, poverty and poor health are experienced by individuals and groups, they are rooted in social conditions and attitudes, and in the way that power is distributed in society. Community-oriented approaches reflect a community consciousness of how people — including teachers, tutors and learners — may experience more or less power because of such factors as gender, income and race.

Rodriguez (1993) points out that power-over can be exercised effectively only if individuals or groups submit to this power. In theory, when people resist submission, power-over loses its effectiveness. Starhawk explains resistance by contrasting it with rebellion; where rebellion involves defying a reality, resistance presents alternatives to a reality.

Community-oriented approaches are sites of resistance when they present alternatives to conventional discourses about literacy, language and education, about power and about how power can be shared. They can also invite teachers and learners to engage in resistance as they engage with each other in literacy teaching and learning.

LITERACY

Freire and Macedo (1987) used the terms *reading the word* and *reading the world* to name two aspects of literacy development. Reading the word refers to reading as it is commonly understood, namely, figuring out words and understanding what is read. Reading the world refers to analyzing experiences and relating them to how society and discourses are constructed.

As a literacy teacher in Brazil in the 1950s, Freire found that the assigned materials and methods were of little interest to the men and women attending his classes after long days of labour. Freire set the assigned resources aside, encouraged people to talk about their problematic issues and then used methods such as problem posing (Nixon-Ponder, 1995) to promote discussion and understanding about the social roots of problems and how to initiate change. These discussions also provided a context to learn reading skills. (Writing the word and the world are also important concepts in community-oriented approaches. I discuss these later.)

Fingeret and Drennon (1997) describe how literacy has been taught as skills, tasks, practices or as critical reflection and action. The first three approaches relate to reading and writing the word; the last is also concerned with reading and writing the world. In the first approach, literacy is understood as a set of technical skills that, once learned, can be used with any materials in any situations. This approach separates reading from its context and leads to instruction and learning activities that focus on decoding and encoding. In the second approach, literacy is viewed in terms of tasks to be accomplished, such as filling in a form, following a recipe, or finding out when a bus arrives. Although this approach recognizes the role of context, it is assumed that tasks are the same across different contexts. Neither the skills nor tasks approach accounts for the social aspect of literacy.

In a literacy-as-practices approach, skills are necessary but of limited value without an understanding of the dialects and meanings of different contexts in which they are used. Barton (1990) notes that the dominant understandings of literacy practices are based in the school domain, and that school literacy practices differ from those of everyday life. In a study about writing practices of Adult Basic Education students, some participants noted, "Down at school I enjoy writing the paragraphs and doing English" or "In school, writing is mostly answering questions, doing assignments" (Woodrow & Norton, 1996, p. 10). Programs that focus on school-based practices and related skills may consider literacy learning as remedial. Community-oriented approaches recognize literacy learning as a lifelong endeavour. They can offer alternatives for adults who need or want structured support to extend their literacy practices.

At the Learning Centre where I work, teaching and learning about reading the word reflects all three approaches — skills, tasks and practices — although the orientation is towards literacy as practices. When working with participants to organize a student conference, I observed how eagerly some phoned other programs, wrote letters, sent faxes and recorded registration fees. One woman, who usually chose not to engage in writing activities, worked through three drafts of a letter as I coached her to think about her audiences and what they needed to know.

In the role of volunteer receptionists at the Learning Centre, students practice communicating with people who phone or drop in. When one of the receptionists volunteered to answer phones in another organization, she had tutorial support as needed to extend her practices in this new context. As another example, Centre participants interviewed staff and volunteers in neighbourhood agencies. In doing so, they practiced asking questions and gathering information in a range of settings.

It can be a challenge to bring authentic and relevant literacy practices into programs. This sometimes has to do with teachers' fluctuating energy and imagination, but also reflects the realities of participants' lives, their current uses of literacy and the beliefs and experiences of both teachers and learners about what counts as literacy and learning. For example, when I asked a participant what she would like to do with reading and writing outside of the Learning Centre, she replied that she wanted to read and write *in* the Centre. Perhaps she understood my question as a suggestion that she move on from the program, maybe she didn't share my views about literacy learning, or perhaps she is confident about how she engages in her everyday literacy practices. While some adults have a clear sense about what practices they would like to learn, others are drawn to literacy programs for more general reasons.

Fingeret and Drennon (1997) support a literacy-as-practices approach because it recognizes that meanings change across context. However, they suggest that meanings in specific situations may be accepted as unproblematic. Literacy-as-critical-reflection encourages readers to analyze and reflect about contexts, to consider needs and possibilities for change, and to plan and take action towards change.

For example, many people feel anxious or fearful about asking questions when visiting a physician. In a literacy-as-practices approach, learners might talk and read about their health concerns and rehearse questions to ask the physician. In a literacy-as-critical-reflection approach, learners might engage in similar reading and rehearsal. However, they would also be invited to analyze personal experiences and feelings of fear in relation to power differences between physicians and patients. Preparing to ask questions would be considered one way to change the power relations.

As another example, participants at the Learning Centre call themselves students (hence my use of the term). Participants also refer to the Centre as "school," while emphasizing that it is not like other schools they have experienced or heard about. These contradictions can be a starting point for critical reflection.

Literacy-as-critical-reflection includes, but goes beyond "critical literacy." Critical literacy has to do with making judgments, based on consideration of available experience and information. When literacy-as-practice moves into literacy-as-critical-reflection, it bridges reading the word and the world.

GOOD PEDAGOGY/CRITICAL PEDAGOGY

Where Fingeret and Drennon (1997) compare literacy-as-practice with literacy-as-critical-reflection, Horsman and Gaber-Katz (1990) compare good pedagogy and critical pedagogy. They use the concept of language experience stories to focus their comparison. One important element of language experience stories is that they use learners' language and meanings. This makes them easy to read for the authors and for others who share the authors' language and experiences. Thus, language experience stories are a basis for good pedagogy.

Good pedagogy becomes critical pedagogy when it is carried out with the awareness and intent to challenge prevailing discourses and power relations. For example, adult learners frequently believe that their experiences and knowledge do not count in the world of writing. Darville (in Woodrow & Norton, 1997) suggests that the roots of such self-doubt include a deep-seated cultural prejudice that people with limited education have little of interest to say. This prejudice is supported when learning materials have nothing to do with the learners' own worlds.

Community writing offers a challenge to these prejudices. Through community writing, people who may not think of themselves as authors meet in groups to "share their writing, listen to, respect, respond to, revise, and sometimes home-publish their work" (Shohet, 1999, p. 2). Publishing learners' writing is fairly common practice in literacy programs.

When the intent of publishing is to affirm learners' work, build self-esteem and provide interesting reading for others, it is good pedagogy. Publishing enters the realms of resistance and critical pedagogy when it also aims to bring learners' languages and experiences into the public sphere and to share and build community knowledge. Such publishing challenges conventional views about who produces knowledge and about whose voices are heard.

PARTICIPATORY EDUCATION

Like the term community-based, *participatory education* carries a range of meanings. According to Jurmo (1989), participatory literacy education means that adult students have "higher degrees of control, responsibility and reward vis-à-vis program activities" (p. 17). Participatory education may be applied primarily in the classroom, when teachers and learners share decisions about content and teaching and learning practices; beyond the classroom, when learners have roles and share in decisions about program operations; and beyond the program, as learners are supported to take part in community activities.

Auerbach (1993) distinguishes between participatory education and learner-centred approaches. She acknowledges that learner-centred approaches presume a sharing of responsibility and power among teachers and learners for decisions about curriculum, and she welcomes this shift from approaches that are based in predetermined or teacher-directed curriculum. However, where participatory education is concerned about collective action towards social change, learner-centred approaches often focus on individual change within the status quo.

Auerbach argues for an understanding of participatory education in terms of its origins in popular education and literacy-as-critical-reflection. Popular education developed from community-based efforts to engage people in "critically analyzing their social situations and organizing to act collectively to change oppressive conditions" (Arnold, Barndt & Burke, 1985, p. 5). In Canada and the United States, literacy and popular education are frequently linked through the work and writing of Paulo Freire. Sauve's (1987) account of critical participatory education stands out as a Canadian reference, with its rich description, reflection and linking of theory and practice. Description of other Canadian examples follow.

In 1989, a group of women in the Winnipeg Journeys program drew together around their common experiences of living with welfare (Norton, 1992). Using popular education approaches, a facilitator helped the group identify and clarify issues and questions. Often questions were answered in the group but when additional information was needed, the women did research and reported back. Equipped with extended knowledge, the women took action to address problems, such as access to special needs allowances and social workers' unscheduled home visits.

Working together, the Journeys' women developed a better understanding of the welfare system and gained confidence to speak up with social workers. To inform others and raise awareness about welfare issues, they decided to write a play (The No Name Brand Clan & Lester, 1990). They performed the play 24 times to audiences totaling 1,300 people. The play was also used as a catalyst and resource when welfare issues came up in a participatory literacy and health group at the Learning Centre. Seeing their own experiences in the script, Learning Centre women subsequently read and discussed the play at a Poverty in Action Conference (Norton & Campbell, 1998).

Informing others and raising awareness also provided an impetus for the Samaritan House Participatory Action Research (PAR) Group (1995) to publish a book about discrimination. The PAR Group describe participatory action research as "a way of finding out how ordinary people experience a problem or problems in their own lives and how they can take action for change" (p. 2). The group shared their own and others' experiences of discrimination, analyzed their common experiences, and planned action for change. They felt that writing a book was the best "way for us to speak up for ourselves" (p. 12).

Apart from examples like these, participatory education has been most publicly understood in Canada as learner involvement. A number of publications have documented ways that learners have been involved at local, provincial and national levels (Cameron & Hall, 1998; Campbell, 1992; Movement for Canadian Literacy Learners' Advisory Network, 1997;

Ontario Literacy Coalition, 1991; Williams & Knutson-Shaw, n.d.). Learners report a number of benefits to active involvement, including increased confidence and self-esteem and opportunities to develop and practice literacy. As with other forms of participatory and community-oriented education, having a voice and sharing power are among the recurring themes and struggles of learner involvement.

Voice

... the ability to express ideas and opinions with the confidence that they will be heard and taken into account (Stein, 1997, p. 7).

When a group of learners at the Centre identified speaking up as a challenge, we read stories about being silenced, looked at causes and considered alternatives. This learning led to Lil Gallant and I speaking together about silence and voice at a regional learners' event. The following excerpt from Lil's talk grounded my presentation and introduces discussion here.

When I was fifty, I decided to go back to school to see if I could pick up where I left off .... A social worker told me about the Learning Centre. I went to check it out. The atmosphere and the students made me feel comfortable .... I felt that everybody was equal, that nobody was better than anyone else .... I felt I could fit in.

Before I came to the Learning Centre, there were times when I thought that I didn't fit in. When I was with educated people, I felt intimidated. When they used big words, I was scared to ask what they meant. I thought they would think I was stupid. Sometimes I might disagree with someone or think they were wrong, but I wouldn't say anything. I would just sit there in silence (Gallant, 1999).

Lil Gallant's experience of being silent is not uncommon among adults who enter literacy programs. In Campbell's (1994) research about participatory practices, learners told how they would "just keep quiet and go along with what everybody else was saying and doing" (p. 68). Further, speaking out is frequently named as an outcome of learning in literacy programs. As an example, Herman (2000) wrote, "I was kind of shy. Now I can read and write a lot. I also speak up more" (p. 1).

Some people cite shyness as the cause of their silence; others, like Lil, talk of being afraid. Campbell (1994) argues that shyness is learned, that students' fear of speaking may reflect past experiences when "... they were not heard because they did not speak the dominant language of academics and professionals such as doctors, teachers and social workers" (p. 73). Both Campbell and Gallant name language differences as a cause for silence; gender, race and other socially constructed power differences can have the same effect. Ellsworth (1989) suggests that awareness of differences in people's power will consciously or unconsciously influence decisions to speak. Situating voice in the context of power relations helps explain why any one of us, in our various roles, may feel silenced at different times. It also accounts for why whole groups in our society are not often enough heard and listened to.

Sharing power

Sharing power among teachers and learners is a basic principle of participatory and community-oriented education, whether it is taken up as critical pedagogy or learner involvement. The sharing of power challenges traditional teacher-learner relations, so it may not come naturally or easily for teachers or learners.

Starhawk (1987) describes sharing power, or power-with, as one's influence in a group. It is "the power of a strong individual in a group of equals, the power not to command, but to suggest and be listened to ..." (p. 10). In a project to organize a student conference, I learned that to share power I had to acknowledge the power-over that is inherent in my position as a paid coordinator and teacher. I also learned to acknowledge and to share my knowledge and ideas as part of the group process, while accepting that the group might not agree with or accept what I offered.

The conference project also helped other group members to develop power-with as they had support and challenge to learn new literacy practices. They experienced having influence and being listened to. As a member of the conference committee, Lil Gallant learned through other students' influence. Now she is sharing her influence with others.

> Now I ask questions and I speak up. I learned to do this from watching other students speaking. When I saw them, I thought to myself, I should have done this years ago. I also learned from workshops at the Centre and outside the Centre .... Sometimes I notice other people who

don't speak up for themselves. Maybe it's because they are frightened like I was. I try to help people feel safe and I tell them that they have a voice; they should be heard (Gallant, 1999).

BORDERLANDS

The title for this chapter came to me one day on a run. Having come across the term in my reading (Giroux, 1992; Smith, 1994), it occurred to me that community-oriented approaches take people into the borderlands between what is and what might be. My hope is that community-oriented literacy programs offer alternatives to what is. As learners, volunteers, and staff experience more equitable power relations within programs, we may see new possibilities — what might be — for resisting power-over and creating more equitable relations outside programs.

The chapter has been written in the borderlands between theory and practice, in snatched hours over the course of a year. Between these hours, the writing coloured my work and my work was subsequently drawn into further writing. I also drew on knowledge and insights shared by others through their writing, in conversations and by example. When contradictions between my perspective and practices became apparent, I was challenged to change practices or revise my writing. Eventually, my writing had to end, but the practice continues as work in progress.

REFERENCES

Arnold, R., Barndt, D., & Burke, B. (1985). *A new weave: Popular education in Canada and Central America.* Toronto, ON: Canadian University Services Overseas Development Education and Ontario Institute for Studies in Education.

Auerbach, E. (1993). Putting the P back in participatory. *TESOL Quarterly, 27*, 543–45.

Barton, D. (1990). Understanding everyday literacy. In J.P. Hautecoeur (Ed.), *ALPHA 90. Current research in Literacy* (pp. 167–177). Quebec, PQ: Direction générale de l'éducation des adultes.

Battell, E., & Nonesuch, K. (Eds.). (1996). *If you could see me now. Stories by women who survived abusive relationships.* Salt Spring Islands, BC: Key Consulting.

Beder, H. (1996). Popular education: An appropriate educational strategy for community based organizations. *New Directions for Adult and Continuing Education, 70*, 73–83.

Cameron, J., & Hall, J. (Eds.). (1998). Learner events in British Columbia. Castlegar, BC: Selkirk College.

Campbell, P. (1992). *Building the network, learning to lead. A workshop for adults in literacy and adult basic education programs.* Calgary, AB: The Alberta Association for Adult Literacy.

Campbell, P. (1994). Participatory literacy practices: Exploring social identity and relations. *Adult Basic Education, 6*, 127–142.

Collins, M.C. (1996). *The first twenty-five years. Laubach Literacy in Canada, 1970–1995.* Saint John, NB: Laubach Literacy Canada.

Ellsworth, E. (1989). Why doesn't this feel empowering? Working through the repressive myths of critical pedagogy. *Harvard Educational Review, 59*, 297–324.

English Express. Edmonton, AB: Alberta Learning.

Fingeret, H., & Drennon, C. (1997). *Literacy for life. Adult learners, new practices.* New York: Teachers College Press.

Freire, P., & Macadeo, D. (1987). *Reading the word and the world.* South Hadley, MA: Bergin and Garvey.

Gaber-Katz, E., & Watson, G. (1991). *The land that we dream of. A participatory study of community-based literacy.* Toronto, ON: Ontario Institute for Studies in Education.

Gallant, L. (1999, Oct.). Unpublished paper presented at the Winning with Words Conference of the Alberta Association for Adult Literacy Student Development Project, Athabasca, AB.

Giroux, H. (1992). *Border crossings. Cultural workers and the politics of education.* London: Routledge.

Godin, J. (Ed). (1996). *Working in context. Federal, provincial and territorial actions in support of literacy in Canada.* Ottawa, ON: National Literacy Secretariat.

Hamilton, E. & Cunningham, P. (1989). Community-based adult education. In S. Merriam, & P. Cunningham (Eds.), *Handbook of adult and continuing education* (pp. 439–450). San Francisco: Jossey-Bass.

Herman, Y. (2000). *Then and now.* Edmonton, AB: Learning at the Centre Press.

Horsman, J. (1990.) *Something on my mind besides the everyday.* Toronto, ON: Women's Press, 1990.

Horsman, J., & Gaber-Katz, E. (1990). Is it her voice if she speaks their words? *Voices Rising, 4*, 1, 22.

I remember. (n.d.). Yellowknife, NWT: NWT Literacy Council.

Isley, P. (1985). Policy formation in adult literacy volunteerism. Issues and ideas. *Adult Literacy and Basic Education, 9*, 154–162.

Jurmo, P. (1989). History in the making: The case of participatory literacy education. In A. Fingeret & P. Jurmo (Eds.), *Participatory Literacy Education* (pp. 17–28). San Francisco, CA: Jossey-Bass.

Movement for Canadian Literacy Learners' Advisory Network. (1997). Project proposal. Ottawa, ON: Movement for Canadian Literacy.

Nixon-Ponder, S. (1995). *Using problem-posing dialogue in adult literacy education. Teacher to Teacher*. Kent State University, OH: Ohio Literacy Resource Centre. (ERIC Document Reproduction Services No. Ed 381 677)

The No Name Brand Clan & Lester, T. (1990). *Under the line. A witty down to earth look at life on welfare*. Winnipeg, MB: Popular Theatre Alliance.

Norton, M. (1992). Literacy, welfare and popular education. In J. Draper, & M. Taylor (Eds.), *Voices from the literacy field* (pp. 139–154). Toronto, ON: Culture Concepts Inc.

Norton, M., & Campbell, P. (1998). *Learning for our health: A resource for participatory literacy and health education with women*. Edmonton, AB: The Learning Centre Literacy Association.

Ontario Literacy Coalition. (1991). *From energy to action: Learners involved in literacy*. Toronto, ON: Ontario Literacy Coalition.

Rodriguez, C. (1993). *Educating for change: Community-based student centred literacy programing with First Nations adults*. Salmon Arm, BC: K'noowenchoot Aboriginal Adult Education Resources, Okanagan College.

Samaritan House PAR Group. (1995). *Where there is life there is hope: Women literacy students and discrimination*. Brandon, MB: Literacy and Continuing Education Branch, Department of Education and Training.

Sauve, V. (1987). *From one educator to another. A window on participatory education*. Edmonton, AB: Grant MacEwan Community College.

Shohet, L. (1999). Community writing. Connecting literacy and the literary. *Literacy across the Curriculum, 14* (Suppl.), 3–4.

Smith, M. (1994). *Local education: Community, conversation and praxis*. Buckingham, UK: Open University Press.

Starhawk. (1987). *Truth or dare. Encounters with power, authority and mystery*. San Francisco, CA: Harper.

Stein, S.G. (1997). *Equipped for the future: A reform agenda for adult literacy and lifelong learning*. Washington, DC: National Institute for Literacy.

Williams, C., & Knutson-Shaw, B. (n.d.). *Learners as leaders. A manual for student involvement*. Vulcan, AB: The Write Break Adult Literacy Project

Williams, H. (1997). Traveling with English Express. In B. Burke, (Ed.), *English Express*. Edmonton, AB: Alberta Learning.

Woodrow, H., & Norton, M. (1996). *Propriety and possibilities: Writing in adult basic education programs*. St. John's, NF: Harrish Press.

Patterns of Participation in Canadian Literacy Programs
Results of a National Follow-up Study

*Ellen Long with Sandy Middleton**

Here we outline key findings from a national follow-up study in 1999, based on phone interviews with 331 individuals, giving us a unique opportunity to look at the conditions that promote or deter participation in literacy education. These research findings are preceded by an overview of the importance of studying patterns of participation, a review of selected literature, and a description of the study's research design. The study was conducted by ABC Canada in partnership with Literacy BC.

WHY IS IT IMPORTANT TO STUDY PATTERNS OF PARTICIPATION?

Canadians are now more educated than ever before. However, dramatic social and economic changes over the last few decades have required increasingly higher levels of basic literacy skills in the general population. In the past decade, the Canadian government established a National Literacy Secretariat and has engaged, along with other industrialized nations, in extensive measurement of adult literacy rates. According to Statistics Canada (1996), 38 percent of Canadians have difficulty with everyday reading and writing tasks.

There is serious debate about the particular reasons why adults need solid basic literacy skills. Literacy advocates and practitioners tend to

---

* This article was prepared with the research assistance of Leanne Taylor.

emphasize issues of personal and political empowerment (Hoddinnott, 1998), while government and business are apt to focus on factors related to labour force development and national economic performance (Bloom, et al., 1997; IALS, 1996). Learners themselves tend to speak about literacy's practical daily applications and the intrinsic satisfaction and personal confidence that come with increased skills (Bossort, Cunningham & Gardner, 1994). There is also debate about whether low levels of literacy skill are the cause or the effect of poverty. Whatever the debate or perspective, however, a basic level of literacy skill among adults is accepted as fundamental to social and economic well-being.

A groundwork for nation-wide research

The Canadian literacy movement has become considerably more sophisticated in its outreach and public awareness work, and people are becoming more aware of adult literacy issues and options. In 1995, ABC Canada launched the multi-media, national LEARN campaign which, along with local outreach efforts, has increased awareness about literacy programs and where to find them (Long, 1996). General awareness of literacy issues has increased significantly over the last decade (ABC Canada and Decima Research, 1999).

Despite the need for higher literacy levels in the general population and increased outreach efforts, recruitment and retention of learners remain major challenges. Only a fraction of eligible adults have ever enrolled in a literacy program, and among the enrolled, attrition rates are high (Quigley, 1997). Presently, there is little representative Canadian research that examines the complexity of patterns of participation and the shape and nature of the underlying issues.

The value of systematic follow-up with learners, both to improve practice and to influence public policy, has long been recognized. However, chronic shortages of staff and resources have caused literacy practitioners to focus on providing services. When follow-up is done, it is typically with people who have completed or dropped out of programs. Little is therefore known about the full range of possibilities that can occur once individuals make initial contact with a literacy group.

Two attempts to track calls to a Canadian literacy referral line have been documented. The first, commissioned by the Literacy Partners of Quebec (Aaron, 1997), followed up with callers to an English-language referral line. The second, by Literacy BC (1999), was a longitudinal study tracking calls to the provincial toll-free number. The current national study is improved because of these foundational efforts. The Literacy BC study was especially influential in shaping the research design of this study.

In early 1999, 55 literacy groups across Canada did the groundwork for this follow-up study by asking each eligible caller (someone who contacted by phone or in person) the same question: Would you mind if someone called you back in six months to see how it's going? With permission, we were able to contact many people at one time to address some important questions at a national level. For example

- After calling a referral line, how many people then call a literacy provider?
- How many callers ultimately enrol in programs?
- What are the reasons some callers do not enrol?
- What proportion encounter waiting lists?
- What do people think about the programs?
- How many stay in the programs?
- What are the factors associated with not enrolling or with dropping out?

This national, systematic study provides an unprecedented opportunity to look at the conditions that promote or deter successful participation in literacy education.

A CRITICAL REFLECTION ON PATTERNS OF PARTICIPATION

This section reviews key literature about participation in adult literacy and upgrading programs, covering the broad range of factors that influence enrollment and attrition. This growing body of literature still remains largely descriptive and unconnected to larger theoretical frameworks. The concepts discussed are piecemeal and contradictory, making it difficult to compare or determine patterns. Much of the existing literature discusses factors affecting participation as if they were independent, ignoring their interrelationships. The overall picture remains fragmented.

What motivates participation?

Views of participation in adult literacy programs have only recently progressed beyond a deficit perspective, in which those not participating in programs were labelled "motivationally deficient" (Beder, 1991). In the most extensive motivational study reported, Beder and Valentine (1990) demonstrated that students are motivated by a wide range of goals. These researchers developed a typology of ten broad dimensions of motivation through in-person interviews with a random sample of 323 students enrolled in Adult Basic Education (ABE) programs in Iowa. The range of motivations included extrinsic benefits, such as vocational mobility and economic need, and intrinsic benefits, such as enhanced participation in community life, and increased ability to meet family responsibilities and negotiate life transitions. Demographic factors such as age and gender should also be considered with respect to motivation (Ziegahn, 1992).

That motivation is multidimensional and that literacy is seen as a means to diverse ends is supported in Canadian research (ABE Outcomes Steering Committee, 1996; Advanced Education Council of BC, 1997; Malicky and Norman, 1994).

Motivation is far from the only factor determining whether or not individuals participate in literacy programs. Indeed, many of the same reasons that motivate people can also deter them.

Factors influencing participation are complex, numerous and much debated. Overall, they can be grouped into three broad, interrelated categories: socioeconomic-circumstantial, cognitive-emotive, and program-related. Multiple factors may be operating simultaneously though differentially, depending on the person and the situation.

Socioeconomic-circumstantial factors

Social, economic and political factors can make participation in formal education difficult for people with low literacy skills. The lower one's socioeconomic status, the lower the rate of participation in *any* type of formal learning activity (Statistics Canada, 1997; McGivney, 1990). Not surprisingly, formal income support to attend programs significantly increases people's ability to participate in literacy education and "something as basic and as inexpensive as a bus pass can make the difference between a person's attending a program or not" (Hoddinnott, 1998, p. 103).

Circumstantial factors relate to individual life situations, from the general (hours of work) to the specific (a chronic health problem). Lack of time is the barrier frequently cited by potential learners; what this generally means is they are "too busy" finding work, working long hours or shift work, and negotiating other life priorities like childcare and community involvement (Perin and Greenberg, 1994; Thomas, 1990).

Research on people who drop out of programs provides extensive evidence of the impact of socioeconomic-circumstantial factors (Literacy BC, 1999). As Thomas states, "everything in a person's life has to be almost in place to make [participation] possible" (p.82) and many students may be just one circumstance away from dropping out. Being of limited means diminishes one's ability to absorb sudden changes; even a minor car repair can be a financial crisis. Furthermore, in the face of other urgent needs, the benefits of improving literacy skills may seem inconsequential. That those who drop out frequently return or intend to return confirms the influence of socioeconomic-circumstantial factors on participation (Thomas, 1990).

Research suggests that people with low literacy skills are keenly aware of the social, economic and political forces besides literacy that shape their lives (Fagan, 1988). In light of systemic factors, improving one's literacy skills may seem a weak tool against economic displacement or poverty, educational inequality, and other social conditions (NAPO, 1990; Ziegahn, 1992). Achieving a higher literacy skill level may be less important than having credentials (Hoddinnott, 1998), especially in the current context of underemployment, where highly credentialed people are increasingly filling jobs previously occupied by those with fewer formal credentials. This may be one of the reasons why a longitudinal study by Malicky and Norman (1994) found that the initial job-related optimism of more than 80 percent of the 94 learners ended with discouragement in reaction to the realities of the labour market.

Cognitive-emotive factors

Well documented in the literature, the cognitive-emotive factors influencing participation refer to the broad range of psychological orientations, attitudes, expectations and perceptions of adults with low literacy skills — often reported in terms of low self-confidence and fear of failure (Hayes, 1988; Malicky and Norman, 1994). One of the most powerful is the stigma of low literacy. Attending a program discloses one's level of literacy; adults who have internalized a sense of stigma may opt instead to hide their low literacy skills (Martini and Page, 1996).

People also direct their lives and make choices based on their experience and values. Quigley (1990) argues that to see nonparticipation strictly as a barriers issue is to "effectively diminish a perceived capacity for human agency among nonparticipants" and to "reinforce stereotypes of illiterate adults as fearful, suspicious victims of socioeconomic circumstances who are incapable of utilizing the educational opportunities extended them" (pp. 104–105). He argues that there may be a certain logic to nonparticipation; for example, in a study of 20 nonparticipant adults in Pittsburgh, Quigley (1992, 1997) found that many actively rejected, not learning and education, but school itself and a schooling system founded on middle-class values. McGivney (1990) and Thomas (1990) also found that adults from working-class backgrounds who participate in literacy programs may experience considerable cultural conflicts. These findings challenge us to see nonparticipation from a new, more critical perspective.

Program-related factors

Any exploration of participation patterns must also critically examine program-related factors and ask, Are programs visible, available, accessible, and effective? Many adults do not participate because they are not aware of programs or how to find them (Long, 1996). In some communities, there are no programs (Hoddinnott, 1998). Where they do exist, literacy may be taught at an inappropriate skill level, with inappropriate instructional approaches (Literacy BC, 1999; Rodriguez and Sawyer, 1990), or held at awkward, inflexible class times (Beder, 1990). Unfavourable physical conditions, complicated and depersonalized enrollment and registration procedures and difficulties finding course information are also significant barriers (ABE Student Outcomes Steering Committee, 1997).

Resourcing issues can create low staffing hours, shortages of tutors, reductions in telephone services and program follow-up, lack of services for people with learning or physical disabilities, long waiting lists, insufficient childcare options, inadequate facilities, and fees for tuition or learning materials (Aaron, 1997; White and Hoddinnott, 1998).

Where do we go from here?

Patterns of participation are not easily compartmentalized. Much of the participatory research presents factors in narrow terms, ignoring the significant overlap and interrelationship among them. A single issue (childcare, for example) can relate to all three categories: unaffordable or unavailable childcare is a socioeconomic-circumstantial barrier; an assumption that the program is "not for single parents like me" is a cognitive-emotive barrier; and lack of on-site childcare is a program-related barrier. Future research should direct us towards shaping clear theoretical models and integrated explanations of participation in literacy programs.

HOW DID WE STUDY PATTERNS OF PARTICIPATION?

We undertook a six to eight month telephone follow-up with a large, representative sample of individuals attempting to access literacy services. Help with sampling methods was enlisted through Statistics Canada. From a pool of 314 groups working in cooperation with ABC Canada's LEARN campaign, a random sample of 60 stratified by province and territory was drawn. The sample included community-based providers, school boards, community colleges, phone referral lines, government agencies, literacy networks, and urban and rural groups. Of the 60 groups, 55 (92 percent) agreed to ask eligible callers in January and February of 1999 for permission to be called back. Eligible callers included potential adult learners and family/friends calling on behalf of potential learners.

In total, the 55 groups collected 505 eligible names and phone numbers. The Institute for Social Research (ISR) at York University in Toronto, Ontario, made up to 20 calls to each number, reaching 331 people for a response of 67 percent. Most of those we could not reach had likely moved: their numbers were out of service with no forwarding number. Because our findings are missing the most transient portion of the overall sample, enrollment figures may be overinflated and the impact of socioeconomic-circumstantial factors underestimated.

Of the five groups not included, two affect our sample's representativeness: French Quebec is not represented because the organization through which all French calls are directed declined to participate; the Yukon, because of a technical erro in obtaining permissions to call back. The Northwest Territories received no learner-related calls during the study period; Nunavut was not yet formed. With these exceptions, the selection method and the willingness of so many groups to participate provided good overall representation.

Interviewers from ISR were trained to ensure sensitivity in making the follow-up calls. The interview questionnaire was adapted from the survey developed for the Literacy BC tracking study, further strengthened according to the lessons they learned. Our questionnaire was also informed by the current literature on participation; several education surveys, including a recent one by the National Research Network on New Approaches to Lifelong Learning (NALL) (Livingstone, 1999); extensive consultation with our advisory group of practitioners and academics; and pilot interviews with 12 eligible participants.

WHAT DID WE FIND OUT ABOUT PATTERNS OF PARTICIPATION?

After making an initial call to a literacy group, callers arrived at various outcomes for complex reasons. Understanding the reasons behind various types of participation will allow insights into issues of practice and policy.

Of the 331 individuals contacted, 85 percent were potential learners and 15 percent were family/friends of potential learners. The information recounted here pertains to potential learners themselves, whom we refer to as "callers" regardless of who placed the initial call.

Who are the potential learners?

More than three-quarters of those in the sample were first-time callers. Overall, slightly more potential learners were women (53 percent) than men. Although callers' ages ranged from 16 to 79, most (82 percent) were less than age 45 and were fairly equally distributed across the age groups of 18–24, 25–34, and 35–44 years. Those more than age 45 were strikingly underrepresented (18 percent), especially considering that literacy rates for people more than age 45 are generally lower than in younger age groups (Statistics Canada, 1996).

English was the language spoken most fluently by 80 percent of callers. More than three-quarters of callers received their early education in Canada. The level of formal education achieved by callers ranged from 7 percent in grade levels zero to four; 28 percent in grades five to nine; 35 percent in grades ten to thirteen; 16 percent with a high school diploma; and 12 percent at least some post-secondary. Most of those with post-secondary education received all or most of their education outside Canada and have the most fluency in languages other than English.

More than half of callers had either full- or part-time employment; 28 percent were on social assistance. Close to 40 percent reported living in households with incomes of less than $20,000 a year.

Why did people contact the literacy groups?

Callers in early 1999 were looking for help with reading and writing (40 percent), getting a high school diploma or credits (28 percent), math alone or as a component with reading and writing (12 percent), employability skills (8 percent), English as a second language (7 percent) or something else (7 percent) such as assistance with a learning disability.

In response to an open-ended question about motivation (Figure 2.1), somewhat unexpectedly more callers reported extrinsic motivators as their main reason for wanting to participate in programs. That is, more people cited motivators related to general educational improvement, personal well-being, and daily skills/social well-being/family (58 percent combined) than motivators related to jobs and upgrading for retraining (42 percent combined).

Most people readily identified multiple reasons for wanting to participate. The reason mentioned most often was personal and social well-being (cited by 46 percent of callers), followed by general educational improvement (42 percent) and job-related factors (35 percent). These results suggest that programs focusing on a narrow range of vocational objectives will not meet the main goals of most callers to literacy groups.

FIGURE 2.1
Main motivation

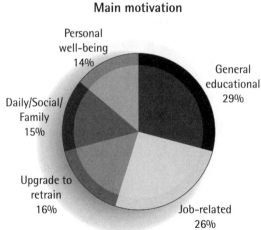

What happened after people made the initial call?

After placing the initial call to a literacy group in early 1999, 47 percent of callers went on to sign up for a program and 53 percent did not. Literacy BC found a similar rate of enrollment (52 percent). It is important to remember that these figures reflect the experience of those who agreed to be called back and who were still at the same address at the point of followup.

As in the Literacy BC study, program-related factors were the main deterrent to enrollment for the largest percentage of callers (43 percent). After program-related reasons, socioeconomic-circumstantial barriers were reported by the next largest group of those who did not enrol (31 percent). Cognitive-emotive reasons were the least likely (15 percent) to be cited as the main reason for not enrolling.

Figure 2.2 gives a detailed breakdown of program-related factors, which include not being called back by the program (reported by 20 percent of this group), long waiting lists (14 percent), inconvenient class locations (13 percent) and times (6 percent), and having to pay for the program or tutor (7 percent). Other program-related factors include wrong program content, for example, a lack of available math classes or instances when a caller wanted high school credits but couldn't get them (11 percent); or wrong program structure, for example, a small group setting where only large class settings exist (11 percent).

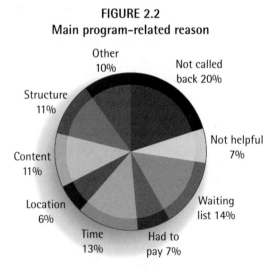

FIGURE 2.2
Main program-related reason

Of those citing socioeconomic-circumstantial reasons as the main barrier to nonenrollment, more than half were dealing with work-related conflicts; we could reasonably expect this to be interrelated with the issue of when programs are offered. Thirty-six percent spoke of childcare and other social responsibilities. Women were more likely than men to cite these reasons as their main barrier.

When given the opportunity to provide more than one reason for not enrolling, the number of times various factors were mentioned went up considerably. Money problems were mentioned most frequently (47 percent), followed by inconvenient time (33 percent); conflict with job hours (37 percent); inconvenient location (31 percent); long waiting period (30 percent); care of children (31 percent); worry or nervousness about studying (34 percent); unfriendly or unhelpful contact with program (28 percent); and care of aging parents (15 percent).

What experiences do people have once they sign up for a program?

Of those who signed up, 45 percent reported studying one-on-one with a tutor, 42 percent in a classroom with a teacher, 10 percent in correspondence courses, and 3 percent in another form of self-study. Disturbingly, 8 percent of those who signed up were still on waiting lists at the point of follow-up. Of those who had finished or were in a program, the great majority (88 percent) reported having positive experiences. More specifically, people felt that programs were at the right level for them and the content was what they had wanted.

When asked to state one thing they would change about the program, participants identified nothing at all (42 percent), smaller classes or more individual attention from the teacher or tutor (17 percent), more relevant material (13 percent), more knowledgeable teacher or tutor or a faster pace (9 percent), and a better time or location (8 percent). A striking area of dissatisfaction was the hours per week spent with a teacher or tutor: Whereas 32 percent of people reported meeting for one or two hours per week, only 12 percent said that this was ideal. In fact, 33 percent would like to be studying for more than 16 hours per week; only 22 percent of people were studying that amount of time.

Why did people drop out of programs?

Of those who enrolled, 31 percent had dropped out by the point of follow-up. Contrary to some other research, we did not find that people
were more likely to drop out in the first weeks of a program than later.
What we did find was that those who dropped out sooner were more
likely to report program-related reasons than those who left later.

Socioeconomic-circumstantial factors were the main reason for the
majority (56 percent) of those who dropped out of programs. The most
typical scenario was conflict with work and work hours, followed by
family and social obligations.

Of those who dropped out, 27 percent cited program-related factors
as their most important reason. These factors include program cancella-
tion or problems with the content or level of programs. Very few people
(6 percent) cited cognitive-emotive factors as the main reason for dropping out. Other reasons (10 percent) included, for example, employment insurance stipulations that do not allow program attendance.

As with motivation and nonenrollment, most people readily cited
multiple reasons for dropping out. The reasons reported by the largest
percentages of those who had dropped out related to jobs (47 percent),
financial worries (35 percent) and childcare conflicts (29 percent).

More than three-quarters of those who dropped out said they would like
to sign up again in the future, which confirms Thomas's (1990) conclusions
that people tend to *drop in and out* instead of permanently dropping out.

RECOMMENDATIONS ON HOW TO IMPROVE ENROLLMENT OUTCOMES

When people contact a literacy group, there are many possible outcomes. Our research confirms that patterns of participation are mediated by a highly complex set of factors operating simultaneously. While
most callers cited multiple reasons for their decisions, some patterns
were discernible. Nonenrollment, for example, is predominantly affected
by program-related factors; dropping out, by socioeconomic-
circumstantial factors. Cognitive-emotive factors seldom constituted
the main reason for non-enrollment or dropping out. A limitation of this
study is that our sample size was not large enough to provide provincial
or regional breakdown of these, or any other figures. Since this study, by
definition, did not include individuals who have never contacted a

literacy group, we must be very cautious about generalizing our findings to their experiences.

The bad news from our study is that a large proportion of callers did not enrol because of program-related factors. The good news, however, is that some impediments could readily be addressed through immediate program and policy initiatives. For example, if people are sitting on waiting lists six to eight months after contacting a literacy group; if programs don't meet the needs of potential learners regarding time, length, structure or level; if return calls are not being made by literacy groups; or if contact is unfriendly, then *obvious recommendations can be made about issues of funding, programming and professional development.*

Addressing socioeconomic and circumstantial factors is more difficult. Close to half of callers directly stated that their financial situation made it difficult to be in a program. Indeed, while 40 percent of callers lived in households with incomes of less than $20,000 a year, only about 11 percent of Canadian households have incomes this low (Statistics Canada, 1997b). In this context, the *fees charged by some jurisdictions for basic education programs should be reconsidered.*

Mediating the full impact of socioeconomic and circumstantial factors on participation cannot be accomplished by the literacy field alone; these factors are related to issues of broader public policy, but focused policy initiatives could be effectively expressed. For example, childcare conflicts was a clear factor for 35 percent of those who did not enrol, and 29 percent of those who dropped out. Further, of those with children, half of the women and a quarter of the men said they would have called earlier if there had been on-site childcare. What this explicitly indicates is the *basic childcare provision could greatly increase enrollment and decrease drop-out rates.*

Work-related factors were strikingly important to enrollment and drop-out rates, confirming the need for a continued focus on promoting workplace programs. But it would be simplistic to stop there when we know that those with lower levels of literacy are more likely to do work that is unpredictably or inflexibly scheduled, intermittent and precarious. There is a clear need for programming to accommodate the work patterns of those with low literacy skill levels.

The questions raised by socioeconomic-circumstantial and program-related factors have no easy answers. There are constant tensions within the literacy field about how best to program for the target population of people with low literacy skills, considering their range of different experiences and realities. The debate (even within the same person) vacillates between a vision of complete flexibility to accommodate the uncertainty and pressures characterizing people's lives, to one of more rigorous expectations. The role of volunteers and trained professionals in program delivery is also debated, as well as how to ensure that people "get enough to make a difference." The overall debate is complex and plays out differently in various parts of the country — almost always against the backdrop of complicated funding issues.

It is most encouraging that more than three-quarters of those who dropped out or didn't enrol in the first place said they would seek help again in the future. Much needs to be done to help ensure a more positive outcome when they do call again.

REFERENCES

Aaron, Mandie. (1997). *Student services in adult literacy: Increasing awareness for successful outcomes*. Referral Systems in Quebec. Montreal, PQ: Literacy Partners of Quebec.

ABC Canada & Decima Research. (1999). *Attitudes of Canadians toward literacy: A decade in review*. Available from ABC Canada, 1-800-303-1004.

ABE Students Outcomes Steering Committee. (1997). *Onward and upward: Moving towards a goal with adult basic education. The Adult Basic Education (ABE) Student Outcomes Project*. Vancouver and Victoria, BC: Advanced Education Council of BC and Ministry of Education, Skills and Training.

Advanced Education Council of BC. (1997). Stepping stones to the future: Highlight of the Adult Basic Education Student Outcomes Project.

Beder, H. (1990). Reasons for nonparticipation in ABE. *Adult Education Quarterly*, 40(4), 207–218.

Beder, H. (1991). *Adult literacy: Issues for policy and practice*. Malabar, FL: Krieger Publishing.

Beder, H.W., & Valentine, T. (1990). Motivational profiles of adult basic education students. *Adult Education Quarterly*, 40(2), 794.

Bloom, M., Lafleur, B., & Squires, R. (1997). *The economic benefits of improving literacy skills in the workplace*. Ottawa, ON: Conference Board of Canada.

Bossort, P., Cunningham, B., & Gardner, L. (1994). *Learning to learn: Impacts of the Adult Basic Education experience on the lives of participants*. Victoria, BC: Ministry of Skills, Training and Labour.

Fagan, W.T. (1988). A survey of a sample of adult illiterates in an urban area of Canada. *Prospects*, 18(3), 395–403.

Hayes, E.R. (1998). A typology of low-literate adults based on perceptions of deterrents to participation in adult basic education. *Adult Education Quarterly*, 39(1), 1–10.

Hoddinnott, S. (1998). *Something to think about please think about this. Report on a national study of access to Adult Basic Education programs and services in Canada*. Ottawa, ON: Ottawa Board of Education.

Literacy BC. (1999). *It guided me back to learning: A longitudinal research study on calls to the Literacy BC helpline*. Victoria, BC: Ministry of Advanced Education, Training and Technology.

Livingstone, D.W. (1999). *A national study of informal learning practices*. Toronto, ON: OISE/UT.

Long, E. (1996). *The impact of ABC Canada's LEARN campaign: Results of a national study*. Toronto, ON: ABC Canada.

Malicky, G.V., & Norman, C.A. (1994). Participation patterns in adult literacy programs. *Adult Basic Education*, 4(3), 144–156.

Martini, T., & Page, S. (1996). Attributions and the stigma of illiteracy: Understanding help seeking in low literate adults. *Canadian Journal of Behavioural Science*, 28(2), 121–129.

McGivney, V. (1990). *Education's for other people: Access to education for non-participant adults*. A research report. Leicester: National Institute for Adult Continuing Education.

National Anti-Poverty Organization. (1992). *Literacy and poverty: A view from the inside* [research report]. Ottawa, ON: Author.

Perin, D., & Greenberg, D. (1994). Understanding dropout in an urban worker education program 1994: Retention patterns, demographics, student perceptions, and reasons given for early departure. *Urban Education*, 29(2), 169–187.

Quigley, A. (1990). Hidden logic: Reproduction and resistance in adult literacy and adult basic education. *Adult Education Quarterly*, 40(2), 103–115.

Quigley, A. (1992). Looking back in anger: The influences of schooling on illiterate adults. *Journal of Education*, 174(1), 104–121.

Quigley, A. (1997). *Rethinking literacy education: The critical need for practice-based change*. San Francisco, CA: Jossey-Bass.

Rodriguez, C., & Sawyer, D. (1990). *Native literacy research report*. Salmon Arm, BC: Native Adult Education Resource Center, Okanagan College.

Statistics Canada. (1996). *Reading the future: A portrait of literacy in Canada*. Ottawa, ON: Statistics Canada, Human Resources Development Canada and the National Literacy Secretariat.

Statistics Canada. (1997). *Adult education and training in Canada. Report of the 1994 adult education and training survey*. Ottawa, ON: Author.

Thomas, A. (1990). The reluctant learner: A research report on nonparticipation and dropout in literacy programs in British Columbia. Victoria, BC: Ministry of Advanced Education, Training and Technology.

Ziegahn, L. (1992). Learning, literacy, and participation: Sorting out priorities. *Adult Education Quarterly*, 43(1), 30–50.

C H A P T E R 3

Learners
The Heart of the Matter

Heather Richmond

Examining the nature of community literacy by looking at community-based programming and literacy social practices provides a review of some problematic issues and briefly outlines a conceptual framework to understand these factors. Definitions of literacy are then examined and provide a link to Norton's earlier chapter. A critical reflection on the tensions in adult education is undertaken to provide insights into the community-based programming found across Canada. The second part includes short case stories of individual learners and uses a narrative framework and a storymap as the means of analysis.

Writing about community-based literacy, I find myself reflecting on recent research, and on my assumptions about discrepancies between the world of theory and the world of practice. I am questioning who is at the centre of community-based literacy and for what purpose is literacy. As a researcher writing about community-based literacy, I bring expertise about reading theory and practice, and about the myths of literacy as a cure for what is deficit in individuals or communities.

The framework of my literacy beliefs is informed by literacy theories and approaches and by models of adult education and literacy curriculum. Much of this draws on political, ideological, educational and societal values that typify the cross-disciplinary directions in new literacy research. The mission of new literacy studies is to bridge the gap between the literacies of the individual and the community, and those of the school and society. This type of literacy research documents people's own perceptions, understandings, decision-making processes and practices as they read, write and communicate.

DEFINITIONS: LITERACY AS EVOLUTION NOT REVOLUTION

In chapter 1, Norton discusses examples of literacy as skill-based and context-based in the Edmonton Learning Centre. Like Barton (1994), she also sees the learners' literacy as social practices in a particular context. Literacy is a socially constructed concept that is defined in ways congruent with the expectations and attitudes of various interest groups. Most interest groups focus on the "problems of literacy" and define it in ways that problematize the relationships among literacy, education, employment, and culture, as well as those among youth and adults with low level literacy skills, their family and community, and with the literate members of society.

The full impact of literacy as a problem, as well as its definition, lies within an intersecting network of local and societal beliefs linking literacy and education, literacy and employment, literacy and culture, and literacy with daily life in the local community. As the demand for literacy skills increases, the demand for coordinated literacy programs also increases.

Past experiences at home and school

Nadia, a woman learner, documents her early perceptions of home and school. Her home life was fraught as she and her siblings were placed together with a foster family. By the time she was 14 she was, as she says, running the roads and on her own and explains why:

> *I know one thing, it wasn't the schools' fault, it was my parents' fault, [my] foster parents. I remember coming home one day with a good mark on a test and I was so excited to show this mark and when I got there and showed it to them [foster parents] they just looked at it and said, "yeah, it's fine but so-and-so brings them home all the time" and then tossed it, threw it in the garbage. So that kind of really ... it really hurt a lot.*

In New Brunswick learners have participated in federal and provincial programs designed to provide certification in basic adult upgrading, occupational training and other such programs. The approach favoured in these programs is either neo-deficit or intervention prevention (Auerbach, 1995a, 1995b). However, Richmond (1999) investigated adult learners who were all enrolled in a provincially designed, community-based literacy program. This program, known as the Community Academic Services Program (CASP), shares responsibility for literacy problems between the government and other valued segments of society. Thus, in New Brunswick, provincial organizations, local communities and individual learners come together in a community-based program.

Experiences in a community-based program

Weiss, only nineteen years old, is a learner with strong views on both community and public school–based programs.

> I didn't like that [the town high school] too much so I came to the community-based school and I liked it. If you need help, you can get it and the teachers are always willing and ready to help you whenever you want it. I stuck with that for a while but I wanted to go back to regular schooling so I could get my high school diploma. Then I went to Rural High School. The teachers there are fine, they'll help you any time you need it because the school's not as big and there's not near as many people ... I was making 90s and 80s so I could do the school work. But I couldn't handle the social stuff. [Now at a community-based school he adds], when you're around adults all day it rubs off on you and you sort of grow up a little bit.

Traditionally, another means for acquiring literacy skills in Canada is to participate in literacy activities provided by not-for-profit organizations such as provincial literacy coalitions, local literacy councils, Laubach Literacy or Frontier College. These organizations do not provide a coordinated public response to the problem of low literacy levels among the youth and adult population. However, these groups do provide another perspective on community-based literacy, and are based on participatory (Fingeret & Jurmo, 1989) and social change approaches (Auerbach, 1995a; Freire 1994). The educational model here is a transformational one (Miller, Caisse & Drake, 1990). In such a definition, literacy is provided at the grassroots by volunteer tutors and organizers in such places as prisons, halfway houses, youth centres, community food banks, or head start programs.

Recent research tends to focus on school-defined reading skills and educational attainment. In this definition, the dominant group selects knowledge and hands it down and marginalized groups accept, receive and store this knowledge (Freire, 1978; Auerbach, 1995a; Miller, 1988). Others place literacy in a community-based model, where the learners and facilitator construct knowledge based on the needs and interests of both the dominant society and the marginalized one. This new type of literacy definition fits into an interactive model, where learning involves critical thinking, reflection and action. The definitions of literacy are recognized as being situated not only in the organizational structure but also in the participants' social practices.

CRITICAL REFLECTIONS ON TENSIONS IN ADULT EDUCATION

The debate about adult learning and programming centres around whether or not it is the learner's literacy experiences and practices or the educator's authority that is at the heart of the matter. The tensions within adult education, and their implications for policy and program development in adult literacy education, reflect the "competing social and political values" (Stierer & Maybin, 1994, p. ix). These tensions and debates have much to contribute to our understanding of community literacy as a model of literacy education.

Objectivity or subjectivity?

In an adult education course designed to give certification, the tensions in adult education are usually resolved in favour of educator authority and objective knowledge, and governmental agencies have traditionally resolved these two tensions in adult education in their favour. For example, academic upgrading programs lead to a GED and may be followed by occupational training and ensuing certification. In adult education in community-based programs that do not lead to a certificate, the education is more in line with learner freedom, subjective and experiential knowledge.

When non-governmental agencies, such as Laubach Literacy and Frontier College, provide adult literacy programs, their resolution of these tensions usually leans towards learner freedom, subjective knowledge and individual agency. Such programs rarely involve a formal evaluation of the learner, although the program itself may be evaluated. The curriculum content of such programs is often based on a learner-centred approach described by Conti (1989).

Learner or institution?

Another question for examination is whether the agency of individual learners or the structure of social institution is the more important context for adult learning (Pratt, 1993). The theoretical framework that underpins much of the discussion of program design for learners focuses on learning as a process. This process requires the human agency of a self-directed learner with direct concerns about social, political, economic, cultural or historical contexts (Pratt, 1993). The human agency side of this tension of adult education has been taken up by Mezirow (1995, 1997) and Cranton (1997) who wrote about transformational learning, the idea being that all adults have developed meaning perspectives based on their experiences and encounters within the various contexts of their lives. All educational programs should provide opportunities for individuals to critically reflect on the origin, nature and consequences of these perspectives and this should be an essential component of any adult literacy program. There is no room here for a deficit approach to literacy. Low level literacy, according to Mezirow and Cranton, is part of an individual's meaning perspectives, as are his or her vernacular literacy practices (Barton & Hamilton, 1998). A literacy program should help the learners to critically reflect on them first, then discover how these affect their life world, and how they could be positively transformed.

CASE STORIES OF INDIVIDUAL LEARNERS

This section summarizes the case stories of four learners in the study by Richmond (1999) that led to the development of the storymap framework shown in Table 3.1. The storymap framework allowed data from the interviews to be categorized using two dimensions: (1) past and present experiences and future intentions; and (2) self, family, community, schooling and work. An abridged form of the data gathered from learner stories is presented first in terms of the storymap; then as a summary of past and present experiences and future intentions. As suggested by Mishler (1986) a narrative core ends each story.

Aleeta

Aleeta's public schooling left her with less than a Grade Nine education, providing a convincing story of her ability to learn. As soon as she left

TABLE 3.1   Schematic Organization of the Storymap

| | The World of: | | | | |
	Self	Family	Community	Schooling	Work
Past Experiences	• Background • Self-identity • Roles	• Roots • Personal history • Events	• Setting the context • Past connections	• Incidents • Sites	• Past work experiences
Present Experiences	• Current status • Level of awareness	• Current support	• Current connections	• Community experiences	• Current work experiences
Future Intentions	• Outcomes • Personal development • Self-identity	• Future support	• Future connections	• Plans for future schooling	• Future work expectations

school she applied for academic upgrading and training at the Canada Employment Centre. While she waited to get into a program, she worked at various jobs. Her time spent working as a receptionist reveals the extent of her coping skills.

> *I always managed to find a job. I'm a very determined person. Once I was a receptionist in a dental office. I did that job for a year and a half and I loved it and nobody ever knew [that I had no education]. I was very good at hiding my [lack of] education. I wanted to prove to myself that I could do this. The dentist had this chart on which every tooth had a name and number. I took that chart home and studied it for the first week. And when I came back I knew it.*

This job lasted about a year and a half, after which she went back to the Canada Employment Centre. The counsellor suggested night school as a way for Aleeta to complete her education.

Narrative core

Aleeta's life is set mostly in small towns in New Brunswick, with a short time spent on an army base in another province. There is no Canada Employment Centre on the base so she has had to travel to a nearby city to get assistance. Her memories of early experiences are set mainly in school. The Community Academic Services Program

(CASP) she attends is located in the community where she lives with her husband and children.

Her character is contradictory; at times she is helpless and seems to be a reader of her own life rather than an actor in it (Randall, 1996). She resented being put in a special class and being labelled by the time she was in Grade Two; on the other hand, she labels her son as having a learning deficit. Earlier in her life she says she knew she was slow and yet she defines herself as literate by knowing that she was the best reader in her class in high school. She predicted that she would always have to work in a restaurant, yet for a year and a half she coped as a receptionist in a dentist's office. As she speaks of her life she reveals herself as someone still seeking an original purpose. She has overcome a number of obstacles: her placement in a special class was overcome when she was able to do other subjects to prepare for junior high. The next hurdle was the work-study program. After high school, she continued to look for better jobs than the restaurant work for which she was trained and all that time, she continued to look for ways to complete her education.

Aleeta seems to lack some awareness about herself and her ability to overcome obstacles on the road to learning; however, her desire and purpose in life has centred around getting her education. She has overcome her fear of being slow and of not being able to learn without "a lot of teaching." Aleeta doesn't want the easy way in life for herself or her children. She has always wanted more challenges and has looked for them. These all point towards her abilities as a problem solver. She is beginning to understand that she is smart and literate, but that she has some sort of learning disability. Her varied abilities are mirrored in her son. As she learns more about his learning and how to help him, it is likely that she will begin to better understand her own way of thinking.

Bea

Bea recounts strong memories of early experiences.

> *I'm scared to go to counselling because of what I might remember. I know for a fact I was molested when I was nine. Out of all my childhood, I can remember four things. I can remember going to the Salvation Army and buying myself a bathing suit and a sweater; I can*

*remember going to the hairdresser and getting my hair washed for
25 cents because it was so long my [adopted] mother wouldn't wash
it; I can remember being molested when I was nine years old, I remember who he was and his name; and I can remember going to my
[adopted] mother's the day the Children's Aid took me there.* 99

Narrative core

The main theme of Bea's story, which is set mainly in her personal
world, is her sense of herself as a survivor. Early on, she was the passive
recipient of events she was unable to control or stop. After she left her
"home" and school in Grade Seven, she seemed to develop a sense of
autonomy. She says herself that when she was doing something for herself, her life was much better.

In raising her two children, she has tried to keep them from the same
kind of abuse that she had suffered. For example, one of Bea's children
faced a potentially abusive incident at the hands of Bea's mother's new
husband. Bea was terrified that history would repeat itself — and was
relieved when the child "had the good sense to get out of there and call
me." She reports: "We took him to court and the whole works." Since
then she has chosen not to speak to her mother. Bea's parting words
to her mother were "What about your two grandchildren? They are
the only ones you have and he has tried to ruin their lives." When her
mother responded, "What about his life?" Bea answered, "If you choose
him over me and your grandchildren, then don't ever bother me again."

Bea's experiences at school cast a pall over her life. Though she was
always literate she did not complete her schooling as she struggled to meet
other more basic needs. Not until she had established a home and raised
her own children was she able to think about continuing her education. In
spite of a difficult childhood, Bea learned independence early, an attitude
that has seen her safely through to adulthood. Her future intentions for
learning more and for working as a secretary are grounded in an experiential reality that she has created and maintained since childhood.

This representation convinces the listener of its trustworthiness — if
it is coherent, whole and if events conform to the conventions of com-
edy, romance, tragedy, and satire (Murray, 1986). Bruner (1987) tells us
that there are only so many stories and that most narratives can be categorized through the use of cultural traditions, archetype and myths.
Connelly and Clandinin (1990) remind the researcher to be mindful of

the events as lived and the events as told. Further, they write that the process of narrative inquiry is, in part, a shared narrative, construction and reconstruction. This idea finds support in Bruner as he writes a life as led is inseparable from a life as told — or — a life is not how it was but how it is interpreted and reinterpreted, told and retold.

Weiss

Weiss finishes his interview by pondering what the future holds for members of his generation.

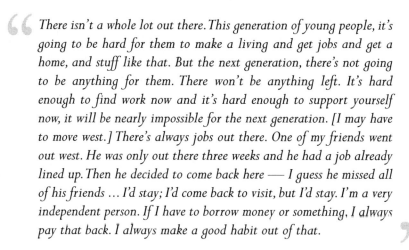

> *There isn't a whole lot out there. This generation of young people, it's going to be hard for them to make a living and get jobs and get a home, and stuff like that. But the next generation, there's not going to be anything for them. There won't be anything left. It's hard enough to find work now and it's hard enough to support yourself now, it will be nearly impossible for the next generation. [I may have to move west.] There's always jobs out there. One of my friends went out west. He was only out there three weeks and he had a job already lined up. Then he decided to come back here — I guess he missed all of his friends ... I'd stay; I'd come back to visit, but I'd stay. I'm a very independent person. If I have to borrow money or something, I always pay that back. I always make a good habit out of that.*

Narrative core

At 19, Weiss's life story has more future intentions than past experiences. The only setting in which we meet Weiss is in the schools of rural New Brunswick. He is the main character in his own story. The only other character who enters his story in any significant way is his uncle whom he looks up to as a role model. The students he met in the high schools, even those he is meeting at CASP, do not play an important part in his story. He mentions only one teacher, an art teacher, who may have influenced his love of drawing. Other teachers have been included in his story to the extent that he perceives them as helping or hindering his school progress.

Weiss is the protagonist in this tale. He is a young hero just beginning his quest, an archetype frequently encountered in male life stories (Randall, 1996). He presents himself as wiser than others his age and as trying hard to live up to certain standards. He wants to do things with his life and knows that his journey is only beginning. He sees himself as independent and as being in charge of creating and managing his own destiny. A major theme running through his story is survival. However, when he speaks of his hopes for his own future and that of the younger generation, he expresses a darker more uncertain feeling. In his study of autobiography, Bruner (1987) says these formal structures may get laid down early in the discourse of family life and persist stubbornly in spite of changed conditions. Basic formal properties of the life do not change easily.

Nadia

During our talk, Nadia mentioned her mechanical ability and her knowledge of motors. She is a bit discouraged about the possibility of becoming a mechanic or a carpenter in the future which is what she has always wanted to do. Some of her so-called friends have told her, "Oh, girls don't do that" and "You'll never get a job." Such reactions make her feel like her foster parents are still with her. Nadia is now considering that she might want to become a kindergarten teacher. She says of herself, "I've got a lot of anger in me and it's pushing me to where I want to go because a lot of people really make me mad. I don't like people using me."

Narrative core

Nadia's story is much influenced by her past life. Her current setting is her marriage and motherhood. She says, "I was a mother with my husband. I didn't need to work, I didn't need an education." She now sees that this existence was dream-like and that she has awakened to her need for education. She wants to prove "Hey, I'm something."

Nadia speaks of being abandoned by the system, defining herself as an orphan, the outsider who didn't know anything (Bruner, 1987). She also defines herself as a victim, someone whose ignorance is not her fault. She describes herself as angry and implies that she is a dangerous character. She seems to inspire fear in those who meet her, and she says, "I don't like people; I don't get close to people; people hurt people." The violence and rejection that characterized her past life are still with her.

Anger drives the action in her story and moves her forward through life. Leaving abusive foster parents who did not care enough and a school that could not help her, to live on the streets at 14 years, has left Nadia with plenty to be mad about. Some equilibrium entered her life when she was first married and her children were small, but this contentment didn't last. As her children became older, she became aware that her lack of knowledge interfered with her peaceful existence. So she decided to go out to do battle once again to make something of herself. Her quest for more learning may be resolved at the CASP. Other issues in her life remain unresolved until she can accept herself. (Bruner, 1987)

LITERACY AS A SOCIAL PRACTICE

The learners' literacy, as described in their narratives, was implicit and subtle. Some of the lessons learned are based on the complexity of the learners' everyday literacies and the role these play both in their lives and in the Community Academic Services Program (CASP) curriculum. The learners' own narratives offer a series of texts that are consistent with the literacy needs of their lives. As Knowles has observed, adult education programs that "do not value the person's experiences do not value the person" (Droegkamp & Taylor, 1995, p. 35). The use of learners' stories and experiences as texts contributes greatly to the development of learners' interests and hence to their development of literacy (Mace, 1992, 1994a).

Everyday social literacy practices amongst learners occurred daily at the Community Academic Services Program (CASP) and in their families and communities. The meanings constructed in relation to everyday texts and literacies included discussions of television soap operas, current best sellers, and their current negotiations for meaning with their children and partners. Barton and Hamilton (1998) point out that the vernacular literacies of learners absorb and incorporate the dominant literacy forms, transforming the dominant forms for their own everyday purposes. The CASP curriculum could benefit from searching out and incorporating both learners' stories and their vernacular literacies.

Making use of learners' interests

The post-literacy interests of the learners suggest another source of literacy learning that could be used by the CASP curriculum. Weiss wants to drive a truck cross-country, Bea to survive her past and work as a secretary, Nadia to be somebody. The CASP offers her an opportunity to write. The CASP in the words of one learner was "a meeting place — to learn." This evokes the notion espoused by Belenky (1996) of public homeplaces where learners can re-enter the world of adult learning, and develop their voice and literacy interests at the same time.

Parents helping to motivate children

The family connection in the case of the CASP is problematic. The learners who are parents expressed concern about their children in school and struggled to be a part of their children's schooling. The schools do not appear to have changed much from the days when the learners themselves attended and did not finish. Many in this study felt that since they had returned to CASP, their children were more motivated to get an education. An explanation for this may rest, not so much in CASP parents helping with homework or reading to their children, but rather upon the parents' increased knowledge of schooling and of how to advocate on their children's behalf.

For the majority of learners in the study by Richmond (1999), early home, school and personal experiences were not a good fit with school-based literacy. By ignoring the social, cultural and economic contexts of these learners, the system failed them, leaving them out of the educational mainstream. The learners found themselves excluded and marginalized, a condition most humans do not want for themselves. Most of the learners enter the CASP wanting to "Get my education." The phrase "getting an education" seems to be related not so much to their ability to read and write, but to their right to be included. In New Brunswick, the GED, a Grade Twelve diploma, or the Adult High School Certificate endows the learner with the right to be included in the world of work or the world of occupational skill training, and hence to be included as a productive contributor to the economics of the dominant literacy.

NEW DIRECTIONS FOR LITERACY RESEARCH

Consideration of a learner's experience as the basis of the curriculum finds support in reading research. Here as in adult literacy education the focus is on literacy becoming more concerned with context and meaning making. Whole language proponents, such as Goodman (1991), and others concerned with socially constructed knowledge (Bruner, 1994) are a reflection of the general trends found in the social sciences away from positivistic and objective generalities, specific to a single discipline or context "towards being more reflexive, focusing on the particular and of being interdisciplinary" (Barton, 1994, p. 7). In order to become literate, the learner, whether child or adult, must construct meaning and learn reciprocally (Smith, 1988). In this view learners use their own experience as the basis for their literacy.

Many learners in the study under discussion (Richmond, 1999) expressed strong interest in learning about computers — although most do not have computers in their homes or use them in their daily life. Mace (1992, 1994a) would describe this as a post-literacy interest, one that could lead to significant learning. According to Street (1984), the need for technology could be used within the learner's curriculum to enable rather than cause the learner to gain literacy. Other post-literacy needs expressed by the New Brunswick learners include the use of television as a part of the technical and communicative knowledge sought. Almost all the learners (95 percent) in the study reported watching television (Richmond, 1999). Parents also reported that television affects their children's learning. Television therefore may be viewed as an "everyday text" that may not always be approved of by the dominant literacy group (Barton & Hamilton, 1998). Television literacy brings other worlds into the family home and needs to be acknowledged as a social practice in people's lives.

Other researchers in the new literacy studies examine literacy from an everyday point of view. Barton (1994, p. 3–4), for example, considers the breakfast table literacy events that go on each morning — listening to the radio, reading the newspaper, engaging in conversation, writing a note to the teacher, or writing a reminder to oneself — as all being literacy practices. He views literacy as social, with literacy events and practices embedded in every context and situation.

The learners in this study experience literacy events and perform literacy practices at home, in the adult literacy program and in the community. Each literacy event or practice is differently structured by the social institution in which it takes place. The grocery list written at home to be read while shopping would not be appropriately written at the adult literacy class. In the adult education classroom, literacy events and practices would be reflective of the uses of literacy in that particular social institution: for example, solving math problems, reading a piece of prose, or writing the answer to a comprehension question.

Barton points out that there are many literacies in an individual's life, each "... associated with different domains ... home, school, church and work — they give rise to different practices" (Barton, 1994, p. 39). The domains of home and school figure greatly in the study of learners' and community literacy. The new literacy recognizes the literacy inherent in the individual rather than blaming the individual for having deficits. Learners "bring with them culture specific literacy practices and ways of knowing" (Auerbach, 1995a, p. 651). These multiple literacies are to be recognized and valued, not changed.

DISCOVERING LITERACY AND POST-LITERACY NEEDS AND INTERESTS THROUGH LEARNERS' STORIES

The policy maker, the curriculum designer, the facilitator or tutor all need to listen to the learners' stories to bridge the gap between literacy as a tool of the mainstream, and understanding the post-literacy needs of the low literate learners. Knowledge of how adults learn and principles therein can serve as a guide to policy and educational planners. Education research into adult learning theories has much to offer (Belenky, Clinchy, Goldberger & Tarule, 1986; Mezirow, 1997). These principles and theories have led to the design of both non-formal and formal adult education programs.

The learners' stories describe subjective literacy knowledge. The work of literacy researchers, such as Auerbach (1995a), Barton (1994), Barton and Hamilton (1998), Fingeret and Jurmo (1989), Mace (1992, 1994a), and Street (1984), describe a wide range of literacy concepts that can be understood as received literacy knowledge. Integrating these subjective and received sources of literacy knowledge into constructed knowledge leads to such ideas and recommendations as the following.

- *Learners must develop their own stories before they can develop their literacy skills.* This enhances self-knowledge and increases self-esteem. Self-knowledge comes from examining the hidden assumptions of one's meaning perspectives and self-esteem comes from feeling valued and successful. The CASP curriculum could benefit from activities designed to promote the development of learner narratives through critical reflection on one's life experiences and the circumstances of one's life.

- *Learners must be encouraged to develop interests that will initially motivate their literacy learning and later will provide post-literacy motives for continuing to better their lives.* Individual interests must be discovered and encouraged first and the desire to become literate will follow from these interests. The CASP curriculum could benefit from activities designed to help learners explore their own interests and needs rather than initially engaging in learning based on the objective knowledge approved by the dominant and authoritative social and political groups.
- *The vernacular literacies characterizing the learners' homes and communities could be used to encourage interests in literacy learning.* For example, local stories and newspapers could bring multiple literacies into close contact with the dominant literacy of the school and workplace along with the learners' personal experiences to encourage the construction of meaning and whole language learning.

REFERENCES

Auerbach, E. (1995a). Deconstructing the discourse of strengths in family literacy. *Journal of Reading Behavior, 27*(4), 643–661.

Auerbach, E. (1995b). Which way for family literacy: Intervention or empowerment. In L. Morrow (Ed.), *Family literacy: Connections in schools and communities.* New Brunswick, DE: International Reading Association.

Barton, D. (1994). *Literacy: An introduction to the ecology of written language.* Oxford, UK: Blackwell Publishers.

Barton, D., & Hamilton, M. (1998). *Local literacies.* London, UK: Routledge.

Belenky, M.F. (1996). Public homeplaces. In N. Goldberger, J. Tarule, B. Clinchy, & M. Belenky (Eds.), *Knowledge, difference and power.* New York: Basic Books.

Belenky, M., Clinchy, B., Goldberger, N. & Tarule, J. (1986). *Women's ways of knowing: The development of self, voice, and mind.* New York: Basic Books.

Bruner, J. (1987). Life as narrative. *Social Research, 54*(1), 11–32.

Bruner, J. (1994). From communicating to talking. In B. Stierer & J. Maybin (Eds.), *Language literacy and learning in educational practice.* Bristol, PA: Multilingual Matters.

Connelly, F. & Clandinin, D. (1990). Stories of experience and narrative inquiry. *Educational Researcher, 19*(5), 2–14.

Conti, G. (1989). Teaching styles and the adult basic educator. In M. Taylor & J. Draper (Eds.), *Adult literacy perspectives.* Toronto, ON: Culture Concepts Inc.

Cranton, P. (Ed.). (1997). *Transformative learning in action: Insights from practice.* San Francisco, CA: Jossey-Bass.

Droegkamp, J., & Taylor, K. (1995) Prior learning assessment, critical self-reflection, and reentry women's development. In K. Taylor & C. Marienau (Eds.), *Learning environments for women's adult development: Bridges towards change.* San Francisco, CA: Jossey-Bass.

Fingeret, A., & Jurmo, P. (Eds.). (1989). *Participatory literacy education.* San Francisco, CA: Jossey-Bass.

Freire, P. (1978). *Pedagogy in process: The letters to Guinea-Bissau.* New York: Seabury Press.

Freire, P. (1994). *Pedagogy of hope.* New York: Continuum.

Goodman, K. (1991). Whole language: What makes it whole? In B. Miller & R. Hubbard (Eds.), *Literacy in process*. Portsmouth, NH: Heinemann.

Mace, J. (1992). *Talking about literacy: Principles and practices of adult literacy education*. New York: Routledge.

Mace, J. (1994a). Literacy interests or literacy needs? Contexts and concepts of adults reading and writing. *Convergence, 27*(1) 57–67.

Mace, J. (1994b). Reflections and revisits. In M. Hamilton, D. Barton, & R. Ivanic (Eds.), *Worlds of literacy*. Clevedon, UK: Multilingual Matters.

Mezirow, J. (1995). Transformation theory of adult learning. In M.R. Welton (Ed.), *In defense of the lifeworld: Critical perspectives on adult learning*. Albany, NY: State University of N.Y. Press.

Mezirow, J. (1997). Transformative learning: Theory to practice. In P. Cranton (Ed.), *Transformative learning in action: Insights from practice*. San Francisco, CA: Jossey-Bass.

Miller, J. (1988). *The holistic curriculum*. Toronto, ON: OISE Press.

Miller, J., Caisse, J., & Drake, S. (1990). *Holistic learning: A teacher's guide to integrated studies*. Toronto, ON: OISE Press.

Mishler, E. (1986). The analysis of interview-narratives. In T. Sarbin (Ed.), *Narrative psychology: The storied nature of human conduct*. New York: Praeger.

Murray, K. (1986). Literary pathfinding: The work of popular life constructors. In T. Sarbin (Ed.), *Narrative psychology: The storied nature of human conduct*. New York: Praeger.

Pratt, D. (1993). Andragogy after twenty-five years. In S. Merriam (Ed.), *An update on adult learning theory*. San Francisco, CA: Jossey-Bass.

Randall, W. (1996). Restorying a life: Adult education and transformative learning. In G. Kenyon & J. Ruth (Eds.), *Aging and biography: Explorations in adult development*. New York: Springer Publishing Co.

Richmond, H. (1999). *Family and community literacy*. Unpublished doctoral dissertation, University of Nottingham, UK.

Stierer, B., & Maybin, J. (Eds.). (1994). *Language, literacy and learning in educational practice*. Clevedon, UK: Multilingual Matters.

Street, B. (1984). *Literacy in theory and practice*. Cambridge, UK: Cambridge University Press.

The Dominant Literacy
Subdued Lives

William T. Fagan

While literacy should be a cohesive factor within society, it often becomes the basis for divisiveness. Rather than providing for behaviour around reading and writing experiences that lead to more productive lives on the part of all, it sometimes gives an advantage to upper socioeconomic levels of society. In this chapter I attempt to provide an understanding of the co-existence of dominant literacy and subdued lives within the context of coastal communities of Newfoundland and Labrador. This understanding is based on the literacy experiences of people from times past, and on literacy opportunities and their implications for people in the present. The quotes, which provide a personal dimension to these experiences, come from those who participated in workshops or interviews by Woodrow (in press) or Fagan (1998). This chapter further extends the definition of literacy as social practices as espoused in Norton's earlier chapter. The experiences described here, while based on a Newfoundland and Labrador context, have implications for a range of geographical and social settings.

HISTORICAL VIEW ON PRACTICES

A senior in a Newfoundland outport was noted for saying, "You can't know where you're going to if you don't know where you're coming from." In order to understand how literacy currently influences and impacts the lives of people, and what the trend might be in the future, it is important to understand life and literacy in times past.

Life in coastal communities

Newfoundland and Labrador coastal people may be considered a proto-type of the natural features of their communities. Ruggedness and strength, resistance and daring are evident in both. The Newfoundland and Labrador coast is noted for its stark headlines, reefs and shoals. While it is also dotted by safe harbours and security, the sudden changes in wind and wave conditions often provide a challenge too great for some people in reaching this security. Life in coastal communities can be considered a paradoxical existence. There was stability in uncertainty, celebration in hardship, and independence in servitude.

As seniors reflected on times past, they agreed, "There were lots of fish," "Fish was not a problem." Not only were there lots of fish, but the means for catching them had changed little over generations. As each generation came of age, it was simply a matter of deciding to participate in the life of their forebears or look elsewhere. People have always moved away from coastal communities, but they went to seek greener pastures, or search for adventure and challenge. They were not "forced out" as are young people of today. While fish was in abundance, prices were not. Not only were prices low, but the people were part of a credit system, which was a form of servitude to the merchants. One senior described it as fol-lows, "You'd go to the merchant in the spring and he'll let you have your supplies ... but you had to sell all your fish to him." Not only did they owe their income from each voyage for food and other supplies, but the mer-chant set the prices of fish and goods so that, in most cases, "fish was low and flour was high." Under such conditions, it is not surprising that peo-ple were resourceful and they narrated the uses one could get from the sacks that flour came in: pillow cases, dish cloths, slips, underwear, table cloths, bed spreads, and sheets. People were also resourceful in being jacks of all trades. Whatever needed to be done to build or maintain hous-es, boats, or other structures could be done locally. The boat was an extension of people in this regard. It was used not just for fishing, but also for bringing salt, wood, and other provisions. People grew up being cooperative and supportive of one another. Life was hard but life was simple. Technology had not intruded. There was no sophisticated fishing equipment. "All you had was a compass and a clock. You got to steer off for a certain length of time and hope that you'll find your gear."

A person's worth was measured by honesty, reputation, and pride in what the individual had worked for. "Honesty is the best policy, see. You know you could go anywhere from Labrador to St. John's. Once you're knowed, you're knowed. What do the Bible tell you about a good name; it's better than all the riches." They shied away from loans because "then if I can't pay for it I won't have nothing then because there'd be someone come and take it."

Changes came. People readjusted and continued as had generations before. The prosperity of some communities declined and others replaced them as supply centres. This happened in some areas when salt fish processing gave way to fresh fish processing. Confederation with Canada in 1949 brought many demands for more literacy through the completion of forms for family allowance and other social benefits. Those who couldn't write turned to those who could and in their cooperative spirit they solved the problem and kept living. However, technology was what completely changed their lives, a change they are still wrestling with. One person aptly used the expression, "There's no point jumping into a puncheon if a barrel will do" (a puncheon equals four barrels). With encroaching technology, people were more inclined to jump into puncheons.

Education

Education in coastal communities in times past mirrored the people who lived there. They were resourceful in education and measured it by its need. They accepted what was within their grasp. They availed themselves of the services of others when needed. One informant summarized the role of school in this way, "Schooling was important to get enough to be able to read and write and the main thing was being a hard worker." Each generation acquired the skills of hard workers as "learning apprentices." There was much truth in the saying, "It takes a community to educate a child." The community was the teacher. One person explained the process in one particular instance:

> And the first little one I built [model boat], my grandfather showed me some of it, and there was an old gentleman that lived across the harbour; his son built a little boat before he went overseas and I copied from that one. The old gentleman told me how to do it, how to mark it off, to get the shape of the boat, and then my grandfather gave me an idea on how, what we call scarfing the boat, putting the head and the stern and that on to it, and from there I went on my own.

Partly because of how people learned necessary skills, and partly because of the nature of the work, a lot of formal education was not necessary. Stories were told of men who could not write their name but who "could use a compass and get through the worst kind of weather" or who "could not be fooled in figures when it came to calculating bills." Schools that did exist in coastal communities were, in many cases, one room schools. The basis of schooling was "reading, writing, arithmetic, respect, and discipline." The importance of knowing how to read, write and do arithmetic among a fishing crew was explained by one senior this way: "You know you got to have somebody in your crew who had education because you wouldn't get neither cent. You'd be rogued to death. You'd be robbed to death." Progress in school was determined by the reading book you were in, usually the Royal Readers. In addition to the basics, there was useful knowledge such as the uses of wool. Related to useful knowledge were lessons in manners which were based on readings. One senior could still recite a poem used for this purpose.

> "Spread jam on my bread," said Fred.
> His mother gave him a cross look.
> And Fred's face grew red and his head sank on his breast.
> He felt he had been rude.
> "Please, mother," he now said, "Spread some jam on my bread."
> So his mother spread some jam on his bread with a smile.

The sons and daughters of fishers recognized the limits of their opportunity for education. In some cases there were exceptions, thanks to the Grenfell Missions for those who lived in communities that they served. In one case, a gentleman, who lived in the Mission orphanage, was able to get a good education, and in other cases, the Mission sent promising students to the United States to train as teachers, nurses, or technicians. But in most cases, further education was for the elite. "Only one who'd go to college or anything was a doctor's son or someone like that, a merchant's son. No such thing as a fisherman's son going to college at that time and getting any education." "They [fishers] didn't have the means to send you for one thing and then you were a fisherman's son and you weren't supposed to know anything, you know."

But to conclude that there was little literacy or education occurring within the communities would be erroneous. Non-formal education was alive and well. Because their livelihoods were tied to the control of outside forces, such as the world of trading conditions, prices, and the like, people kept informed of pertinent information. They read the *Family Fireside* newspaper and union flyers, and listened to the Fisherman's Broadcast on radio. If there is such as thing as "training one's memory," they did so superbly. Years afterwards, seniors could name dozens of politicians, union, business and other people who had, in some way, an impact on their communities. Some people attended night school, or a cooperative school established by a field worker enlisted by the Grenfell Mission. The latter also provided a study club. People in the community knew who were readers and writers and availed of their skills. There were stories of several people gathering at the house of a reader, who would read for hours. "Some of the older fellows couldn't read, you know, but they could tell you after you read it to them. They could tell me better than what I remembered." Those who could write wrote to politicians or others on behalf of the community. Most of the seniors who were interviewed still read, and named a range of reading interests, from biography, to fiction, to spiritual text.

Literacy was measured according to its need within the community and according to the expectations of the people. The people lived sub-dued lives that were matched by their possession of a subdued literacy. They were aware of its limits. They knew that literacy of dominance was possessed by those who controlled many aspects of their lives — the merchants, the politicians, the clergy.

A CRITICAL REFLECTION
ON COMMUNITIES IN CHANGE

Change is inevitable. In such times people look for "threads of hope." Unfortunately, such hope is often tempered by "counter threads" limit-ing a person's ability to adapt to and capitalize on change.

Life continued in rural Newfoundland and Labrador, much as it had for generations before, until July 2, 1992. At that time, John Crosbie, minister of Fisheries and Oceans, announced a two-year moratorium on the northern cod fishery in Atlantic Canada. Other groundfish closures were to occur, and by 1994, the future for employment in the fishery was bleak, with mounting evidence that commercially exploitable levels of this resource would not return until the end of the century.

This drastic, but necessary action by the federal government did not take the fishers by surprise. What it again demonstrated was a division between the dominant literacy of bureaucrats and the pragmatically meaningful literacy of the local people. The fishers had "read" the signs of codfish depletion for years prior to July 1992. They had attempted to make their views known to the bureaucrats but were ignored because those who read books and studied figures in an official capacity were the recognized authority. The local fishers went so far as to try and use the dominant literacy of the legal system and took court action against the federal minister of the environment. Pat Cabot was called on as an expert witness, and stated that he "was convinced we are going to end up with a watery desert" (Woodrow & Ennis, 1999, p. 22), which is exactly what happened.

The closure generated massive changes in the lives of individuals and in the fabric of community life. In areas where two-income earners were affected by the closure, women managed the severe reduction in household income by robbing Peter to pay Paul. A hush settled over small communities with a traditional dependence on groundfish (that is, fish like cod and haddock that swim close to the bottom of the sea). Relationships changed, as people spent more time together inside their homes. Animosities developed between those recognized for the income replacement program and those who were disqualified or not eligible. After all, didn't everybody depend on fish in coastal communities? Weren't jobs tied to the economic health of the fishery?

Thread one: Income, adjustment support and paper work

At the time of the announcement of the cod moratorium, a Northern Cod Adjustment Recovery Program (NCARP) was announced, and replaced in 1994 by The Atlantic Groundfish Strategy (TAGS). Special units were created with Human Resources Development Canada (HRDC) and the Department of Fisheries and Oceans (DFO). Almost $2-billion was spent as part of this government strategy.

In 1993 the Task Force on Adjustment in the Atlantic Fisheries concluded that a future sustainable fishery would require only one-half of the industry workforce that had participated prior to the moratorium. Consequently, the NCARP and TAGS programs offered industry workers access to a range of programs including career planning and counselling, early retirement, licence buybacks, mobility assistance, skills training, academic upgrading, and income support. To be eligible for income support, people must be actively involved in labour adjustment efforts.

Each of these initiatives immersed the fishers and their families in a range of bureaucratic literacy practices. Paper work replaced hard work. People were required to provide responses to questionnaires, complete survey forms, read letters that defined their eligibility and status as clients, and write letters appealing bureaucratic decisions. For those beginning to participate in alternative fisheries, logbooks reporting on their catches had to be completed, and species-specific licence documents that stretched over 14 pages complied with. These data could have been gathered through other means, including records of employment and annual income tax returns.

Additional paperwork appeared to be an essential feature of bureaucratic literacy — literacy of control and regulation. People experienced a rapid change in the relationship of literacy practices to economic development. According to bureaucratic decision, a fishery of the future would consist of multi-species operations. Fishers would need to prepare to fish in deep waters in boats costing from $200,000 to $500,000. Very few fishers could finance this expansion, and banks were not in the habit of lending money to fishers. Purchasing and outfitting those boats with gear and technology often meant a return to the economic relationships of their elders. In these contemporary times, fishers would have to commit their product to buyers who financed their expansion into a new fishery.

Arch, an 85-year-old retired fisher, noted that when he started fishing on his own, there wasn't any paperwork or licences associated with the fishery. But before "I knocked off, there was a money purse full of licences." Now his sons own the business, and the captain has an office on land. "He's got everything there. You got to be almost a lawyer to run it." Frank, a young skipper in his mid-thirties, has doubled the number of files he keeps on his family's fishing enterprise. "You almost want a brief case. When I go fishing that's what I do — take the brief case."

The increased paperwork became a rationale for promoting enrollment in education programs. The fishery was to become professionalized and the level of professionalism accorded to the fishers would be decided by a Professional Fish Harvesters Certification Board.

Thread two: Life skills programs

Counsellors from the federal programs contacted their list of displaced fishers and plant workers about their future goals. Mildred, a 50-year-old plant worker, was told to attend a life skills program. She and others were taught how to get along with their co-workers and bosses. Mildred did not understand the program's relevance to her life, past, present, or future. These were skills that she and her co-workers had learned in the home from their parents and displayed on the job every day.

> It almost made you feel that because you were a fisher you were stupid; because you were a fisherman or plant worker you were uneducated, but that's not true. We didn't have the same type of education but we weren't uneducated in your standards, in our morals, and in our way of life. We knew what we had to do. We were taught better than ever we could have been in school.

In earlier generations, people in coastal communities co-existed with dominant literacies. They were aware of the power of dominant literacies, and of the select few who could avail of them. By and large they were able to manage their lives through their own literacies. The lack of access to dominant literacies mostly affected those who wanted to move beyond their communities and the fishing lifestyle. However, in the 1990s, people were brought into confrontation with dominant literacies. They did not see the relationship of their imposition and their practice. Lorna was repeatedly called by her counsellor and told she must either attend an ABE program or participate in a community volunteer project. She opted for the latter and when she went to see the counsellor, she narrated the following.

> I am president of the Dart's League, a leader with the Sparks and Brownies, a member of the Firettes, and am responsible for calling the men on my husband's roster who is a volunteer fireman. I am a member of the Winter Carnival committee, and the Summer Recreation committee, a volunteer worker at the arena canteen, a member of my church women's group; we meet every Wednesday. I am a member of the 1996 High School Graduation committee and I am busy making decorations for the graduation.

He looked at her and said, "But we must have something which is official."

Thread three: Adult Basic Education programs

For those who had not completed high school, the route to skills training for work outside the fishery, or retraining within the fishery, was an ABE program. There was no distinction within this program for the two groups of participants. An ABE certificate was an essential "pass" to a next step. Women and men who had led rich, complex, and successful lives were now destined to return to a classroom situation, a situation which they had chosen to leave many years before, whether to earn money in the fishery, or because school was not a rewarding or successful experience for them. While they had been living in a world that focused on the application of practical knowledge versus the acquisition of knowledge from books, they now had to return to the latter type of learning situation.

Some took the plunge and enrolled. Of these, many found it a valuable experience, mostly in terms of personal gain. For many, it was an opportunity to prove to themselves that they could do it; they could complete a certificate that for many reasons had been denied them when they attended regular school. They developed more confidence in themselves. They were more inclined to speak out on community matters. Some were able to give more help to their school-age children. All were role models for their children. Some were able to share their skills in helping others write up their lives for government, through the completion of forms. Some, after completing the diploma, found work, particularly in the tourist industry. But while they learned to complete resumés, few saw a high school certificate as a direct route to a job.

A lot of people just did not see the relevance of academic upgrading to life or to their goals. Unfortunately, in many cases, there was little relevance. ABE or similar programs are bureaucratically designed. They tend to constitute "rites of passage" as opposed to connecting education with people's lives and goals. It sometimes became a matter of book knowledge versus world knowledge. Learners within the ABE programs questioned how memorizing the types of rock, or the circulatory system of the body was to help them become carpenters, or better fishers. Technology was epitomized as the fountain of knowledge, yet most of the displaced fishers and plant workers blamed modern technology for their plight. One person phrased her concern this way: "The knowledge is in the technology now. When they have the technology to tell one species from another, the fishery don't have a chance." Another person made the following observation: "This generation may have a lot of knowledge but they won't have as much knowledge in their head as the old people had. Modern technology killed us, along with our greed."

One assumption that underlies academic upgrading programs, whether ABE or GED, is that program enrollment equates with improved literacy standards. But in ABE programs there may be very few courses focused on helping the participants become competent and critical readers and writers. As the seniors demonstrated during their interviews, literacy must be balanced with a knowledge of people and environment, and with a lot of common sense. Becoming critical participants through reading and writing is not learned solely from books, but from a combination of texts, environment, and lived experience. Learners through academic upgrading programs must acquire those very skills that give dominant literacy the edge. The learners must be able to acquire those very same literacy skills that enable them to meet the bureaucrats on their own terms. This point is constantly emphasized by Delpit (1988), a literacy activist among low-income African-Americans, and other disadvantaged groups. The myth that certification equals a satisfactory level of literacy functioning must be shaken.

The overall success of this post-cod moratorium experience in improving educational (literacy?) standards is debatable. Prior to TAGS funded programs, the percentage of funding-eligible people with up to Grade Eight level of education was 41.1. The percentage of people in this group after the programs had finished was 36.7. For those with some secondary education, the percentages before and after the TAGS programs were 29.0 and 25.9. Overall, over 60 percent of adults eligible for participation in these programs still had not completed high school. It seemed as if there was a general resistance to dominant literacy. People who had integrated and interwoven literacy as part of their everyday lives were not convinced that the rigidity of an education program with books, memorization, and tests was to their advantage. There was a clash between the literacy of bureaucracy and their own literacies.

For those who enrolled, especially the young, without long-standing ties to the fishery or their communities, it was an opportunity to move on. However, a negative or counter thread to this was that the "youngest and most educated" were leaving coastal communities in Newfoundland and Labrador. If, as the literature on literacy points out, generational cycles have a profound effect on the literacy development of the next generation, then the implications here are self-evident. The very success of the young created mistrust and despair in the next older generation. People were convinced that the whole mismanagement of the cod fishery, and the resulting moratorium and rules and regulations were part of a plan to de-populate coastal parts of the province. The slogan that higher education means work became vacuous when one questioned where the work was. There was no work in the communities or in the province. As one person said, "To get a job at home, you'd want a dozen ABE's. There's no work and that's it." And they watched the younger generation go.

VISIONS FOR THE FUTURE

This chapter has come full cycle from where people were to where they might be going. While the data are based on the stories of people in coastal communities in Newfoundland and Labrador, it is a reasonable generalization that there are similar stories in other parts of the country — stories of farmers, miners, and factory workers who have experienced the interruption of a traditional way of life. The problem with vision is that conditions are still in flux, making the vision of a future blurred. However, from what we have learned, there are some general issues in literacy that can be addressed.

Challenging the deficit view of literacy

It is perhaps an anomaly that while coastal (and other) communities have experienced great change, schools and formal literacy programs have tended to remain stagnant. Literacy in the past was largely viewed by schools and educators from a deficit perspective and this view strongly persists. Schools are organized along vertical lines. Children enter kindergarten and progress through a vertical system to Grade Twelve and then to post-secondary. Screening begins at kindergarten and children who are not doing well are remediated to compensate for a deficit within the home and community. On a recent visit to a school, a teacher was discussing a group of kindergarten children from a low-income area and indicated that they were in a remedial class for their ABCs. Those who drop out of school, or who receive a certificate without adequate competency in reading and writing, eventually enroll in adult literacy programs. There they are helped to overcome their deficit by mastering the basics of literacy, hauntingly similar to those taught in Grade One, though embedded in adult-oriented text.

The richness of the lives of adults is neither understood nor taken into consideration. The horizontal nature of literacy, in which many literacies are happening simultaneously among people across communities, is ignored. The work of researchers/educators like Barton and Hamilton (1998), Heath (1983), Woodrow (in press), and Fagan (1998) is either unknown or unheeded. People's lives are embedded in literacy and vice versa. Barton and Hamilton (1998) have grouped these literacies into five categories: organizing one's life, communicating, using literacy for leisure, document-ing one's life, and seeking information. Heath (1983) has pointed out that these literacies are ignored because they do not correspond to the literacies valued by the school. Literacy programs, both school and adult, must shift their perceptions of literacy from a set of skills people do not have, but need, to that of multiple literacies abounding in communities and families.

Recognize literacy practices

Closely related to the previous point is the need to acknowledge the lit-eracy practices that occur in communities. Woodrow (in press) and Fagan (1998), in participant-observer workshops, alerted the partici-pants to the myriad of literacies that occur in communities on a daily basis, as well as those that have a historical basis. For example, in one community, photographs taken by participants showed laneways with names like Pride's Drong or Drong's Hill. The person who could give a meaning for "drong" was the one with the least success in academic lit-eracy, a drong being a road or laneway from a main road to gain access to fishing premises on the waterfront. Literacy texts can no longer include only the printed material of traditional literacy. The communi-ties must be a source of text, whether the functional meaning of road-way signs, or signs and slogans of a political or social nature. Literacy practices must be merged with literacy knowledge.

Unless literacy is practiced there is no literacy. The literacy practices that are currently illustrated in communities are the models for how lit-eracy is practiced. It makes sense that in literacy programs, learners become knowledgeable of what literacy is for. Learners must be provided the opportunity to become critical users of reading and writing. They must be able to weigh the uses of reading and writing against the observed needs within their lives. They must be able to become participants in dom-inant literacies, not by being controlled by them, but by using them to give themselves vision, to take ownership of the present and future.

Literacy as imagination

In a recent teleconference organized by Woodrow, involving experts from North America, Britain and many local participants, one of the liveliest sessions was one on poetry by Francis Kazemek. Poetry is one form of literacy not grounded in fact or function, but entailing enjoyment and imagination. Poetry writing and reading is a valid literacy practice.

Literacy as imagination engenders a magic that seems to cast a spell on those who participate. This is true for seniors as for children. One senior, whose interview data were used in the first part of this chapter, said, "I get up at four o'clock in the morning when I get a good book." During the teleconference the participants shared how poetry writing and reading sparks their imagination and creates magic for them.

> "I experience magic when I become the story I am reading."
> "When I finish a book, I miss the characters for a day or two."
> "Magic occurs when we want to express a strong feeling or emotion."
> "The magic of literacy is that we begin in our own language, in the language that we know, and the language of the people that we know in our community."

Literacy learners must become knowledgeable and experienced in the broad perspective of literacy — from the boring treatise, to the latest by-law, to the exciting story, to the newly created poem. Experiencing literacy as imagination takes time, but to deprive learners of this time is to interrupt an important facet of literacy. Perhaps, all writing has a magic to it as suggested by one participant.

> Gently coaxing words into my mind
> Caressing them, discarding them
> Like shattered pieces of pottery.
> Picking them up again and trying to piece them together.
> Words.
> Pieces broken.
> Write, right now.
>
> Jeanette Winsor

(Reproduced with permission from the author)

RETROSPECTION

It is unfortunate that a corollary to dominant literacy is subdued lives. In historical times in coastal communities in Newfoundland and Labrador, people knew their place in terms of the dominance of literacy. They knew that only the privileged or lucky could aspire to a life beyond the fishery. Consequently, they made the best of what they had and became experts at doing it, including the utilization of whatever literacy skills or literacy resources were available to them.

In contemporary times, people were offered an opportunity to participate in accessing a dominant form of literacy but through a bureaucratic process and for bureaucratic purposes. Actually, it may be called "controlled literacy," rather than "dominant literacy" since their use of it was controlled by others. If ordinary people are to acquire dominant literacy, this literacy must allow them to take ownership of their own lives. This means being competent in engaging in literacy practices that are meaningful in terms of their daily lives. In addition, they must acquire those literacy skills and competencies that enable them to understand, challenge, and act on literacies originating at bureaucratic levels.

End note

I am indebted to Helen Woodrow for much of the data on which this chapter is based. Her literacy practices project, including interviews, literacy practice workshops, and teleconferences, contributed significantly to the chapter content. I was privileged to participate with Helen in the workshop and teleconference experiences. Data also came from projects and interviews from my own research. While I take responsibility for the selected content and its organization within the chapter, I acknowledge Helen's contribution through informal talking, questioning, challenging, and through feedback on what I have written.

REFERENCES

Barton, D., & Hamilton, M. (1998). *Local literacies: Reading and writing in one community*. London: Routledge.

Delpit, L. (1988). The silenced dialogue: Power and pedagogy in educating other peoples' children. *Harvard Educational Review, 59*, 280–298.

Fagan, W.T. (1998). *Literacy and living*. St. John's, NF: ISER Books, Memorial University.

Heath, S.B. (1983). *Ways with words: Language, life and work in communities and classrooms*. Cambridge, MA: Cambridge University Press.

Woodrow, Helen. (in progress). *Literacy practices in coastal communities in Newfoundland and Labrador*. St. John's, NF: Educational Planning and Design.

Woodrow, H., & Ennis, F. (Eds.). (1999). *Sea people: Changing lives and times in the Newfoundland and Labrador fisheries*. St. John's, NF: Harrish Press, 1999.

The Demographics of Low Literacy

Susan Sussman

I am not a "numbers" person. Everything I still remember about math, I learned in high school. Nevertheless, this chapter chronicles my journey through the land of literacy statistics, highlighting discoveries that surprised me along the way. At one time I would have thought that nothing could be more dull or inaccessible than literacy statistics. However, my journey has proven otherwise, leading me to question many of my assumptions and much of what I see as commonly held beliefs on the subject of literacy. It has transformed my understanding of Canada's literacy challenges.

I am employed by the Ontario Literacy Coalition (OLC), a provincial non-profit association of individuals and organizations who share a commitment to promoting and increasing literacy in Ontario. As OLC's executive director since 1993, I've been invited to make more than 100 public presentations to a wide variety of audiences. At nearly every presentation, I have been asked to talk about literacy statistics describing the size and shape of literacy problems in this province. Thus, my foray into the land of literacy statistics began as just another business trip fueled by my professional responsibilities.

I invite you to join me as I retrace my route. In the first section, I describe some signs I saw along the way that led me to look at literacy statistics from a demographic perspective. In the second section, I explain decisions I made about how to categorize the demographic data. Findings of this analysis are presented in the third part. Finally, the chronicle of my journey concludes with reflections on the findings and the implications I see for the future.

SIGNS ALONG THE WAY

First sign: avoid cracks in credibility

Much of what is currently believed by policy makers about adult literacy rates in Canada is based on the findings of the International Adult Literacy Survey (Statistics Canada, 1995). Current ideas about the causes and consequences of low literacy appear to be closely linked to the available analyses of IALS data. Policy responses also have followed from these analyses.

The IALS data help advance the notion of literacy as a continuum. Participants in the survey were assigned to one of five literacy levels, based on the probability of their ability to perform increasingly complex reading tasks (Level One being the lowest level, and Level Five the highest). Survey tasks were designed to resemble the kind of literacy demands encountered in everyday life. These were taken from three distinct literacy domains (prose, document and quantitative). Prose domain tasks require the ability to understand and use information from texts. Document domain tasks require the ability to understand and use print information in various formats, including forms, schedules, maps, tables and graphics. Tasks in the quantitative domain require the ability to apply arithmetic operations to numbers embedded in print.

According to the experts who have interpreted the survey results, people ranked at Level Three or higher have reading skills to cope with most everyday demands in our knowledge-based society, while those below Level Three probably do not. People at Level One are already suffering negative consequences associated with their limited literacy skills, such as low income and higher levels of unemployment. Those at Level Two are soon likely to find themselves unemployed and unemployable, as low-skilled jobs are increasingly automated and the majority of new jobs in Canada demand higher literacy skills.

I am explaining all of this to an audience of social service providers and educators in Ontario. The title of my presentation is "EverythingYou Ever Wanted to Know about IALS." The audience appears to be engaged, eagerly awaiting the statistics. With the flick of a switch on an overhead projector, I display a bar graph showing the distribution of Ontario's adult population by literacy levels. A man in the audience raises his hand. "I'd like ask a question and maybe make a comment if I may," he says. He is a senior level administrator in the local school board. I pass the microphone to him, encouraged by his keen interest in the presentation. He says, "My math skills aren't perfect, so let me check. The graph shows that 19 percent of adults in Ontario are at Level One and an additional 28 percent are at Level Two. Have I got that right?" I nod approval. "And, do I understand that you're telling us that because all those people are below Level 3 they probably have inadequate literacy skills for everyday life?" "Yes, that's what the survey says," I reply, encouraged by his clear grasp of my message.

"Hogwash!" he says. His voice, amplified by the microphone, shakes with anger. "The claim that 47 percent of the adult population has literacy problems defies common sense, logic and all my years of experience with the public. If that's what you're selling, I don't buy it." The audience is dead silent, and I think to myself that before my next presentation I'd better find a different way to talk about people at Level Two. I also think that next time maybe I should change the title of my presentation to "IALS: Handle with care."

I have made scores of similar presentations since that Tuesday morning. In nearly every one, someone in the audience expresses the same skepticism as the school board administrator. On good days, someone else in the audience rushes to my aid, adamant in their personal observation that today's youth obviously lack skills and that the schools are obviously doing a lousy job.

Second sign: Danger ahead − flagging demand

On a gray Thursday afternoon in late September, OLC staff are collating a report about priorities for future field development initiatives across the province. It summarizes what Ontario's literacy practitioners have identified as their own needs for training, resources and other types of support, during a consultation process. This document will influence decisions about the kinds of special literacy projects that will be funded by the provincial and federal governments.

The "need to attract new students" once again ranks among the top three needs identified by the field. This need has shown up as a top priority in every similar consultation conducted by OLC over the past five years. Reflecting on the pattern, I recall several literacy workers recently confiding that they are having trouble meeting their "student-contact-hour targets." These targets are like production quotas, negotiated with funders and documented in their funding agreements. Then I recall something I read seven years ago about problems associated with attracting adult literacy students.

Writing about Quebec's experience, Hautecoeur (1990) has described the paradox of "generous supply and flagging demand for literacy programs." Though Quebec's provincial program was ostensibly designed to allow school boards to expand their literacy training services in keeping with the demand, "the people presumed to have an imperative and urgent need are simply not showing up" (p. 166).

Is it just a coincidence that both Quebec and Ontario have had difficulty with recruiting students? How long-standing and widespread is this problem? Why do so few adults come forward to literacy programs, when so many are struggling with literacy each day?

Third sign: Warning — Deconstruction zone

It is an evening in early November and I'm at home flipping channels on the TV. On an educational channel I see a familiar mop of red hair. Slowly I recognize that the hair sits atop the head of Dr. David Foot, an economics professor at the University of Toronto. In 1982, when I was working as a management consultant, I collaborated with Foot on an education research project. In recent years, his ideas about the impacts of Canadian demographic patterns have become well known.

Foot's TV appearance inspires me to look at his most recent book. In it he argues that demographic information can help us understand and predict the demand for goods and services.

> *Demographics explain roughly two-thirds of everything.... Demography is the most powerful and ... underutilized tool ... to understand the past and to foretell the future (Foot, 1998, p. 8).*

The penny drops. I think to myself, if we want to improve our ability to recruit new students, obviously we need to know more about who and where potential literacy students may be. For example, how old are they? Where do they live? Are they currently employed? In other words, what are the demographics of low literacy?

Conventional presentations of the results of the IALS have focused on overall percentages of the adult Canadian population found at each of five literacy levels. For example, Calamai (1999, p. J1) reports that "48 percent of adult Canadians have some trouble with everyday reading, writing or numbers" and that "80 percent of Canadians over 65 have low literacy skills." But what about the demographic patterns within literacy levels and the implications of these patterns for policies and practices aimed at addressing low literacy? My journey begins in earnest when I decide to go back to the IALS data, this time to see if a demographic analysis sheds any light on the phenomenon of "flagging demand" for literacy education.

ASSUMPTIONS PAVE THE WAY

Analysis focuses on demographic patterns within Level One

Statistics Canada (1996) provides a wealth of data about people at five different levels of literacy proficiency, within three distinct literacy domains. At the lower end of Level One adults are unable to read anything at all in either English or French; at the upper end of this level, they are able to answer simple questions about something they've been asked to read. My reasons for focusing on Level One follow.

CREDIBILITY

The credibility of claims about Canada's literacy problems are usually called into question whenever we suggest that *nearly half* the adult population has inadequate literacy skills. When Level Two is included in the analysis of low literacy, the resulting figure is 47 percent of all adults in Ontario, age 16 years and over.

PRIORITIES

I assume that efforts to recruit literacy students are intended to target those in the community who are most likely to be in need of improving their literacy skills. The National Institute for Literacy (1998, p. 4) suggests that adults at Level One tend to be most disadvantaged by limited literacy, and that "We consider those score at the lowest level [Level One] to be most urgently in need of nationwide attention." Statistics Canada's (1996) findings about Canadians supports the view that adults at Level One are clearly the most disadvantaged.

PERSONAL RECOGNITION OF LIMITATIONS

I assume people are unlikely to sign up for literacy programs unless they see the need to do so. One of the most curious findings reported by

Statistics Canada (1996) is that the large majority of people at all levels say they are not limited by their reading skills either at work or at home. For example, with respect to tasks in the document domain, 90.8 percent of Ontarians at Level Two, 96.6 percent at Level Three, and 98.6 percent at Levels Four and Five rate their own skills for reading at work as excellent or good. A sizeable percentage of people acknowledging difficulty with reading are found only amongst those at Level One. At that level 42.1 percent rate their skills as excellent or good, while 26.2 percent rate their skills as moderate or poor and 31.7 percent have no opinion on this topic. The same pattern holds with respect to reading in daily life (document domain). We see that 90.3 percent of Ontarians at Level Two, 97.3 percent at Level Three, and 99.9 percent at Levels Four and Five rate their skills for reading in daily life as excellent or good. Although 54.6 percent at Level One also rate their reading skills for daily life as excellent or good, 45.4 percent rate their own skills as moderate or poor. (Queen's Printer for Ontario, 1998, pp. 34–37)

CONSEQUENCES OF LOW LITERACY

I assume employment-related problems might motivate a person to seek opportunities to improve his or her literacy skills. Statistics Canada (1996) reports that people at Level One are more likely than those at Levels Two or Three to be unemployed or receiving social assistance benefits. Specifically, 26 percent of those in the labour force and at Level One (prose) are unemployed, compared with 10 percent of those at Level Two and 10 percent of those at Level Three (Statistics Canada, 1996, p. 47). Similarly, 37 percent of those at Level One (prose), between the ages of 16 and 65, receive income from social assistance, compared with 28 percent of those at Level Two and 27 percent of those at Level 3 (Statistics Canada, 1996, p. 49).

Comparison of Level One adults who are under and over age 55

Within Level One there appears to be huge differences between cohorts under and over age 55. For example, the percentage of each age group at Level One ranges from 10.4 to 16.5 for all cohorts 55 years and under. In contrast, 36.7 percent of Ontarians ages 56–65 and 43.1 percent of those 65+ are at Level One. I wonder if the phenomenon of "flagging demand" is linked to how low literacy is distributed by age, coupled with perceptions of the purpose and priorities of Ontario's literacy programs.

EFFECTS OF AGE ON LEARNER MOTIVATION

Anecdotal evidence suggests that older workers, such as those age 55 and over, face myriad age-related barriers when seeking new jobs. While it may be necessary for older workers to improve their literacy skills to increase their odds of re-employment, improvements in literacy skills alone may not be sufficient to enable them to overcome all the other barriers that limit their opportunities. Furthermore, laid-off older workers are generally more likely than others to have accumulated personal savings that they can draw on until a company and/or government pension kicks in. Given both factors, an older worker may be less motivated than one who is younger to invest time or money in literacy skills upgrading in order to secure employment.

Comparison of Level One adults by mother tongue

It is a commonly held belief that Canada's literacy "crisis" is essentially a born-in-Canada problem. It is also suggested that low literacy is something significantly different from English as a Second Language (ESL). These two beliefs limit who is recruited and admitted into Ontario's adult literacy and basic skills program. Provincial guidelines state that "English-as-a-second language (ESL), (and) Actualisation linguistique en français ... activities are not funded by the Literacy and Basic Skills (LBS) Program" (Ontario Ministry of Education and Training, 1999, p. 7).

Lacking a clear definition distinguishing ESL activity from literacy activity, this guideline is currently interpreted by some in the Ontario literacy community to mean that anyone without English or French as their mother tongue is to be referred to an ESL program and not to be served by the provincial literacy program. Thus their efforts to recruit new literacy students are not likely to be designed to target those at Level One who fit the ESL category, and those that do attempt to enroll may be turned away.

FINDINGS

I began this chapter acknowledging that I am not a numbers person. Nonetheless, in my work as an advocate for literacy, I rely heavily on quantitative data about the dimensions of Ontario's literacy challenges to support claims I make about literacy problems and recommendations I offer for policies and programs to address problems. For this reason I have committed myself to understand and critically consider the numbers that I use. For a detailed account of the methodology, see Sussman (1999).

In May 1999 a consultant working for Statistics Canada was asked to independently produce demographic estimates for Level One, using conventional statistical methods. While some small differences were observed between his estimates and my own, the general directions of findings from both estimates were consistent and both sets of estimates were widely circulated in the literacy community.

The demographic patterns revealed surprised me. These estimates suggested that probably only half of Ontario adults at Level One are under age 55, while the rest are older; and that roughly four in ten Level One adults speak English or French as a second language, while the rest are native speakers of an official language. The total number of Level One adults in Ontario between ages 16 and 55 who are native speakers of English or French appears to be much smaller than the number suggested by global, more inclusive percentages reported in the IALS. For example, the IALS reports that 19 percent of all Ontario adults age 16+ are at Level One. My estimates suggest that only three in ten of all those Level One are under age 55 and have an official language mother tongue.

REFLECTIONS AND VISIONS FOR THE FUTURE

The analysis reported in this chapter calls into question many commonly held beliefs about Canada's literacy challenges. For example, it raises questions about the notion that Canada's literacy crisis is "*not* primarily an issue of immigrants or seniors" (Calamai, 1999, p. 1). It calls into question the logic of positioning literacy primarily as a labour force development issue. It sheds new light on assumptions about the responsibility of our current education system for low literacy rates amongst adults. It also suggests the need to explore the correlations between low literacy and disabilities and to look at related implications for policies and programs. Last but not least, this chapter raises questions about the extent to which the available quantitative data can help us understand the dimensions of low literacy in this country.

Effects of first language and birth place on literacy skills

Ontario's adult literacy and basic skills program, according to guidelines issued in 1999, specifically excludes ESL activities. If it is assumed that low literacy in Canada is essentially a born-in-Canada problem and it is believed that literacy education and ESL instruction are two different things, there may be some justification. However, this analysis suggests the possibility that as many as two of five adult Ontarians at Level One *do not have a Canadian official language as their mother tongue.* If this is the case, then the following inconsistency emerges: while people with English as a second language are included in the statistics used to call attention to and secure resources for Canada's literacy problem, the policies and programs established to address our literacy problems are not always accessible to them. Concerns about fairness are obvious. By excluding ESL learners from programs, yet including them in our statics, we are seriously limiting the extent to which literacy programs can be expected to "bring down the rates" of low literacy, as measured by an instrument like the IALS.

Effects of age on motivation to upgrade literacy skills

Ontario's literacy and basic skills program targets low-literate adults who need to improve their literacy skills in order to get or keep jobs. Designed and administered by the province's Workplace Preparation Branch, the program is positioned as an important part of a labour market development strategy. It is certainly true that many low-literate adults in Ontario between the ages of 16 and 55 will need to upgrade their literacy skills in order to gain or maintain employment. However, this analysis also suggests that roughly five of ten adult Ontarians at Level One may be age 55 years or over. Those who are genuinely concerned with the negative impacts of low literacy on people's daily lives will want to pay attention to the needs of this group as well.

Literacy policies and programs that emphasize employment preparation over other goals or needs may not attract or be appropriate for low-literate older adults. On the other hand, issues related to health and independence are likely to be primary concerns for this group. For example, Roberts and Fawcett (1996, p. 33–34) point out that low-literate seniors are more likely to be at highest health risk, more likely to require assistance to complete everyday tasks such as reading government information and filling out forms, and less likely to be able to independently access social assistance, health-care information and a variety of other health-related programs. The links between literacy and such issues should be an equal concern for policy makers and program deliverers.

Effects of today's schools on adult literacy

With school bashing almost a national sport in Canada, Ontario's adult literacy problems are often assumed to result from and to reflect on the failures of our education system. Yet, Statistics Canada (1996) reports that years of education is the strongest predictor of literacy levels and this analysis provides additional evidence in support of schooling.

This demographic analysis suggests that low literacy is *not* concentrated amongst young recent graduates. As already noted, people over the age of 55 appear to comprise more than five of ten of all those at Level One; more than six of ten at Level One are either over 55 or do not have an official language mother tongue. Obviously, today's schools cannot be held responsible for the low literacy rates amongst today's older Ontarians; nor does it seem reasonable to hold the schools solely responsible for literacy rates amongst non-native English or French speakers.

Correlations between low literacy and disabilities

Once those with English or French as a second language are subtracted from the pool, the number of Ontarians remaining at Level One between the ages of 16 and 55 drops dramatically. These estimates suggest the number remaining probably corresponds to no more than 10 percent of all Ontario adults in that age group. This calculation gives rise to two new questions. What is the prevalence of all congenital and acquired disabilities that could affect literacy skills (for example, learning disabilities, visual and hearing handicaps, developmental delays, acquired brain injuries, and mental illnesses)? Current estimates of the prevalence of major learning disabilities alone range from 2 percent to 5 percent of the general population (personal communication, Carol Yaworski, January 23, 2000). How many people included in Level One have some form of disability complicating their learning needs? To what extent do existing literacy policies and programs meet the needs of people with such special learning challenges? Ontario's policy makers and literacy practitioners need answers to these questions to help them understand and respond appropriately to a trend towards an increasing number of learners with special needs enrolling in their programs.

Limits of the available data

In March 2000, I requested permission to include demographic estimates produced and distributed by Statistics Canada in May 1999, in this chapter. After lengthy negotiation, permission was denied with the explanation that the sample of Ontarians included in the IALS was, in fact, too small to provide statistically reliable answers to the demographic questions being posed (i.e., what portion of those at Level One in Ontario are under age 55 and have an official language mother tongue?). That surprising turn of events calls into question the validity of both sets of estimates — those I produced on my own using data reported in the IALS and the census, and those subsequently produced for and by Statistics Canada. By extension, it also calls attention to some limitations of IALS data.

Without a doubt, the IALS has been instrumental in keeping the issue of literacy on the public agenda by showing that a large percentage of Canadians clearly struggle with low literacy. However, if the sample used for the IALS is too small to tell us *which people* are most likely to want or need help with literacy, then the survey does not give us the information needed to support the development of programs. This represents a very significant gap in the knowledge needed to improve literacy rates. The design of appropriate strategies to address the issues of low literacy requires an understanding of the characteristics of the potential market for literacy programs and services.

Last sign: Exit at the fork in the road

There have been three kinds of responses to my research. A majority of literacy workers and students are interested, receptive and encouraging. They say that the findings are consistent with their own experiences. A minority of practitioners and policy makers are upset and alarmed. They say that immigrants, seniors, and adults with disabilities are not the government's current priority. They fear that public and political support for literacy will erode if people see low literacy as mostly a problem for these marginalized groups. A small number of statisticians are critical of the way I arrived at my estimates, eschewing any discussion of the policy and practical implications that arise from a demographic analysis of people in Level One.

I understand and share the anxiety of literacy workers who worry about future support for literacy, but I remind myself that many professionals and volunteers got involved in literacy work precisely because they wanted to help people who are marginalized. I also remind myself that the purpose of this analysis was to help explain and address the challenge of flagging demand for literacy education. It seems to me that in the long run, support for literacy education, as well as morale amongst literacy practitioners, is likely to erode if literacy programs can't continue to attract new students. The statistician's response has helped me better understand why so many people are skeptical of statistics, believing that numbers can and will be manipulated to make any case.

This analysis was undertaken to help preserve, strengthen and build momentum for effective literacy policies and programs in Ontario, and the findings reported here can and should be used in that way. Fewer than 4 percent of all adults at Level One in Ontario, regardless of who they are, are currently being served by Ontario's Literacy and Basic Skills program. Clearly the number of people struggling with low literacy is huge, as is the unmet need for effective interventions. If our policies and programs are expected to result in a significant reduction in the incidence of low literacy, we must know *more about the people* who are likely to need help, but who are not receiving help from existing programs — the potential "market" for literacy policies and programs. Our policies and programs must be market-driven.

As we come to the end of this journey, the road forks in two directions. One that veers downhill, away from a demographic analysis of low literacy, is for those unable or unwilling to question the commonly held beliefs that have shaped our efforts to date. The other goes uphill. It leads towards all those people whose daily lives are most clearly compromised by the struggle to access, organize and use print or written information, regardless of whether or not they fit the profile for existing literacy programs. Understanding how their lives are impacted by low literacy, and finding effective ways to improve their circumstances, may take us to places we have never been before. I know which way I'm going.

REFERENCES

Calamai, P. (1990). *Broken words: Why five million Canadians are illiterate.* Toronto, ON: Southam News.

Calamai, P. (1999, August 28). The literacy gap. *The Toronto Star,* pp. J1–J3.

Foot, D. (1998). *Boom bust and echo 2000: Profiting from the demographic shift in the new millennium.* Toronto, ON: Macfarlane Walter & Ross.

Hautecoeur, J. (1990). *Generous supply, flagging demand: The current paradox of literacy.* Quebec City, PQ: Alpha 90.

National Institute for Literacy (1998). *The state of literacy in America: Estimates at the local, state, and national levels.* Washington, DC: Author.

Ontario. Ministry of Education and Training. (1998). *Adult literacy in Ontario: The International Adult Literacy Survey results.* Toronto, ON: Queen's Printer for Ontario.

Ontario. Ministry of Education and Training. (1999). *Literacy and basic skills (LBS) program guidelines.* Toronto, ON: Author.

Roberts, P., & Fawcett, G. (1998). *At risk: A socioeconomic analysis of health and literacy among seniors.* Ottawa ON: Minister of Industry.

Statistics Canada (1996). *Reading the future: A portrait of literacy in Canada.* Ottawa, ON: Minister of Industry.

Sussman, S. (1999). *From staying the course to turning around: Options for OLC's voyage into the new millennium,* Toronto, ON: Ontario Literacy Coalition.

SECTION SYNOPSIS

Defining Reality
The Struggle for Voice
in Adult Literacy Education

B. Allan Quigley

Plato's dialogue, *The Phaedrus*, tells a story that holds prophetic meaning for literacy education today. Socrates is having a discussion about writing, and is asked if it is "proper" to write? In answer, Socrates recalls an Egyptian tale of how the god Theuth discovered the art of writing and enthusiastically shared his discovery with Thamus, the king of Egypt.* Far from sharing his enthusiasm, the Egyptian king flatly rejects writing. He argues that this new discovery will only separate people from knowledge. Writing, he predicts, will

> *cause men [sic] to lazily neglect their memories and allow them to substitute an unassimilated knowledge of symbols for personally gained knowledge of things"(Callaghan, 1938, p. 150).*

Centuries later, people have indeed been separated from knowledge and, in particular, from knowledge that has been deemed "official knowledge." Nowhere is this more acutely obvious than in adult literacy education. In this respect, teachers and tutors find themselves in a unique, even pivotal, situation. Although they can see and engage with the experientially lived knowledge of learners, honouring this knowledge is not part of the literacy teacher's job description. To the contrary, it is typically understood that knowledge of real worth is the codified knowledge found in approved texts — the official knowledge deemed

---

* In some translations Thamus is not a king but a god.

necessary for jobs, educational advancement, social recognition, and, sadly, even for self-esteem. In ways Plato never could have imagined, official knowledge is manufactured, legitimated, codified, and disseminated today through systems that typically require literacy for access. With more than a little irony, the lived-knowledge that the Egyptian king wanted to honour is now largely dismissed in Western culture. As adult literacy educators know all too well, those with the least official knowledge are also the least honoured in today's society (Quigley, 1997).

Can anything possibly be different in the 21st century? These chapters on community-based literacy suggest that the future can be different from the past for our learners, and perhaps for society too in this postmodern era. If there are two consistent themes in these chapters, they are the struggle over whose voice *should* be heard and what knowledge *should* be honoured. Norton's chapter describes how "the distribution of power in society" is a central point of critique, reflection, and action in her literacy program. She gives a compelling argument for the importance of connecting or reconnecting with oneself through one's lived-knowledge. Richmond takes connecting/re-connecting and honouring lived-knowledge a step further. She discusses how her literacy study explored the richness and regenerative power of learners' case stories through interviews. She advocates that "learners must develop their own stories before they can develop their literacy skills."

These complementary chapters echo Olson's observation that "literacy has to be seen in its oral milieu" (Sinclair, 1988, p. 18). Simply choosing to ignore the oral milieu — shrugging off context and lived-knowledge — can have serious consequences for literacy, as is painfully clear in Fagan's chapter. The atrocities he describes in Newfoundland communities in the name of upgrading leave me with the singular image of Lorna, a potential student, seated in front of a bureaucrat listing the multiple community volunteer and leadership activities she is currently engaged in. Like an Orwellian nightmare, she is then told, "But we must have something which is *official* [emphasis added]." Here is an example of the darker side of literacy history — a history that includes the struggle for literacy during slavery in the US, the retributions against adult educators such as Paulo Freire, and the fact that it was illegal to be illiterate under the 1919 *Decree on Illiteracy* in Russia (Eklof, 1987; Quigley, 1997). Official knowledge is indeed power, to adapt Francis Bacon's aphorism, and it can be used to denude people, whole communities, and entire countries from their personal and collective lived-knowledge. The lesson from these chapters, I think, is that it is essential to be clear about what we are doing in the field of literacy, how we are doing it, and why.

Long and Middleton give some guidance for future policy and programs in their chapter. They provide new findings on participation in literacy programs and point to the significance of learners' intrinsic motivation to learn. They also conclude that "programs focusing on a narrow range of vocational objectives will not meet the main goals of most callers to literacy groups." Sussman's chapter deconstructs some of the policy imperatives that seem to follow inevitably from statistical studies on illiteracy. She challenges the field to consider the unasked question: Is it possible that those who have indicated a low literacy level in the International Adult Literacy Survey (IALS) should not be painted with the same policy brush? Even more challenging: Is it possible that some of these adults may not want — or need — our programs? In fact, this was precisely the response given by many participants in the Canadian IALS (Statistics Canada, 1996, p. 12) and the American National Adult Literacy Survey three years earlier (Kirsch, Jungeblut, Jenkins, & Kolstad, 1993, p. xviii). Sadly, we have a history of assuming that every adult's lack of official literacy is a problem to be fixed — even if they tell us otherwise. Moreover, one-size-fits-all governmental programs have long been assumed to be the single, best tool for the job. These chapters are questioning why the millions of adults in this country who are designated low-literate are not given a meaningful voice in the programs and policies designed to help them.

I believe these authors are helping to build new hope for literacy policy and practice in Canada. One way of understanding the struggle inherent in adult literacy education, and how the ideas within these chapters are helping in the struggle, is to see the dynamics of literacy through a model developed by Niemi and Nagle (1979): "In every educational setting, an inevitable tension persists among three sets of needs" (p. 141). There are "the needs of learners, the needs determined and defined by professionals, and those needs as deriving from [institutional and societal expectations]" (p. 141). Literacy in Canada is no stranger to this triangle of tensions. However, there has been a healthy shift away from the official knowledge curriculum decided by the governmental representatives of society and dutifully delivered by our field. Program-created knowledge determined *with* learners, as in the case of practitioner action research (Quigley, 1997) and learners' lived-knowledge, as discovered and discussed by the authors in this book, are becoming much more common in Canada.

Our history of official literacy can be seen as beginning in the halcyon 1960s when "institutional and societal expectations" began to be defined through the Adult Occupational Training Act and implemented by the Canada Manpower and Immigration Commission. The subsequent decline of program funding after a 1977 senate review ultimately led to today's condition of gross underfunding. Our field has become highly dependent on such funding and, with a history of roller-coaster governmental policies and uncertain resources, many who have stayed with the field over the long haul have agreed that our field is closer to a network of charities than a profession (Quigley, 1997). What once promised to be a field of professional adult education with a solid infrastructure is now being run on the strength of volunteer goodwill. It is now being rightfully accused of the exploitation of women since women comprise most of the underpaid/unpaid workforce that carries this field on a daily basis (Luttrell, 1996).

However, the positive side of this history is that the shift from the dominance of governmentally sponsored programs and curricula to the growth of community-based programs across Canada has meant that literacy practice has been able to move towards a much truer realization of learner and community needs. What we have lost in funding quantity, we may well have found in pedagogical quality and service to our learners.

As we enter a new century, I believe the central issue for literacy educators will continue to be the struggle for voice. These chapters bring hope. So do the times we live in. There is reason to believe that our postmodern age will be more open to new voices than ever before in literacy history. Today, the grand solutions — the meta-narratives — of scientists, economists, governments, and educators are no longer as acceptable as they once were. As Aronowitz and Giroux (1991) argue, today's challenges to the old conventions are bringing a new openness for a

> *plurality of voices and narratives … [and] for different narratives that present the unpresentable"* (p. 22).

If those dedicated to literacy do not challenge the old discourses, do not question official knowledge, and do not present the unpresentable, who will?

REFERENCES

Aronowitz, S., & Giroux, H. (1991). *Postmodern education: Politics, culture and social criticism.* Minneapolis, MN: University of Minnesota Press.

Callaghan, W. (1938). *An outline of Plato's republic and dialogues.* Boston, MA: Student Outlines.

CBC Radio *Ideas* (1998) Literacy: The medium and the message. Available from CBC Transcripts, P.O. Box 6440, Station "A", Montreal, PQ.

Eklof, B. (1987). Russian literacy campaigns. In R. Arnove & H. Graff (Eds.), *National literacy campaigns.* New York: Plenum Press.

Kirsch, S., Jungeblut, A., Jenkins, L., & Kolstad, A. (1993). *Adult literacy in America: A first look at the results of the National Adult Literacy Survey.* Washington, DC: US, Department of Education.

Niemi, J., & Nagle, N. (1979). Learners, agencies, and program development in adult and continuing education. In P. Langerman & D. Smith (Eds.), *Managing adult and continuing education programs and staff.* Washington, DC: National Association for Public Continuing and Adult Education.

Luttrell, W. (1996). Taking care of literacy: One feminist's critique. *Educational Policy, 10*(3), 342–365.

Quigley, A. (1997). *Rethinking literacy education: The critical need for practice-based change.* San Francisco, CA: Jossey-Bass.

Statistics Canada. (1996). *International Adult Literacy Survey. Reading the future: A portrait of literacy in Canada.* Ottawa, ON: Ministry of Industry.

Workplace Literacy

FRAMING CHAPTER

Workplace Literacy
The Contested Terrains of Policy and Practice

Adrian Blunt

Workplace literacy has become a central focus for literacy policy and practice following two decades of shifts in social and economic policies to ensure that businesses have skilled labour to compete in the new global economy (Blunt, 1995a). In Canada, as in other technologically advanced countries, literacy skills are now more important to the economy than ever before (Hardwick, 1996). New manufacturing technologies and electronic information communications systems, requiring advanced literacy, have replaced many mass production processes of the post World War II era that required little literacy. Further, employers are demanding that all employees have higher levels of literacy although, as will be discussed later, there are differences of opinion about the evidence to justify these demands. This overarching context of economic, workplace and labour market change has stimulated debates over definitions and understandings of literacy, its social value and applications, and particularly, workplace literacy policy and practices.

This chapter maps the terrain of workplace literacy discourses and situates the interests of major stakeholders, such as employers, labour, government and the community, within these discourses. Utilizing a critical adult education perspective, I argue that historical tensions between two competing perspectives have influenced, and continue to influence, practice and research. The first perspective views literacy as essential to social development, the maintenance of democratic institutions and the achievement of social equity and justice. This perspective informs an emancipatory literacy education focusing on social outcomes and is located in community-based programs managed by non-governmental organizations (NGOs) and publicly funded institutions to respond to individual, family and community needs, including employment. The second perspective regards literacy as a component of human capital, that is, as an essential skill required of the labour force, upon which production and service effectiveness and efficiency are dependent. Human capital is enhanced through increased literacy functioning of individuals; therefore, literacy serves as an occupational skill. This technical-rational view informs a literacy education that has an economic and individual focus, and workplace literacy education has emerged from this technical-rational paradigm.

Frequently, the two paradigms are in tension, particularly in the context of competition over limited public resources for literacy programs and services. The paradigms are ubiquitous and influence all research and writing on adult literacy, making it difficult to maintain a balanced or neutral discussion of literacy work. This has resulted in a polarized literature with emancipatory literacy authors attacking technical-rationalism using ideological arguments and theories of social change while the technical-rationalists largely ignore the emancipatory literature and focus on their own pragmatic issues. As Venezky (1990) has stated, and I amend for the purposes of this discussion, "At issue here is not the meaning of literacy to the individual, [or to the employer,] but its meaning to society."

CRITICAL REFLECTIONS ON DEFINING LITERACY: GROUNDING PRACTICE

The two prevailing paradigms of literacy outlined above have served as foundations for two broad corresponding categories of adult literacy definitions. Although the categories are not fixed and absolute, they are mutually discrete and closely associated with the two dominant social science research paradigms. *Constructivist* literacy definitions are derived from the qualitative research tradition to serve the emancipatory paradigm, and *functional* definitions are derived within the quantitative research tradition to serve the technical-rational paradigm.

Functional definitions

Within the technical-rational paradigm researchers require definitions operationalizing literacy as a quantifiable variable for evaluations and surveys, or quasi-experimental studies, of persons in samples drawn from geographic areas, worksites or occupations. Functional definitions serve to guide data collection and analysis and ensure that results are generalizable. They enable researchers and planners to categorize persons by literacy level based on, for example, scores from tests (Statistics Canada, 1991). The most recent functional definition used to assess literacy in Canada, and other member countries of the Organization for Economic Co-operation and Development (OECD), is a relative concept given meaning in relation to the demands of society and the individual's aspirations. Participating in the 1994 *International Adult Literacy Survey* (IALS), Statistics Canada agreed that literacy is the "ability to understand and employ printed information in daily activities, at home, at work and in the community — to achieve one's goals, and to develop one's knowledge and potential" (OECD & Statistics Canada, 1995, p. 3). For many years, before mass survey tests, the years of schooling completed was used as a proxy measure of a person's literacy attainment. Eight years of schooling, or less, was the criterion for functional illiteracy and more was the indicator for functional literacy (Thomas, 1983).

In addition to providing estimates of populations with certain levels of literacy, and describing their socio-demographic characteristics, we have learned three important things from efforts to quantify undereducation and literacy levels: (1) little can be gained from statistics of literacy in isolation from their context (Venezky, Wagner & Ciliberti, 1990); (2) statistics are an important weapon in the policy domain where the struggle to direct scarce public literacy resources towards social or human capital goals occurs (Blunt, 1995a); and, (3) undereducation in Canada is essentially a social rather than an economic problem (Livingstone, 1999).

Constructivist definitions

Working within the emancipatory literacy paradigm, researchers agree that literacy is a socio-political construct and "reading and writing are meaning construction processes and abilities" (Macias, 1990, p. 18). The literacy context is therefore a crucial consideration in the construction and choice of definitions. Researchers working in the emancipatory paradigm employ qualitative methods, for example, case study and ethnography, where the purpose of definitions is to guide observation and analysis of literacy in use and to uncover literacy functioning in specific social contexts. Such research enriches our understandings of the literacy learner's experience and the social dynamics of literacy programs (Fingeret et al., 1994).

While rich description is seen as helpful by program planners and instructors, policy analysts and program evaluators, on the other hand, prefer the concreteness of numbers and statistics generated by quantitative studies. The dominant discipline in public literacy policy analysis is labour economics; consequently, labour market and adult education policy studies are dominated by empirical indicators derived from macro-level studies, rather than micro-level quality of life studies.

All studies tend to sustain the paradigms in which they are conducted rather than critically challenging the assumptions underlying them. Consequently, the numerous definitions, viewpoints, and disagreements on the social and economic impacts of illiteracy have not heightened awareness of the assumptions underlying literacy definitions as they define the need for and shape programs. All definitions originate from historically specific social contexts and have multiple social implications.

Changing conceptualizations of literacy

A further complication in defining workplace literacy is that over time conceptualizations of literacy change. While reading, writing, and numeracy abilities were once the only criteria considered, today's criteria include aspects of visual literacy: understanding and manipulating schematics, figures, diagrams, models and other abstract representations of information. A second example is computer literacy: understanding and using desktop, portable and handheld computers to perform word-processing, data entry and information-retrieval functions. As applications of literacy are extended, the concept itself is extended to include the contexts of the new applications. A number of agencies have published lists of critical skills thought to be required of the Canadian workforce today. For example, Employment and Immigration Canada and the Conference Board of Canada have produced *The Employability Skills Profile* (Employment and Immigration Canada, n.d.) identifying a range of communication and interpersonal skills where literacy is essential to the acquisition of the employability skills.

Because language pervades all thought and action, literacy can be conceived of as language in action. Many researchers, therefore, claim that language-based approaches and social applications of literacy are ideological. This conclusion around constructivist literacy definitions is important because it establishes the foundation for an emerging critical adult literacy practice and research sensitive to the range of literacy contexts. Critical literacy work begins with the understanding that definitions reflect the ideological agendas of literacy stakeholders and actors making decisions about what literacy is: who will have access to opportunities to acquire it; who will manage literacy programs; what literacy will be used for; how it will be used; by whom; and in what contexts (Baynham, 1995).

WORK AND LITERACY: HISTORICAL GROUND

Gatekeepers of literacy

In 18th century England, the interests of the middle and upper classes in maintaining social privilege and control over work were openly expressed in texts, and access to these was virtually restricted to members of their own class. However, today's labour educators have access to such texts and use them in their courses to depict the historical interests of the business community in restricting workers' access to literacy. Mandeville, for example, wrote in 1714 that "Reading, writing and arithmetic are very necessary to those whose business requires such qualifications, but ... they are pernicious to the poor, who are forced to get their daily bread by their labour.... Should a horse know as much as a man, I should not desire to be his rider" (Hopkins, 1985, pp. 24–25).

By the 19th century, following the Industrial Revolution, when most work still required little or no literacy, employers continued to oppose the literacy ambitions of the working class. However, employers did value the role of the emerging public school system for its potential to prepare docile factory workers willingly performing repetitious, poorly paid tasks and accepting social roles that perpetuated inequitable class relations (Graff, 1987). Social reformers at this time were frequently imprisoned to prevent their writings from reaching the masses and to silence their calls for political reform and social change (Neuburg, 1971). It was only with the arrival of large factories and when greater efficiency in the management of workers required the establishment of a workplace bureaucracy, that employers sought a small number of literate workers to supervise, monitor and control the majority (Vincent, 1989). At this time the Mechanics Institutes were being organized in England to raise workers' literacy levels and to gain a voice in the organization of work. However, the Institutes' efforts to democratize and humanize the workplace failed (Vincent, 1989, p. 150).

Evidence from global literacy work now confirms that literacy itself is not a trigger for people's development and empowerment. Rather, literacy through complex networks within civil society contributes to the acquisition of knowledge and power by individuals and groups, which, in turn, leads to more effective development and expansion of human potential, leading to greater participation in decision making and social action within certain opportunity-filled contexts. Extended periods of time are required for the incremental benefits of literacy to accrue and impact on the structural barriers restricting access to equity and social justice.

The efforts of emancipatory literacy workers need to be considered within the same historical context revealing literacy to be a centuries-old occupational skill. What has changed over time are the occupations and social class of those workers requiring literacy, not the interests of those who value literacy for its potential to maintain and change social relations. The workplace has become contested terrain because literacy is sought there to an unprecedented degree while stakeholders' inherited economic and social interests strive to control those literacy applications.

Business stakeholders

Today business leaders argue that high levels of workplace literacy are required of all employees on the grounds that production and service efficiency in a competitive global market requires it while relatively cheap, undereducated labour is available offshore. Canada's more highly educated, expensive labour force is now needed to perform information-enhanced production and service work in new flexible work environments. This requires continuous training, adaptation and self-management calling for well educated workers, previously thought to be a threat to business autonomy. Yet employers have some concerns that the highly literate workers needed as problem solvers in the workplace may think critically in ways considered threatening to corporate autonomy and interests. Employers' goals for workplace literacy programs, therefore, are often limited to achieving an effective and efficient skilled workforce for increasing production and service efficiency. Some evaluation studies suggest that such priorities may contribute to employers making decisions in the name of training — but which actually result in training grants becoming wage subsidies (Muszynski & Wolfe, 1989).

Labour stakeholders

In addition to supporting programs to ensure their members' continuing employment, labour seeks to gain greater organizational capacity and workplace democracy. Literacy programs are an opportunity to extend the reach of labour education preparing workers to assume labour organization responsibilities. Labour interprets the agenda of business to be in control over what is learned and the uses made of literacy, both in the workplace and in the community. Unions believe that, if employers can ensure literacy is taught to be applied in only mechanistic and uncritical ways, the need for workers with information-processing and communications skills will be met, and labour's goal to achieve greater workplace democracy will be thwarted. Workplace literacy would therefore "domesticate" rather than emancipate workers (Lankshear, 1987).

An additional concern of labour is the quality of the training provided. Studies have documented the willingness of some employers to treat government training grants as wage subsidies and provide low level, non-transferable skills (Muszynski & Wolfe, 1989). Labour recognizes that if workers are to derive the maximum benefit from public investments in workplace literacy, unions must be active program partners.

Community stakeholders

It is in the interest of communities to support workplace literacy programs as a means of ensuring employment continuity, maintaining family incomes, and sustaining the capacity of the local labour force to perform work. It is also in a community's interest that businesses earn profits to sustain economic enterprises and the ability of employees and businesses to pay taxes and service costs that, in turn, sustain community infrastructure and the quality of life for all residents. The democratic development of communities and institutions of civil society are also dependent on a literate, informed and engaged citizenry. The interests of non-labour force community members are linked to whatever occurs in the workplace through economic and social contracts negotiated and maintained by institutions in the larger society. Mutuality of interest therefore requires the negotiation of all social relations, including applications of literacy, defining responsible employers as good corporate community members and responsible community members as good employees.

Territorial struggles in academe

Tensions between the two literacy paradigms, constructivist and functional, extend into academe where they create a divisive climate influencing literacy instructor training, faculty research and community service. For example, at the University of Saskatchewan, the extension division and the graduate department hold differing views that influence both the courses and programs each unit offers and the research conducted by their respective faculty (Blunt, 1995b). The academic program is oriented towards an adult education for social change and an emancipatory literacy perspective while the extension division holds a human resource development and labour market service perspective. In this case, rather than promoting healthy debate and stimulating research and practice, little cooperation occurs between the two units to support literacy leadership, practice and research. I suspect this situation may be similar in other provinces.

CANADA'S LITERACY POLICY PRIORITIES: SHIFTING GROUND

In the early 1960s, the federal government had no concerns about the nation's levels of literacy and returned a UNESCO survey form "with a curt notation that the question did not apply since illiteracy was not a problem" (Moon, 1961). This assessment was made from a technical-rational perspective. As the nation's economy was based on natural resource extraction and agriculture, a highly literate workforce was not required. If literacy had been viewed from an emancipatory perspective, the government's response could have acknowledged the gap between its rhetoric on building a democratic egalitarian state and achieving universal literacy.

During this period, the federal government provided training allowances to enable those with low skills to attend upgrading programs. *The Basic Training for Skills Development* (BTSD) programs were to upgrade the academic skills of adults who could not meet the Grade Ten or Twelve entry level requirements for trades training or employment. Unemployment and poverty were to be reduced by increasing literacy and thereby strengthening local labour forces and communities. At this time, literacy was widely regarded as a basic human right, a means for the marginalized to achieve full participation in society and the labour market.

Keynesian economic policies and training

Through the 1970s, advocacy to expand the provision of ABE and BTSD was ineffectual and as Dickinson (1979, p. 29) reported "on any scale of national or provincial priorities, adult illiteracy does not even appear on the list." The situation worsened when the Department of Employment and Immigration altered priorities away from the undereducated towards "those who may more readily and quickly benefit from training" to the point that Labour Canada (1979, p. 122) acknowledged, "Adult literacy in Canada is a serious social and economic problem which is largely being ignored." These cuts to literacy budgets were an early consequence of several major studies' training policies, which set the parameters for public investments in literacy education (McLeod, 1994). These studies argued for policy changes as existing programs focused on the short-term reduction of unemployment rather than long-term employment creation, low level rather than higher level skills training, and institutional training rather than training in the workplace. Increasingly training policies became instruments of labour market and national economic strategy for managed, as opposed to boom and bust, development (Dunk, McBride & Nelsen, 1996). These policy shifts reduced opportunities for the under-educated by reducing budget allocations for ABE and BTSD programs, a move strongly opposed by some parliamentarians who said, "The federal government appears to have lost sight of its commitment and, more seriously, its duty to provide basic adult education to the illiterate Canadian" (Federal Task Force Report, 1981, p. 72).

By the mid 1980s, influenced by Thatcherism from the United Kingdom and Reaganomics from the United States, the Conservative government introduced the Canadian Jobs Strategies (CJS) that largely deinstitutionalized federally funded training and forced post-secondary institutions into the training market to compete with private trainers. Where functional illiteracy had once been targeted as a barrier to employment to be addressed by community-based programs, the policy now shifted to focus on increasing manufacturing and service efficiency and workplace training. Today public funds are focused on supporting business competitiveness. The unemployed and other adult learners must purchase training using their Unemployment Insurance (UI) benefits and personal resources.

In summary, technical-rationality is now the dominant paradigm in literacy policy and spending-priority decision making, and because policies are grounded in ideologies, the effects on communities, labour markets and the workplace are not politically neutral.

CANADA'S LITERACY CRISIS: UNCERTAIN TERRAIN

The question of whether or not the workforce lacks the literacy skills required to meet current job demands is at the centre of a major difference of opinion. Claims by the business community and its advocates that there is a literacy crisis (DesLauriers, 1990) have been widely accepted by governments and the media. However, the evidence advanced to support this view has been challenged (Boothby, 1993; Willinsky, 1990).

Undereducation or underemployment?

Some critics argue that the fundamental problem with today's labour market is underemployment not undereducation. That is, we are experiencing a failure of the economy to develop good jobs requiring higher levels of education, rather than the failure of the education system to provide graduates capable of performing available and future jobs (Livingstone, 1999). One explanation for underemployment can be found in employers' efforts to reduce training costs. Historically, Canadian employers have invested less in training than their U.S., Japanese and European competitors (Muszynski & Wolfe, 1989) and consequently have enjoyed some economic advantage. Now, however, they are forced by increased competition and technological change to invest more heavily in training and are seeking training programs that are cost-effective. As the highly educated have more experience as learners, and are likely more highly literate than the lesser educated, they have the potential to be trained most cost-effectively. So, to reduce training costs, employers hire, and retain, workers with higher levels of education and literacy than are actually required on the job (Thurow, 1975).

To further complicate matters, as successive generations improve their literacy they use it at increasingly higher levels, thereby requiring those who later work with them to function at higher levels too. As Vincent (1989, p. 16) points out, "Every rise in welfare benefits enlarges the population in poverty; every advance in the use of literacy increases the numbers defined as illiterate."

Where do we stand?

Regardless of evidence from the literacy crisis debates, it is clear that workplace applications of literacy have expanded. Today more workers engage in reading, writing and calculating on the job than has been the case historically. More print-based materials, including operations manuals, memoranda, graphic representations of data, and trade magazines, to list only a few, are found in today's workplaces and employees are expected to use them effectively. In addition, with e-mail, fax, and word processing more workers use written communication in their work. Also, increasing numbers of employees are engaging in self-directed learning activities requiring high levels of literacy. Yet the same surveys that claimed the existence of disturbingly high levels of functional illiteracy report that the great majority of workers categorized as functionally illiterate believe that they themselves have no serious literacy deficits and perform their work satisfactorily.

This divisive literacy crisis debate is also obscuring the need to clarify the question of literacy for which workers and for what job tasks? Frequently, programs are planned on the basis of insufficient knowledge about literacy applications. Does workplace literacy today require only higher levels of the traditionally understood forms of literacy taught in schools, that is, larger vocabulary, enhanced capacity to derive meanings from text, and ability to write more complex texts? Or does work require a different kind of literacy, a specific work-related literacy? Diehl and Mikulecky (1980) concluded that on-the-job reading differs significantly from school reading, leading them to differentiate between three types of reading: "reading-to-learn" (remembering information from the text), "reading-to-do" (applying information in a text immediately), and "reading-to-assess" (skimming text to select useful information). School-based reading emphasizes the first type, reading-to-learn, while work-based literacy emphasizes reading-to-do and reading-to-assess. Researchers have also concluded that little transfer of general reading ability to work situations occurs (Askov, 1989), but this line of inquiry needs to be extended to clearly identify generic skills and to determine ways to maximize transfer between contexts and applications. Nor has there been adequate research to identify workplace conditions maximizing on-the-job literacy learning. How the workplace can best be conceptualized as a site for learning still remains to be defined.

WORKPLACE LITERACY PRACTICE, CHALLENGES AND RESEARCH: MAPPING THE GROUND

The last two decades have been a period of growth in workplace literacy programming and knowledge building. Both deductive and inductive research now contribute to the identification of elements for successful practice, and articles that synthesize and integrate research findings are establishing a strong knowledge foundation for future practice accessible through new electronic information dissemination centres (see NALD, 2000).

Partnerships and programs

Research indicates that successful workplace literacy programs in Canada are established through partnerships of employers and labour, and frequently by triumvirates of employers, labour and public education institutions, or private training groups (Lewe, 1994). Resources are frequently contributed from one or several levels of government. Employers and unions may agree to share in contributing facilities, texts from the worksite and paid leave. Educational institutions or private training groups contract to provide needs analyses, instructors, program administration and evaluation services. Workers' interests, in particular, are served when public education institutions also assess learner achievement and award-recognized, transferable credentials. Because of the history of complex relations and tensions between the main stakeholders, close collaboration and transparency in decision making are essential aspects of partnership (Lewe, 1994; Darville, 1992).

Contexts for learning

One important concern of employers is that school districts' and post-secondary institutions' ABE programs do not focus on applications of literacy within the context of specific work tasks and do not result in the transfer of needed literacy skills to jobs (Askov, 1989). However, it remains a misconception among instructors, and learners in these programs, that mastering literacy in a classroom context ensures the substantial transfer of literacy to the worksite. As previously mentioned, literacy abilities only partially transfer from one context and format to another (Mikulecky, 1982; Mikulecky & Ehlinger, 1986; Philippi, 1988).

That only a little transfer occurs from general reading ability to specific uses of literacy (Sticht et al., 1987) provides strong justification for worksite, as opposed to community-based, programs, especially when employers and employees can demonstrate that applications of specific levels of literacy are required to perform particular work tasks, and incumbent employees do not function at the required levels of literacy to perform the tasks effectively and efficiently.

A common concern of labour and emancipatory literacy activists is that the corporate sector's narrowly conceived view of literacy for efficiency and profit may be uncritically accepted by workplace literacy instructors, whose practice might then result in the limited teaching of functional literacy skills that "can become an exercise in domestication" (Lankshear, 1987).

However, the worksite remains only partially conceptualized as a site for learning. Recent work by Livingstone (1999) reveals that extensive, informal workplace learning is occurring, but with little effort to the identification of social relations, resources and work processes supporting learning. Rubenson and Schuetze (1992) have drawn on the work of European researchers using action regulation theory, to propose a line of inquiry linking workers' developmental needs for control (or agency) with knowledge and skills acquisition, productivity and work experience. If the current emphasis in public education on the development of lifelong learning skills is to benefit the economy, among its range of likely beneficial effects, educators and work designers must collaborate to clearly identify work contexts that enhance informal and non-formal literacy learning.

Learning needs identification

Research confirms that successful programs occur when thorough needs analyses are performed. Systematic job observation, interviews with workers, and careful content and skills analysis of all forms of communications and job-related reading materials are essential components of a needs analysis (Taylor & Lewe, 1991). Ineffective programs are frequently preceded by hasty literacy audits relying on "official" versions of literacy practices and miss crucial literacy practices operating as part of the social organization of work (Baynham, 1995). Programs implemented on the basis of inadequate needs assessments tend to reflect aspects of classroom-based literacy education, including vaguely defined ability levels, generalized learning outcomes identified by employers and the use of textbooks and readers.

ENVISIONING COMMON GROUND

Current thinking continues to be constrained by past thinking about literacy definitions and applications. A recent reconceptualization of literacy from the perspective of adult literacy applications presents one opportunity to build bridges between the currently divisive paradigms. Lytle and Wolfe (1989) propose four conceptual categories of literacy applications: literacy as *skills, tasks, practices* and *critical reflection*. The categories are not intended to be perfectly discrete, yet each allows one major application of literacy to be highlighted and considered in relative isolation from other legitimate applications.

- Skills include the academic skills of reading, writing and numeracy.
- Tasks include functional applications of literacy to daily life tasks encountered at home, in the community and at work.
- Practice refers to contexts where literacy is used to create and understand professional and cultural texts.
- Critical reflection includes applications of literacy emphasizing social justice and equity.

[The category of literacy as *skills* includes the academic skills of reading, writing and numeracy and the category of *tasks* includes the functional applications of literacy to daily life tasks encountered at home, in the community and at work. Literacy as *practice* refers to contexts where literacy is used to create and understand professional and cultural texts. Finally literacy as *critical reflection,* includes applications of literacy which emphasize social justice and equity.]

Each of the four categories allows literacy intentions and behaviours to be abstracted from the concrete actualities of social relations to focus on one particular aspect of utilization. In practice, the categories are inseparable and a literate person will need to call on each of the four applications during daily living. This schema is helpful in reconceptualizing the field of literacy in ways that acknowledge how literacy applications intersect because people are multiply constructed as workers, consumers, community volunteers, parents, environmentalists, and informed citizens functioning in multiple social contexts.

Adult literacy policies in Canada today are largely founded on a view of citizen as *Homo economicus,* an actor whose salient criterion is an economic calculus, and who is educated for productive roles in the commercial world (Daly & Cobb, 1988). Functional literacy, related to aspects of Lytle and Wolfe's literacy as *tasks* and *practice,* is now a recognized aspect of human capital. Literacy workers have been enlisted in the development of a labour force to optimize private economic interests while ignoring, or remaining unaware of, alternative, community sustaining approaches to labour market development. One of the undesirable consequences of narrowly conceived vocational literacy programs is that learners then value and apply their literacy predominantly in terms of private, short-term, economic motives. People are now forced to obtain higher levels of literacy to gain access to jobs only because others have obtained, or are seeking higher levels to gain, an advantage in the labour market. In this case investment in higher literacy likely doesn't contribute to needed human capital, and serves instead as a subsidy to employers paid by individual workers, their families and communities.

A more holistic view of citizen is *Homo literatus,* an actor who thinks as a person-in-the-community, recognizing adults' multiple roles in society, valuing person-within-the-community relations, and acting to meet valid labour market needs. *Homo literatus* may be constructed around renewed social and community values and an interpretation of literacy as social practice. Lytle and Wolfe's literacy as *tasks* and *practice* leaves legitimate space for literacy as *critical reflection.* Envisioning *Homo literatus* through policy instruments would acknowledge that no one literacy practice should be privileged over another and would allow all literacy programs to acknowledge the legitimacy of the full range of desirable literacy applications.

Many of the tensions in workplace literacy policy and practice originate from disagreements over the legitimacy and priority afforded to investment in particular literacy applications. A literacy discourse is needed to recognize that workplace learners are also community learners whose social contexts are shaped by their multiple life-roles and their multiple subjectivities as raced, classed, gendered and sexualized persons. From such a postmodern discourse, policies and practices could emerge to sustain literacy learning and extend applications to the complex economic and social realities of the new century.

REFERENCES

Askov, E.N. (1989). *Upgrading basic skills for the workplace.* Institute for the Study of Adult Literacy, Pennsylvania State University.

Baynham, M. (1995). *Literacy practices: Investigating literacy in social contexts.* Harlow, Essex: Longman.

Betcherman, G. (1993). Research gaps facing training policy-makers. *Canadian Public Policy, 19*(1), 18–28.

Blunt, A. (1995a). The problem of adults with low literacy levels. What problem? A critical review of the research. In L. Wason-Ellam, A. Blunt, & S. Robinson (Eds.), *Horizons of literacy* (pp. 177–196). Winnipeg, MB: Canadian Council of Teachers of English Language Arts.

Blunt, A. (1995b). Adult education research in Saskatchewan. *Canadian Journal for the Study of Adult Education, 9*(1), 63–88.

Boothby, D. (1993). Schooling, literacy and the labour market: Towards a literacy shortage? *Canadian Public Policy, 19*(1), 29–35.

Daly, H.E., & Cobb, J.B. Jr. (1989). *For the common good: Redirecting the economy toward community, the environment, and a sustainable future.* Boston, MA: Beacon Press.

Darville, R. (1992). Collaboration in workplace literacy. In J.A. Draper & M. Taylor (Eds.), *Voices from the literacy field* (pp. 341–352), Toronto, ON: Culture Concepts Inc.

DesLauriers, R.C. (1990). *The impact of employee illiteracy on Canadian business.* Ottawa, ON: Conference Board of Canada.

Dickinson, G. (1979). Adult illiteracy in Canada and British Columbia. *Pacific Association for Continuing Education Newsletter, 9*(1).

Diehl, W.A., & Mikulecky, L. (1980). The nature of reading at work. *Journal of Reading, 24,* 221–228.

Dunk, T. , McBride, S., & Nelsen, R. (Eds.). (1996). *The training trap.* Halifax, NS: Fernwood.

Employment & Immigration Canada. (n.d.). *The employability skills profile.* Ottawa, ON: Author.

Federal Task Force Report. (1981). *Work for tomorrow: Employment opportunities for the '80s.* (Chairman, Warren Allmand) Ottawa, ON: House of Commons.

Fingeret, H., Tom, A., Niks, M., Dawson, J., Dyer, P., Harper, L., Lee, D., McCue, M., & Morley, A. (1994). *Lives of change: An ethnographic evaluation of two learner-centred literacy programs.* Raleigh, NC: Peppercorn Press.

Graff, H. (1987). *The labyrinths of literacy: Reflections on literacy past and present.* Philadelphia, PA: Falmouth.

Hardwick, C. (1996). International survey on adult literacy. *Education Quarterly Review, 3*(4), 23–32.

Hopkins, P.G.H. (1985). *Workers' education: An international perspective.* Milton Keynes, UK: Open University Press.

Labour Canada. (1979). *Education and working Canadians: Report of the committee of inquiry on educational leave and productivity.* Ottawa, ON: Author.

Lankshear, C. (1987). *Literacy, schooling and revolution.* New York: Falmer.

Lewe, G.R. (1994). Understanding the need for workplace literacy partnerships. In M. Taylor, G.R. Lewe & J.A. Draper (Eds.), *Basic skills for the workplace.* (pp. 51–66) Malabar, FL: Krieger.

Livingstone, D.W. (1999). *The education-jobs gap: Underemployment or economic democracy.* Toronto, ON: Garamond.

Livingstone, D.W. (1999). Exploring the icebergs of adult learning: Findings of the first Canadian survey of informal learning practices. *Canadian Journal for the Study of Adult Education, 13*(2), 49–72.

Lytle, S., & Wolfe, M. (1989). *Adult literacy education: Program evaluation and learner assessment.* ERIC Clearinghouse on Adult, Career and Vocational Education. (ERIC Document Reproduction Service No. ED 315 665)

Macias, R.F. (1990). Definitions of literacy: A response. In R.L. Venezky, D.A. Wagner, & B.S. Ciliberti (Eds.), *Toward defining literacy* (pp. 17–22). Newark, DE: International Reading Association.

Macleod, C.D. (1994). *Highlights of federal government training & literacy initiatives (1966–94).* Toronto, ON: ABC Canada.

Mikulecky, L. (1982). Job literacy: The relationship between school preparation and workplace actuality. *Reading Research Quarterly, 17,* 400–419.

Mikulecky, L., & Ehlinger, J. (1986). The influence of metacognitive aspects of literacy on job performance of electronics technicians. *Journal of Reading Behavior, 18*(1), 41–62.

Moon, B. (1961, August 6). Two million illiterates: Canada's obsolete tenth. *Maclean's* magazine. In J.R. Kidd (Ed.), (1963) *Learning and society: Readings in Canadian adult education* (pp. 301–307). Toronto, ON: Canadian Association for Adult Education.

Muszynski, L., & Wolfe, D.A. (1989). New technology and training: Lessons from abroad. *Canadian Public Policy, 15*(3), 245–264.

National Adult Literacy Database (NALD). (2000). [Website] Fredericton, NB. www.nald.ca

Neuberg, V.E. (Ed.). (1971). *Literacy and society.* [A reprint of, W.H. Reid (1800) *The rise and dissolution of the infidel societies in this metropolis* and W. J. Linton (1880) *James Watson: A memoir of the days of the fight for a free press in England and of the agitation for the people's charter.*] London, UK: Woburn Books.

OECD & Statistics Canada. (1995). *Literacy, economy and society: Results of the first International Adult Literacy Survey.* Ottawa, ON: Author.

Philippi, J.W. (1988). Matching literacy to job training: Some applications from military programs. *Journal of Reading, 31*(7), 658–666.

Rubenson, K., & Schuetze, H. (1992). *Learning at and through the workplace: A review of participation and adult learning theory.* Vancouver, BC: University of British Columbia, Centre for Policy Studies in Education.

Southam Press. (1987). *Broken words: Why five million Canadians are illiterate.* Toronto, ON: Southam Newspaper Group.

Statistics Canada. (1991). *Adult literacy in Canada: Results of a national study.* Ottawa, ON: Author.

Sticht, T.G., Armstrong, W.B., Hickey, D.T., & Caylor, S. (1987). *Cast-off youth: Policy and training methods from the military experience.* New York: Praeger.

Taylor, M., & Lewe, G.R. (1991). How to plan and conduct a literacy task analysis. In M. Taylor, G.R. Lewe, & J.A. Draper (Eds.), *Basic skills for the workplace* (pp. 217–235). Malabar, FL: Krieger.

Thomas, A. (1983). *Adult illiteracy in Canada: A challenge* (Occasional paper No. 42). Ottawa, ON: Canadian Commission for UNESCO.

Thurow, L.C. (1975). Education and economic equality. In D.M. Levine & M.J. Bane (Eds.), *The "inequality" controversy: Schooling and distributive justice.* New York: Basic Books.

UNESCO, (1976). *The experimental world literacy programme: A critical assessment.* Paris: Author.

Venezky, R.L. (1990). Gathering up: Looking ahead. In R.L. Venezky, D.A. Wagner, & B.S. Ciliberti (Eds.), *Toward defining literacy* (pp. 70–74). Newark, DE: International Reading Association.

Venezky, R.L., Wagner, D.A., & Ciliberti, B.S. (Eds.). (1990). *Toward defining literacy.* Newark, DE: International Reading Association.

Vincent, D. (1989). *Literacy and popular culture: England 1750–1914.* Cambridge, MA: Cambridge University Press.

Willinsky, J. (1990). The construction of a crisis: Literacy in Canada. *Canadian Journal of Education, 15*(1), 1–15.

CHAPTER 8

Developing a Learning Culture Within Business

Wendell C. Wiebe

The previous chapter has identified the major stakeholders involved with workplace literacy and their respective opinions on this topic. Blunt has correctly identified that business views workplace literacy programs as a means to develop a highly skilled workforce to increase production, which, in turn, will increase profits. The intent of this chapter will be to expand on this perspective of business.

Over the past seven years, I have been involved in the establishment of training and development programs within the context of an aerospace company. In the late 1980s, training activities within this company were initiated in isolation by individual managers to meet their specific business needs. Funds for training came from an unmanaged pot of money that could be accessed to support selected employees to attend various seminars and conferences, at least until the training budget was spent. The training function has evolved from an unmanaged process to a coordinated and consolidated process. For the past three years, a master training plan has been generated with a budget and presented to the executive for their approval and endorsement and it responds to training and development requirements identified by senior management to meet their business challenges. The budget includes management development, professional development for employees, training of employees on new software systems being introduced into the company, re-certification in areas of quality processes, health and safety issues, as well as a workplace literacy program.

The evolution of the training function role has reinforced my understanding that literacy programs, delivered within the context of a business, need to focus on the enhancement of employees' performance. Throughout this chapter, it is my intention to share my own evolving experience and thoughts.

THE BUSINESS CONTEXT

It is vital to understand that training and development programs set up within the context of a business must meet certain requirements. Businesses are established to produce a product or provide a service in order to generate a profit. This is even more significant in a publicly traded company. If the company does not generate the rate of return demanded, investors will buy shares from other companies that will. Managers are being measured by their ability to increase the value of those shares. Business decisions are based on whether an activity will generate the type of return required, and it is within this context that workplace education programs must be justified.

In the manufacturing sector, it is becoming more difficult to maintain profit margins. In long-term business arrangements, suppliers are commonly required to progressively reduce the cost per unit over the length of the contract. This, when combined with global trading, means that to stay in business, companies need to become more efficient in how they operate. Continuous improvement is imperative. Training is an important part of this imperative.

Customer service is another critical aspect of business. As a supplier of component parts for further assembly, a manufacturing company needs to comply with its customers' requirements. These typically are cost per unit, parts manufactured according to their specifications and on-time delivery according to the customers' schedule. In addition, the schedule may change to accommodate the ever changing needs of a given customer. Parts may need to be delivered earlier or later. To perform in this environment, a business culture must develop the ability to respond quickly to change.

Reviewing Bristol's experience

Bristol Aerospace Limited, located in Winnipeg, Manitoba, manufactures aeroengine and aerostructure components and provides services to a broad base of commercial and defence customers throughout the world. Bristol employs 1,150 people and provides a diverse range of manufacturing skills used both in the manufacture of new components and in the repair and overhaul of aircraft. Bristol started a workplace literacy program in 1994, with an extensive basic education needs analysis. The resulting training program helped employees to develop the speaking, reading, writing and math skills required in the aerospace industry. To obtain external funding for the initial pilot, we had to comply with a number of requirements, including courses to be delivered on-site and 80 hours in length. In addition, half the course was delivered on company time and half on the employee's time. The workplace literacy program was offered to employees on a voluntary basis. Since the initial pilot in 1995, the company has covered all costs associated with paying instructors to come to the workplace to deliver the program, and 153 employees have participated.

In 1996, we began to explore the development of technical training specific to the various trades at Bristol. A local college introduced us to a process of Developing A Curriculum, called DACUM, which could help define our training requirements. DACUM consisted of gathering those deemed to be experts from a skills group and having them define the key competencies required in the skilled area. The result was a DACUM chart. This DACUM chart was then compared to existing education programs to determine if there was a match.

We were introduced to Prior Learning Assessment and Recognition (PLAR), an approach for educational institutions to grant credit for knowledge and skills developed outside the classroom. In this way, students can be assessed and obtain credit for what they have already learned, and take only those credits in the program that they require. This approach significantly reduces the amount of time employees are required to be in training to obtain certification and ultimately reduces the cost of technical training. Bristol decided that any technical training program we use would need to have PLAR capabilities.

In the fall of 1998, we embarked on a project to streamline our workplace literacy program to better suit our needs. We wanted it to also prepare employees to be successful in the technical courses being offered. As a result, an analysis of the technical courses was conducted to determine the literacy skills required to be successful and consequently the program was reworked. Not only would this program equip employees for job-specific activities, it would also prepare them for necessary technical courses. This was done to remove any potential barriers that employees may encounter as they pursue an educational endeavour.

Because the workplace literacy program was 80 hours in length, employees indicated that this prevented them from participating. It was either too long or it covered material that was not relevant for their educational needs. So the program was modified to address these concerns by dividing courses into shorter modules and incorporating PLA principles. By doing so, we allowed employees to take the modules of a program, such as math, that they required for their job or for future technical training. By using PLA, the instructor assessed the students' skill level to ensure that they had the necessary skills required for the module being taken. It is our belief that a program must be flexible to the needs of the participants, as well as being consistent with the company's continuous improvement philosophy.

CRITICAL REFLECTIONS ON OUR WORKPLACE LITERACY AWARD

Bristol Aerospace Limited received the 1999 Award for Excellence in Workplace Literacy on April 26, 1999. This award is sponsored by the National Literacy Secretariat, Human Resources Development Canada, and coordinated by the Conference Board of Canada. We were filled with a sense of accomplishment on the day we were informed of our award in the Large Business Category. The training program created at Bristol was recognized as being world class. As part of the process of receiving the award in a formal ceremony, we had to generate a banner highlighting features of our program distinguishing us from other winners.

After some reflection, the following five factors were identified:

1. This training initiative was a collaboration of *management and union*.

2. *All stakeholders were consulted* at each phase of developing training programs.

3. *Beginning with a literacy program,* we moved on to technical training.

4. *Prior Learning Assessment and Recognition* (PLAR) shortened certification time for technicians.

5. *Incorporation of continuous change was* based on learners' feedback.

These five factors were incorporated into the banner, which profiled our program at the 10th anniversary Workplace Literacy Conference — Reaching for Success: Business and Education Working Together in Toronto, April 1999.

THE BUSINESS CASE

Key components required in a business case to initiate a workplace literacy program include the need to justify the program to obtain support and commitment by those who supervise the potential participants of the program, the need to link literacy to existing technical training, and the need to establish a mechanism evaluating the effectiveness of the program.

Initiatives need justification

Since the fundamental purpose of business is to generate a profit, activities will be measured against that criterion. When a new piece of equipment is being considered for purchase, a cost benefit analysis is undertaken to determine if the benefits will justify the initial purchase cost. To enlist the support of senior management for an education program, it is critically important to approach the enterprise with this mind set. One needs to identify the business reason to set up the program. Training initiatives may not always result in clear financial benefits. But training and development programs need to be able to demonstrate results such as increased productivity or reduction of defects. Either of these results will ultimately increase the profitability of a particular product line.

In the early 1990s, Bristol shifted its business focus from a military contractor to a manufacturer of commercial aerospace products and services. To compete in the commercial manufacturing environment, a company must produce in a cost effective manner. Competitors are constantly improving their production processes. In addition, primary manufacturers require suppliers to continually reduce the price charged for goods and services. Consequently, in order to stay in business, companies such as Bristol must develop a continuous improvement philosophy.

Also in the early 1990s, ISO 9000 was becoming the quality standard by which companies were evaluated. Quality standards were not new within the aerospace industry. However, ISO 9000 required industry to document the qualifications of its employees involved in the manufacturing of a product. This aspect was new for Bristol. To address this need for documentation of the employees' qualifications, a training and development program was required. Bristol's technical certification program was then established for this purpose.

In addition, customer quality assurance representatives have begun to raise questions about whether literacy levels of employees affect the quality of their product. Some of our customers have requested that we establish a literacy standard and demonstrate that all employees comply with this level. Because Bristol already has a program to address a lack of literacy skill, we have satisfied their requirements.

These are just a few of the business realities that can be used to justify the establishment of training and development initiatives. To gain support from senior management, training and development initiatives need to be generated as potential solutions for the business issues of the day.

Linking with line management

In order for any training initiative to be successful, it must also have the support from line management. Since our workplace literacy program has, from the beginning, been partly delivered during work hours, there has been a significant impact on production. Line managers are monitored on their ability to maintain a high level of productivity. Since sending employees off to training significantly impacts this measurement, the training function had to consult with them frequently to enlist their support and participation.

Initially, the training function had to promote the benefits of a literacy program, and indicate clearly how those benefits would help line management. Once line management accepted the need for a program, we had to work on lessening the impact on production. Line management agreed to release small numbers of employees from their cell areas, which would reduce the impact on production. In turn, we in the training function had to monitor employee requests for training to ensure that a single cell was not adversely affected. We worked out a way to collect requests for various courses, generate a class list and then distribute it to line managers, and we waited to hear from them before we formally confirmed employees' participation in a course. To date, we have had very few situations where employees have not been given the opportunity to participate in a chosen course. However, it is important to keep line managers involved in the selection process, providing them with a critically important sense of control. Line managers know that if they desperately need to meet a production schedule, they can successfully request that we place an employee on a waiting list for the next course offering.

Linking to technical training

An initial needs analysis in 1994 to determine the literacy skills required in our workplace was followed by the literacy program focusing on the various activities people were being asked to do. Then we embarked on a high-level technical training initiative to upgrade and eventually certify our technicians in their respective trades.

In subsequent meetings between management and union, it was agreed to enhance our literacy program to prepare employees to be successful in these technical courses. In 1998, we completed a literacy analysis of 12 technical courses. The literacy analysis identified knowledge and skills required to be successful in the course. The information gained from this has been incorporated into the curriculum covered in the new workplace literacy program. As new technical courses and programs become available, additional analysis will be done and incorporated into the workplace literacy program.

Evaluating to support justifications

Business activities are justified by a cost benefit analysis. Training is no exception. However, there are some factors that make this difficult. Seldom can training be singled out as the only factor that has improved performance. Regardless of this, a process has to be incorporated to respond to senior management's needs. At Bristol, we have struggled to define a process that is not excessively time consuming.

Instructors of our literacy program are required to identify specific competencies to be achieved in a given program that are measurable and observable. Upon completion of the program, the instructor meets with each participant to review his or her competency level. This assessment information is the property of the employee, who may use it as PLA evidence for credit courses from another educational institution.

In addition, instructors collect information from the employees' and supervisors' perspectives about how the literacy program has impacted their lives. We hope to collect anecdotal evidence of how the various programs have assisted employees in the performance of their jobs. For example, one employee who participated in the English as a Second

Language (ESL) program began to read an English language newspaper during his lunch break. Another, a math student, after reviewing the use of a calculator, gained confidence to solve a calculation instead of asking a co-worker for the answer. Results of the performance enhancements include a noticeable general increase in confidence in the employees' ability to learn. Employees also increase in their willingness to contribute their ideas and participate in problem-solving processes. These are but a few examples, but once a company compiles them, the result makes a significant impact.

INVOLVEMENT OF STAKEHOLDERS

Here I will illustrate the critical need to consult with all stakeholders potentially impacted by the training initiative.

Establishment of partnerships

In 1993, during collective bargaining, the Bristol Company and CAW Local 3005 agreed to establish a joint training review committee. The committee's mandate was to explore the development of training programs for employees being affected by the amalgamation of classifications. Prior to 1993, Bristol had 108 classifications with very specific skill sets. At the present time, we have 24 classifications, which have much broader skill sets. Since 1993, this committee has been responsible for the development and implementation of the Workplace Literacy program. This partnership has established an approach replicated in other situations. In 1996, after delivering three offerings of the essential skills program, the committee explored the need to address technical training. This became the Prior Learning Assessment and Recognition Initiative.

In a collaborative effort, the committee defined the requirements from various perspectives and agreed to link up with a formal educational provider. From management's perspective, the company was not interested in developing a training department with a large number of trainers — it was our mandate to develop partnerships with external providers. From the union's perspective, it was important that the training to be delivered would be recognized outside of Bristol. Due to reduction in the amount of work available, Bristol needed to reduce employment levels. Since people were being laid off, it was important that the training delivered would be recognized by other companies.

Since 1996, partnerships have been established with Red River College, Stevenson Aviation Technical Training Centre, and University of Manitoba's Continuing Education Division. The college and the training centre have technical programs consistent with our requirements, while the university has education programs for management and key professions.

For management and union, working together has not always been easy — it takes a willingness on both sides. If both parties agree on the end product required and collaboratively develop solutions to any existing problems, it can work. However, if either side decides it is no longer going to follow agreed-upon approaches, the partnership will quickly fall apart.

Training needs analysis

In any training and development initiative embarked on, we have found it critically important to define our requirements through a needs analysis process. In 1994, 150 interviews were completed with representatives of various levels of the organization to define the literacy skill requirements of our business. In 1996, as already outlined, we defined our technical skill requirements using the DACUM method. A needs analysis helps to define what it is you want people to learn in a training program.

A needs analysis also provides a way to obtain commitment from all participants. If the end users of the program are involved in the development of the program, they will be less suspicious of it. They will also be much more likely to see the validity of the training program.

In addition, a training needs analysis helps define the parameters of the program and clearly outlines the shareholders' requests. From these parameters, stakeholders can establish learning outcomes that describe the knowledge and skills expected of the learner. This provides structure to the program. Each participant in the workplace literacy program can review these generic learning outcomes and define unique learning goals.

AUTONOMOUS LEARNING

It is important to reflect on the need for learners to take ownership of their learning. Their learning should be a positive experience, programs should be modified to meet their unique needs and learners should have the freedom to choose topics to study. It is also the company's responsibility to prepare employees for any new requirements of their job function.

Learning responsibility

When the basic education program began in 1995, half the course was delivered on the employees' time. Even though this was a criterion to obtain government funding for the program initially, the company has continued this approach. To participate in this training program, employees have had to commit some of their own time. By doing so, they have made a commitment and taken responsibility for their own learning.

Building on success

All learning should be a positive, enjoyable activity. Not all individuals have had this experience. Therefore, we found it was important to make literacy a fun experience. Once someone begins to enjoy the activity you can build on that.

If literacy training is viewed as a satisfying experience, reluctant employees are more likely to come forward for other technical training. Since the certification of our technicians is crucial, employees need to participate willingly in the upgrading of their skills, as a preparation step for technical training.

Program flexibility

In conjunction with making literacy training fun and enjoyable, we need to ensure that it be set up to fit the schedules of the participants. We have to continually remind ourselves that our participants have already completed a full day's work when they enter the classroom. Their departments may be behind in their production schedule for the week, so they may even go back to work after class. Each of these participants has a life outside of work, with the many activities that families typically generate. Training and development must fit within these many factors. This was one of the critical reasons we have modularized our workplace literacy program. Employees customize their programs to ensure efficient expenditure of time. This type of flexibility is a motivating factor.

Choice of topics

The learning outcomes of the workplace literacy programs are determined by the needs analysis. The individual employees can review the learning outcomes to identify which ones they want to focus on during the program. This gives the employees the opportunity to take ownership for their learning, within the parameters identified by all the stakeholders. We have found that once employees start this process, they soon realize there are other topics that they need to learn in order to achieve the results they want.

Preparing for technical training

One of the first professional development programs I coordinated began in the fall of 1992. A number of employees participated in a part-time Engineering Technology program, delivered by Red River College. Most of the participants had been out of school for at least ten years. Their first course in this program was calculus but because their math knowledge was very rusty, successes were slim. The math instructor then revised the program to bring the students to the knowledge level required for them to master the calculus material. The lesson here was to prepare employees taking technical courses.

Our business case for the certification of technical production employees has been described earlier. To ensure that employees were prepared for technical courses, a study was completed in 1998. Employees participating in the reworked workplace literacy program have the opportunity to select topics that will prepare them for future technical courses. We believe this will maximize their future success in the technical training program.

THE CHANGING ROLE OF THE INSTRUCTOR: VISION OF THE FUTURE

I believe that the role of workplace literacy instructors needs to move towards that of a performance consultant, whose mandate is to provide resources to facilitate and document the acquisition of literacy skills of the learners. With a continuous improvement mind set, this role will change to meet the needs of the key stakeholders.

From a classroom instructor to a workplace performance consultant

When our first program was delivered in 1995, the instructors focused their attention on the participants in the classroom. Over time, we have requested that this focus be expanded. We wanted the instructors to talk with the participants' line managers to create a link with line management and foster their support of the initiative. We found that this was not an easy transition for instructors or for line management.

As stated earlier, training and development initiatives are certainly justified by providing enhanced performance. To help foster that orientation, instructors need to become workplace performance consultants with a focus on what the participants have learned. They need to understand that learning transfer from classroom to the workplace is crucial. Classroom activities need to include discussions on how the learning can be applied in the workplace, what are the potential barriers that could prevent this from happening, and what can be done to eliminate them. They also need to understand that this transfer of learning must be measured by a post-course skill assessment to justify ongoing investment in this type of training.

Partnerships need to be developed between participants and their line management who must see the values of the literacy program. Line managers must also work in partnership with the instructors to enhance employee performance. This results in continued support for employees' participation in future programs.

In addition to line management, senior management needs to have evidence that the training expenses, including the employees' salaries while in training, are producing positive results. The documentation of literacy skills acquired and the collection of comments from employees and line managers can reinforce the collective benefits of the program.

Further, when the learning is transferred to the workplace, it must be documented. This will provide the evidence that literacy skills were acquired and are being used in the workplace. This will also provide documentation which may be required to respond to inquiries from Quality Assurance Auditors from our various customers.

In order to become a performance consultant, workplace literacy educators need to understand business. Workplace literacy is more than just literacy training in a workplace. It needs to be linked to performance enhancements, which lead to the business achieving its goals, in other words, a criterion for success. Understanding the business culture within which this training takes place leads to better results.

Instructors need to understand learning styles and strategies in order to enhance a student's learning. They must also be aware of the students' world and the role that training plays in the achievement of business goals.

Continuous improvement is another aspect of the business culture. To stay in business, processes need to be reviewed continuously and to be improved on. If workplace literacy consultants take this same attitude to heart, they will begin to hear what their customers want, whether management, organized labour or learners. Through such an approach, workplace literacy consultants will begin to identify the various issues from the stakeholders and begin to improve the delivery of their services.

Literacy Is a Labour Issue

Ian Thorn

This chapter explores the many reasons why literacy is a labour issue and begins with a brief description of the changing world and the increased demand for literacy at home, in the community, in the workplace, and within our democratic society. In the first part I explain how workers have struggled with workplace change and new literacy demands, and how literacy enhances our personal well-being and our daily lives. The next section presents a critical reflection on literacy, people and the economy. I provide a number of examples of the historical approach by organized labour to literacy programming. Links are made to the earlier chapter by Blunt as I express my agreement, and that of the Labour Movement, that literacy is a social issue.

THE CHANGING WORKPLACE

Technological development has been the most often acknowledged cause of the greater complexity in our daily living, changing workplaces and rapidly increasing literacy demands. However, that is far from the only cause. Regional and world trade agreements and practices have changed where, how and by whom goods and services are produced. As a result, in Canada, some jobs no longer exist, others have changed, and still others have been created. In addition, due to the world trade agreements and the intense global competition for quality, productivity and primarily profitability, we have experienced continuing corporate mergers, downsizing, plant and office closures, multi-skill and multi-task programs, and so on. Coupled with this is the ever so rapidly advancing "information exchange," which has affected the method and speed of communication and information accessibility. The result of all of these factors has been, and will continue to be, extensive lay-off, job content changes, and worker reassignment and relocation. Employees who are laid-off must often obtain new skills to gain new employment. Those who are displaced in the workplace must also gain new skills to retain employment. Such disrupted workers as labourers, tradespeople, skilled processing and manufacturing plant operators, clerical people, managers and engineers find themselves requiring education and training for additional or different workforce needs. However, many will need to develop their learning and literacy skills as a necessary first step towards new employment skills.

An additional issue facing Canadian society is the need to prepare immigrants in Canada for entry and advancement in the workforce. English and French language skills will make available the communication, technical and professional skills that the immigrants possess and practiced in their mother tongue. To leave those skills under utilized is a loss to Canadian society, the workforce, the economy, and the individual immigrant.

ASSESSING OUR PAST GOALS

Wisdom dictates that we periodically assess our past goals, objectives, practices and results.

In doing that, we in the Labour Movement, while recognizing decades of progressive and innovative union literacy programming, acknowledge that in the past, workers have slipped through the cracks because literacy difficulties were not identified by the worker, the union or the employer. This occurred either because the worker didn't want to make a literacy deficiency known or because he or she didn't understand literacy skill needs as a simple and resolvable issue. It may not have been identified by the union or the employer because each party lacked the awareness and understanding of, or the commitment to resolving, literacy issues.

In looking back over close to 30 years as a union officer and national representative, I can recall cases where we failed and where we succeeded. We failed when computerization of a workplace required direct operation of many parts of the facility from a centralized computerized control station, rather than the more manual operation of one part of the facility. The required intensive new skill training was generally much easier for the younger employees. That training also showed that some workers struggled less and were able to succeed quicker than others with their first exposure to the computer and with the need to access, use and pass on much more information, written and oral.

We failed in not recognizing cases of literacy need. It was instead considered to be lack of ability.

I can also recount a case in which a worker moved from Quebec to Western Canada. An issue first perceived as a lack of skill was quickly identified as a second language issue, and resolved. The resolve included a monetary cost to the employer and to the union member, a transition cost to the employer until language skills allowed for the full utilization of job skills, and considerable effort on the part of the union member. However, the result was positive for the member and family, the union and the employer.

The enhancement of our daily lives through literacy

Literacy is a union issue because it affects the lives and opportunities of all workers, union and non-union, off the job as well as on the job. It is a determining factor in the level of an individual's participation in every aspect of our democratic society. Therefore literacy and learning skills development must be for the purpose of enhancing the individual's whole life.

The Trade Union Movement actively promotes literacy development as a democratic societal issue, which is essential to human devel opment, democracy, and the achievement of social equity and justice. Literacy development also has the positive effect of bringing to the workplace a more highly skilled, motivated, and adaptable workforce. Such a workforce will place Canadian business and industry in a much improved position to compete in the international marketplace. The workers, coincidentally, must be compensated according to their contribution to productivity and profitability.

The primary purpose of literacy is for the gaining of knowledge and skills that are relevant to, and applicable in, the learners' whole personal life.

The union's purpose is to provide the skills and knowledge that enable the learner to participate more fully in the increasingly complex daily living and employment situations. These include the ability to assist children with their school and other learning activities and the improved ability to make personal health, economic and employment decisions. Improved literacy skills also enable greater opportunities, successes and contributions in the workplace and a more informed ability to advocate, lead and to participate in decision making in the local, national and international communities.

In our democratic society, those who possess the reading, writing, numeracy and communication skills are those who influence opinion, and therefore decisions before, at and after the vote at the ballot box. This includes the vote for government members, local boards, referendums, union officers, union resolutions and collective agreements. Those who lack these skills, and the ability to readily add to their knowledge and to fully apply that knowledge, are subject to the decisions of others and are therefore denied the basic benefit of democracy. They have, in effect, been disenfranchised.

Literacy and learning skills development must be designed to open doors to the whole world for the learners' personal growth and satisfaction, for their greater successes and more valuable contributions to every activity they wish to pursue. The beneficiaries will be the individuals, their families, their communities, their workplaces, and our world. Literacy is a union issue because it is a social issue and because it is a workplace issue. However, it is primarily a social issue, a human issue.

Literacy is a right of all Canadians

Education is a human rights issue protected by Canadian legislation. The right to an education is included in the 1948 United Nations Declaration of Human Rights (Article 26), which states that everyone has the right to free and equally accessible education and that education shall be directed to the full development of the human personality.

Literacy is basic and fundamental to achieving education.

Therefore, literacy is a Canadian right, a human right.

A CRITICAL REFLECTION ON LITERACY, PEOPLE AND THE ECONOMY

Literacy and education

As education requirements will continue to increase to keep pace with the rapidly changing workplace and daily living technologies, so must literacy and basic skill levels increase to keep pace with changing education needs. The definition of literacy has evolved from that of a basic reading ability to include how adults actually use and process written information to function in society — a necessary skill in industrialized nations.

In Blunt's earlier chapter, he discusses the rising literacy requirements needed for the changing workplace. In supporting this point it is interesting to note that power (boiler) engineers, tradespeople, the factory or process control operators and soon must intake, evaluate, compute, respond to and output vastly more information today than in previous decades. As the workplace uses computers for monitoring, controlling and troubleshooting, CD-ROMs of information have replaced charts and gauges. The tradesperson of yesteryear would generally receive a few pages of instruction for installation, operation and maintenance of a new piece of equipment, but today the equipment is preceded by very significant manuals and often, training periods prior to arrival.

Literacy for the person or the economy

The fact that literacy levels must increase to keep pace is undeniable and is not in dispute among governments, employers, labour or society in general. However, as the dispute plays out between those parties as to "literacy for the whole person which benefits the workplace, or literacy for the workplace which may benefit the worker's life away from work," I submit that the former position must prevail because justice, humanity and democracy require that, and because literacy for the whole person will provide the greater opportunity for real and lasting success.

Individuals are more likely to participate and succeed in a learning opportunity if the goals, objectives and rewards are clearly those of and for the learners, and if the process is designed for their total life activities using materials, which most broadly interest them (e.g., personal, family, hobby, community, union and work). Further, if literacy development is driven by economic, corporate and workforce needs, and if it is preparatory to specific workplace training needs, then the benefit to the worker, the economy or workforce may be only temporary, because continued workplace change and displacement may cause repeated relocation of the worker to a different workplace or industry.

As literacy for corporate productivity, efficiency and profit became a national public policy priority, rather than literacy for the person and social equity, then the basic principles of democracy were violated. Indeed, the policy and practice must be such that economies serve the people rather than the people serving the economies. This is much more true, and becomes much more urgent when we realize that it is the less literate, the less educated and the less well off in every way who would serve the economies of the corporations and their wealthy shareholders. Such a situation becomes even more offensive when it is recognized that those who lack literacy skills and therefore the ability to fully, and with reasonable knowledge, participate in the democratic process are, as stated earlier, disenfranchised.

Who controls our economy ... and our literacy?

The World Trade Organization, within which Canada has relatively little influence, has the power to set policy and practice directing our Canadian government and our economy. It would appear that, unless there is a reversal of government policy, adult literacy development will serve the needs of an economy controlled by foreign and multinational corporations at the will of the World Trade Organization. This being the case, where is our democratic control? Literacy for social justice and equity must prevail. As all stakeholders begin to work collectively and collaboratively towards common goals, the result will be a broader social approach to literacy development.

As the Union movement explores approaches to literacy in the workplace we will want to look beyond the present workforce to the workforce of tomorrow. Indeed, literacy development begins at home with the very young.

Studies have shown that children who have been read to a lot from birth to age five years are most able to take advantage of formal literacy education and are more successful in their formal education. More highly educated parents read more to their pre-school children, thus providing them with cognitive and language skills that contribute to early success in school. Start early, finish strong!

The workforce of tomorrow will have the same literacy gaps until the cycle is broken. That cycle can be broken only through family literacy programs which simultaneously address the literacy needs of the parents and their children. There are such literacy programs, now active in our communities, which promote reading to our children from birth to school age. This is recognized as the most active and beneficial learning period. This approach must be expanded to help make lifelong learning a true reality.

As Canadians become aware of the consequences of illiteracy, organized labour and other social and democratic minded groups are on the front line struggling for a positive response from government and industry — a call for a focus on people's needs, not corporate greed.

Literacy is a social issue and a workforce issue and a union issue, which impacts the economy of the individual, the business community, the country and the world. For the prosperity of each and all, this issue must be addressed by the whole of society so that the priority is on the people — starting with our children. The current need is great. The urgency is that literacy development must progress faster than the increasing demand for even higher literacy skills.

If the literacy priority is for economic gain, those benefits will not likely be shared equally throughout society. History has proven that. However, if the literacy priority is for the benefit of all society, then more people will prosper and consume more, driving the economy to greater prosperity, and the cycle continues. It may be easily perceived here that I subscribe to the demand-side economic principle.

The economy, as presented by government, the business community and the media (national and international), is, of course, the *macro economy*: large worldwide capital ownership, stock trading activities and indices, and the response and activities of large investors, the banks, governments and those generally "unfathomed" organizations like the Bank of Canada, the US Federal Treasury Board, the International Monetary Fund, the World Bank and the World Trade Organization.

This picture is so very far from the realities of the economies of individuals, which range from, again for most of us, "unfathomed" individual wealth of multibillions of dollars to unreported, unrecognized multimillions of individuals in poverty. The macro economy is becoming even less relative to the majority of individuals as the disparity grows between the poor and the wealthy. A great many empirical studies show that worldwide, the top 20 percent of society has gained while the remaining 80 percent has lost. It is clear that there have been economic victims. One must expect that if literacy priority, design and funding are for the benefit of the economy, then only a shrinking few will receive the benefits of literacy training and the fewer jobs that may come with it.

Our own record as a nation is not good. Canada's policy has been based on economic need, on literacy as required in the labour force. The reversal of that unsuccessful policy will lead to greater individual, corporate and national success.

A CALL FOR A NEW ERA

Business, labour, government, and the education system must work collectively and collaboratively towards a recognized common goal of clearly defining the literacy needs of today and tomorrow. We will fail if we do not. This goal requires that government, employers, manufacturers, researchers and developers share with other stakeholders their vision of future technical developments. With that information the life skills and workplace skills that will be required to keep pace with change can be more accurately identified, government agencies would be assisted as they update the Essential Skills Profiles and literacy providers would be able to respond with more relevant needs assessments. The education system, government funding, and the labour community may then respond with the education and training needs, and individuals may respond to opportunities for life and workforce preparedness and career planning.

Such a process took place in the 1980s in northern Alberta with union, business, local government and educators openly sharing information for their mutual benefit and for the benefit of students and others preparing to enter the workforce. Information included the anticipated needs for skilled trades, process operators, equipment operators, clerical, technologists, professional engineers, etc. From that information high schools, colleges, technical schools and trade schools were better able to prepare for and deliver according to skill needs and job availability. Those entering the workforce could then set their objectives and better prepare themselves. Government could allocate funding to the educational institutions and the employer could expect a readily available, trained local workforce.

This process was presented like a trade show where employers, labour unions and educators displayed and informed the public from their booths, which were staffed with knowledgeable people. Public response was very favourable from high school and college students and from local and surrounding communities. The more complex and changing issues of today would require a more sophisticated and continuing process.

The business and corporate community strive, for good business reasons, to forecast, plan and implement ahead of their competitors. Our society, our educators and our people must strive for the same advance readiness. This country will not be on the cutting edge of very much if we have a large percentage of our adult population with poor reading skills. (Senator Fairbairn, 1996, p.17)

THE UNION APPROACH TO LITERACY

The Trade Union Movement, from the local bargaining unit through to the regional, national and international components, has long recognized the need, accepted responsibility, and pursued and presented programs for literacy upgrading among our members and their families.

Union members have been seeking, and continue to demand, more education and training due to the increasingly precarious nature of employment and the rapidly changing requirements of work. Many are seeking basic education in order to access workplace training relative to computers and other information technology.

Literacy development provides the tools for broader activity in the community, the union and the democratic process, that is, the empowerment of the person. Workers need the literacy skills in order to pursue their own agendas. Workers need to be involved in the planning, design, program delivery and evaluation of their literacy development. The programming must be provided equitably to all workers regardless of gender, race, first language, physical abilities or age, and must be based on what the worker knows rather than what they do not know. Prior learning, interests, and activities should be recognized and built upon. Workplace literacy programs should be administered and controlled by the union or by a joint union-management committee. There must not be a cost barrier to the learner since literacy is essential education and should be free. Skills gained must be accredited and recognized by other employers and educational institutions anywhere in Canada. The Communications, Energy and Paperworkers Union has found that when the union took the initiative and brought about change, the security of our members was enhanced and our industries were strengthened. Their experience demonstrates that the key to success is for the union to pursue its own agenda and to play a full role in managing change.

A long history of union literacy programs

Union and joint union-management workplace literacy programs have many things in common. Unions or labour organizations either developed or played a central role in the development of the program and they either control or are equal partners in it. The holistic learning opportunities are relevant to workers, with results that meet their wants and needs, the broader goal of social and economic justice, unionism and the empowerment of the worker. Resources used are primarily particpant interest and workplace based: policies, manuals, union newsletters, by-laws, collective agreements, benefit program documents, etc. The response has been overwhelmingly rewarding to the individual members, their families, their communities and their unions. In fact non-members have also been welcome participants in our union literacy programs.

Basic to our literacy and workforce programs is recognition of the need to develop or refresh learning and study skills for the learner. Courses offered in our programs include basic skills in reading, writing, numeracy, oral and written communication, critical thinking, problem solving and decision making. Others courses include English or French as a second language, technology readiness, research skills, preparation for GED or high school credits or trade certification. Career transition workshops regarding career options, job search, resume writing and job interviews are also presented. Still others provide introduction to computers and the Internet and more advanced computer training. Courses are presented to update or upgrade and develop new transferable skills. Because many of our union courses use peer trainers and rely on workplace coaching, we present Train the Trainer programs.

Each union has its own union education programs, such as for shop stewards, health and safety committees, collective bargaining committees, local union leadership and financial officers. We have begun integrating literacy components into those courses. In 1997 the Alberta Federation of Labour and the Canadian Labour Congress began a process of integrating literacy into their labour studies programs.

Examples of union or joint union/ employer literacy programs

Basic Education for Skills Training (BEST) (Website at www. creativewizardry.com/Best) was established in 1988 by the Ontario Federation of Labour. BEST programs are open to workers in unionized workplaces across Ontario. BEST combines the philosophy of popular education with labour's traditional use of worker instructors. The costs, including the instructor training, are paid by the employer. The employer is also involved, through a joint committee, in the coordination of the program.

Workers' Education for Skills Training (WEST) (Website at www.sfl.sk.ca) is funded by a yearly grant from the Saskatchewan government and by substantial in-kind support from the Saskatchewan Federation of Labour. WEST uses a modification of the Ontario Federation of Labour's BEST model. WEST charges no fee for its services. Employers contribute through coverage of lost time required to train the facilitators and to run the classes.

Workplace Education Project, United Brotherhood of Carpenters Local 1338 (PEI), received funding and assistance from Workplace Education PEI. It is a joint initiative of the provincial education ministry and the federal government that includes representatives from business and labour.

The United Food and Commercial Workers Union (UFCW) Training Centre in Winnipeg opened 1998 (Website at www.ufcw832.mb.ca). It is financed by an Education and Training Trust Fund made up of employer contributions negotiated in collective bargaining. It also received seed money from the UFCW National Training Fund. Instructors and staff are union activists and/or certified teachers from the public education system who practice participatory education technique.

Skills for Tomorrow was funded by the National Literacy Secretariat and conducted for the Union of Needletrades, Industrial and Textile Employees by ABC Canada. The second phase has trained regional interns to promote literacy and to work with local executives to get literacy programs started for UNITE members. Two such programs are the Learning Experience Centre of Local 459 in Winnipeg (Website at www.nald.ca/LEC.UNITE) and the Montreal Joint Boards Skills for Tomorrow Education Centre (Website at www.unite.svti.org).

The Toronto and York Region Labour Council was a pioneer, in the early 1980s initiating the English in the Workplace program. In 1987, the Metro Labour Education Centre (MLEC) (Website at www.mlec.org) was born, offering literacy and adult basic education. MLEC continues to provide free English upgrading, communication skills, and computer literacy to unemployed workers.

Learning and Education Assisted by Peers (LEAP) is the basic skills initiative of the Joint Union Management Program (JUMP) in the BC pulp and paper industry (Website at www.mountainmecca.com/jump/). JUMP is a program negotiated between the government of British Columbia and forestry companies and funded through royalties and stumpage fees. The Communications, Energy and Paperworkers Union of Canada (CEP) and the Pulp, Paper and Woodworkers of Canada (PPWC) with Capilano College, bring the LEAP program to pulp and paper work-places across British Columbia. There are no fees and no tests to pass. The LEAP program combines elements of both the OFL BEST program and the Hospital Employees' Union program. Classes are delivered by peer instructors, with a college resource person available by phone.

Canadian Steel Trade and Employment Congress (CSTEC) (Website at www.cstec.ca) is a joint venture between the United Steelworkers of America and Canada's steel-producing companies. Initial development costs of the program were funded by the unions, companies, Collège d'enseignement général et professionnel (cegep) and provincial and federal governments. Ongoing funding is negotiated with local employers. Federal government support ended on March 31, 1999.

SkillPlan (Website at www.nald.ca/skill.htm) is a not-for-profit society founded in 1991 by the Construction Labour Relations Association and the BC and Yukon Territory Building and Construction Trades Council. The Board includes equal representation from union and management. SkillPlan is funded through cent-per-hour contributions by employers and unions and from fee-for-service work carried out for governments, unions and companies.

Meeting political and economic challenges

The future must be motivated by equity and social justice, rewarding and continuing employment, and the production and provision of high quality goods and services utilizing technological innovation for the "benefit of all people." Making literacy, basic skills education, and job training opportunities readily available to all Canadians for lifelong learning is the key to that future. It is achievable through the efforts and cooperation of all individuals and organizations. Organized labour is committed to its agenda as determined by the membership, and is committed to work with other stakeholders for the "benefit of all people." The demonstrated ability of government, business, unions, educators, and other stakeholders to work in partnership should also be a part of the plan.

As the Trade Union Movement continues to work with other progressive social, environmental, industrial and government organizations for the benefit of working people and their families, we will also continue to work for political change that would be a means to that end.

Multi-partite activity should focus on identifying and forecasting changing literacy needs. The approach and process, from increasing awareness, through program design and development to program delivery, is extremely vital to success. The development of awareness must be among potential learners and among all who can help make it happen. This means union, employer, education, and government leadership at the local and senior levels. From that awareness all parties need to accept the responsibility for their role in the process, followed by a commitment to act.

Throughout this process we must recognize and adapt to the overall and the individual needs and circumstances of the learners. Understanding must be developed for and consideration given to regional and cultural differences, degree of literacy need, and relevant approach and programming. Approach to the worker for input on program development and adaptation is also vital to success. Programs initiated by the union are presented on a confidential basis. In this way the member is able to participate without concern that exposure of a literacy deficiency may negatively effect employment. The union and other workers are in the ideal position to provide first-hand, on-the-shop-floor understanding and experience, which is valuable to the program developers and providers. This type of worker/learner input should be from the earliest point of program development through to delivery. We will promote and use the public education system.

A new vision for the future

We must all strive for a society of lifelong educational opportunities and a society and economy based on the needs and aspirations of all people, devoid of exploitation of children, the poor and the politically oppressed.

The ideal Canadian society is one working collectively towards literacy supremacy, and therefore fair and equal individual opportunity and full and active democratic participation — a Canada that continues to be the best country in the world in which to live while also competing in the global economy. This is achievable when power at the ballot box is greater than the power of any corporation and when the power of education is available to everyone.

The achievement of our desired level of literacy, education and life skills is an issue common to government, organized labour, workers, employers, educators and the entire community. From that achievement we will all prosper. Indeed the most successful and prosperous society and economy will be the one that is the best educated and has the most highly skilled workforce.

Society and the democratic process will gain from more informed and increased participation. There will be prosperity from change rather than desperation and conflict. Individuals and families will gain from job retention, advancement and higher income (spending power), job satisfaction and self esteem. The union will gain from an increased, more informed and participating membership. The employer will gain from a more highly skilled, motivated and adaptable workforce, and from the greater spending power of a more successful employee. The return in investment in job skill training will be increased.

Change is inevitable yet directable. Workers and their unions can and will participate in setting that direction. Change without foresight and collaborative direction means prosperity for some and desperation for others. There need not, must not, be victims of change. That is not progress. Our society's commitment to and action on advancement of literacy, learning skills development, and lifelong and whole person needs education — ahead of change — will bring true progress.

In the words of R. T. (Buck) Philp, a late friend, mentor and colleague:

 Ignorance can be corrected
Stupidity is forever
The desire for learning is the difference

REFERENCE

Fairbairn, J. (1996). *Literacy economy and society.* Calgary, AB: Western Canada Essential Skills Training Network.

The Worker as Lifelong Learner

Sande Minke

It is definitely true, as Blunt argues in the earlier chapter, that literacy has been a field of conflicting ideologies. It is a socio-political construct, manipulated and shaped by academic, business, labour, and community organizations of various types. Historically, literacy has held different levels of importance often related to configurations of power and the prevailing economic structures of the day.

Government policy and programs with respect to literacy can be broadly interpreted as reflecting the shifts and changes within an ideological battlefield. Depending upon one's own set of beliefs, there can be agreement or disagreement with current policy and argumentation for certain kinds of program focus. This type of armchair theorizing that considers the socio-political and historical implications of literacy is useful for everyone because it helps clarify personal assumptions and ideologies about the field of practice.

However, in my role as a government bureaucrat, I don't have the luxury of stepping outside and theorizing about literacy nor the freedom to advocate one ideological position over another. I live in the centre of the battlefield and spend my working life negotiating it. I must take a pragmatic approach, one that attempts to find compromises that best serve the competing needs within the literacy field. And at the centre of all of this are the needs of the learner.

From this position, the premise of this chapter is that workplace literacy must be integrated into the broader literacy delivery system to meet the emerging needs of the adult learner. Three major arguments are presented. The first section discusses the changing nature of the workplace and why adults with lower literacy skills need to upgrade for work. This is followed by an articulation of the key needs of the work-force learner — requirements such as services that are accessible, transparent, and portable and learning that is transferable and portable. The third section illustrates how the Ontario government is reforming its community-based program to better address these emerging needs, and concludes by suggesting ways of further integrating the world of work with adult learning.

WHERE I COME FROM

I have been a literacy field consultant with the Ontario government for almost ten years. Prior to my current role as a public servant, I coordinated a community-based organization that delivered workplace literacy and English as a Second Language (ESL) in a predominantly manufacturing area of southern Ontario. My main duties over those five years entailed promoting literacy in area workplaces by developing responses to identified needs with various stakeholders. During that time I helped create a regional literacy network that brought together the key players in adult education. I also served on the executives of the regional Teachers of English as a Second Language (TESL) affiliate and the provincial literacy umbrella group — the Ontario Literacy Coalition. Before that I worked in literacy, ESL and workplace education in a school board.

My background in the literacy field is shared by several of my colleagues at the Ontario Ministry of Training, Colleges and Universities, while other consultants bring training and education experience from different fields. The performance of our duties, such as monitoring funded agencies, coaching practitioners, and encouraging program development, are not simply directed by government policy. Our actions are informed by our past experiences, by the ongoing interactions that we have with our field of clients and by discussions with each other. It can be viewed as a type of praxis.

Workplace or workforce?

The key element in Blunt's definition of workplace literacy distinguishing it from other types of literacy is its focus on work tasks. Many in Canada call this *workforce* literacy. However, there is a distinction between this term and workplace literacy. In workplace literacy, the stakeholders of business and labour own it in some measure. Although it often focuses on work tasks, it may be much more than that. It usually occurs at the workplace, at some expense to the organization and often with instructors on a contracted basis. To varying degrees, it is integrated into the broader training program and learning culture of a workplace. Workplace literacy, then, is an important piece of our broader efforts to improve the literacy skills of the workforce. The purpose here is not to debate such term distinctions but rather to examine the lifelong learning needs of adults in order to build the foundation for an integrative and holistic system that can serve Canadians with low literacy skills.

The world of work has changed dramatically in the last few decades. Canada's economy has shifted from local to global and from resource-based to knowledge-based. Some of the most plentiful jobs of the past have disappeared; the jobs that remain and the newly created ones are dramatically different. Changing work has become a central concern for every sector of society — employers, labour organizations, governments, and individuals. Employers struggle to remain competitive by consolidating their business, introducing new technologies, downsizing their operations, and merging with other companies. Labour organizations fight to protect the jobs and rights of their memberships while individuals become more entrepreneurial and dedicate increasing time and effort to managing their income potential. Meanwhile, governments focus their policies and resources on sustaining a strong economy by creating the conditions for increased employment opportunities.

A CRITICAL REFLECTION ON TECHNOLOGY, THE WORKPLACE, AND LITERACY

Technology is often viewed as a result of economic activity as well as an instrument of change. To produce advantages in a market system, people have developed technological innovations that have changed the way the economy functions, the available jobs, and the ground rules for participation in the labour force. However, the effects are uneven and are putting greater pressures on some working adults more than others.

The last three decades have seen technological advances across every industry and workplace sector. The use of computers has revolutionized the tasks of all jobs, from robotics and computer-managed manufacturing systems to word-processing and electronic communications. As the generation time for each new development of technology shrinks, rapid changes affect the what and how of our jobs.

Changes in the way that work is organized and the widespread introduction of quality control systems required for International Organization for Standardization (ISO) certification are indicators that the level and range of essential skills required of jobs have increased. A generation ago, shop floor workers in a factory operated their specific machine and communicated problems verbally to their supervisor. Now, they work in manufacturing teams building the entire product unit as a group and managing their work to meet standards defined by ISO, Hazard Analysis Critical Control Points (HACCP), or even the corporation itself.

These ways of working now require new essential skills. Individuals need to be able to read, problem-solve, access and use very different types of information. In the past this may have been someone else's responsibility. Even in the last few years, the reading and writing requirements of a job have increased. Workers now must have skills in research, oral presentation, and group decision-making. These types of skills are being viewed as important as the skill of literacy and they are becoming part of the definition of literacy itself. Literacy has come to mean more than simply reading and writing. As job tasks continue to change, the essential skills requirements also change. The workplace now requires individuals to be able to transfer knowledge from one context to another. Many companies believe that it is the ability to learn and manage change comfortably that they value most in their employees.

The worker as self-directed learner

Having the same job in a lifespan has now changed to having several different careers. Companies are hesitant to invest in workers they see as likely to be gone in a few years, and labour must negotiate upgrading and training into contracts in order to protect the employability of its membership. In response, educators promote lifelong learning by offering evening courses and opening adult learning centres, creating the perception by business that it is reasonable to expect adults to go off to school on their own time. This scenario is much different than it was even a decade ago.

With literacy gaining prominence as a workplace issue in the economy, workers are realizing that their employability is directly related to their literacy skills and the expectation of personal upgrade. As adults search out programs, these need to be responsive. But how are responsive programs created? Identifying the needs of a workforce learner is an important starting point in the process. Learners who upgrade their skills are a diverse group; however, they have a common set of needs. Even though their backgrounds, formal education experiences, learning styles, and articulation of goals vary, they share the same five fundamental expectations.

1. **Accessibility** — Adult learners have limited time to spend on learning. They are working overtime or on several jobs, or are in a rush to find a job as soon as possible. They are caring for children or parents, or heavily involved in community activities. They need programs that are available to them at times and places that are convenient — at work, in their community, and in their homes. Some are interested in a longer program while others can only devote a few hours a week. In other words, learners vary in the amount of time and effort they can commit to learning.

2. **Transparency** — Learners benefit from a clear picture of where to go and what to expect. They don't want to waste time going to the wrong places and finding themselves in strange and uncomfortable situations. Learners need to know how they will be served and how the system works. They need to know about choices.

3. **Effectiveness** — Adults are discerning consumers and view even publicly funded programs as an investment of time and effort. They need to know that learning will impact their daily lives and have immediate application at work. This type of learning has to mesh with their reservoir of experience. They need service providers who can get them on track quickly and meaningfully.

4. **Transferability** — Learners need to acquire skills that serve a variety of purposes, so that after they leave a program they can transfer these skills to new tasks and to new change situations. They also need to understand and talk about the impact of their learning and how it affects their roles as workers, family members and community citizens.

5. **Portability** — Learners come to programs knowing that they need certain skills in order to be hired, or to be eligible for training and promotion at the workplace. They need programs that accredit the learning in a way that is easily understood by the workplace. They need to see how a program fits into the broader education and training system. Learning must be recognized by

commonly understood credentials, so that adults can enter and exit education and training throughout their lives without having to repeat content previously learned.

How governments are responding

Governments across Canada have been responding to these emerging needs of the "learner-as-worker and worker-as-learner" in a variety of ways over the last decade. For example, school-based education systems are being reviewed with an intent of making them more proactively responsive. In Ontario, some program reform initiatives of the K–12 system are of a scale not seen since the 1960s.

Paralleling these initiatives, the Ontario government is also reviewing the extent of their fiscal responsibility in workplace learning. Presently, the apprenticeship program is undergoing reform, and the Labour Market Development Agreement (LMDA) with the federal government continues to be negotiated. This agreement devolves the responsibility for training from a federal to a provincial level and recognizes the need for training to be integrated within the education systems of each province. Ontario is the last of the provinces to have such an agreement in place.

In addition, a policy decision has been made by the Ontario government to recognize the full fiscal responsibility of the primary workplace stakeholders — employers and employees — for the delivery of all in-house training, including literacy. This also means that the province will continue its role in the development of workplace learning cultures. The workplace literacy strategy identifies the ways that literacy in the workplace will be encouraged by the government. It also supports the further development of the publicly funded literacy delivery system to better serve the needs of the workforce.

A VISION FOR NEW DIRECTIONS

The workplace literacy strategy is one element of Literacy and Basic Skills (LBS), the Ontario government's program providing literacy services to adults. Through the significant reform of adult literacy services and the ongoing development in the field, the government seeks to address the five fundamental requirements of learning and working adults.

Employability is the focus of LBS. However, learners often have personal goals that also require a further development of literacy skills.

Therefore, the use of literacy in an adult learner's personal life is a major thrust of the program.

Directions towards accessibility and transparency

At the highest level, there is a need for governments to streamline their literacy delivery systems to become more user friendly. Generally, this is accomplished by redefining their relationships with literacy delivery organizations and the criteria they use to fund services. In Ontario, colleges, school boards, and not-for-profit agencies have delivered separate literacy programs with different budgets, eligibility criteria, and conditions. These have now been replaced by a single LBS program, with uniform eligibility requirements, application processes and reporting mechanisms. In other words, the government's expectations of the service provider are now consistent across the board. Each funded agency knows the expectations of other funded agencies.

While this single LBS program with clear guidelines increases the transparency and efficiency of the system at the provincial level and between the government and the delivery agencies, it also needs to occur at the community level. Through the LBS program, the government of Ontario now requires joint planning and coordination of literacy delivery at the local level.

In practice, this means that all funded agencies within a community are required to identify their specific literacy needs and the services they will perform, such as the constituencies, delivery model and so on. The purpose is not simply to describe who is doing what for whom, but to depict how the services fit together in addressing the particular needs of that community. This will help to ensure against overlaps and gaps. Within this kind of framework, each agency sets achievable goals, identifies the steps needed to get there, and determines how progress towards those goals will be monitored and accomplished. Together, the agencies determine how their service delivery system should be improved, what actions will be taken, and how they will measure their steps forward.

The result of such a process is a comprehensible plan for literacy delivery within a community, providing a blueprint for the delivery agencies — a guide for their activities and a standard against which they can measure their performance. It also enhances the transparency of the system as a whole. Taxpayers will be able to see clearly how the system is working, and clients can easily find out which agency best suits their requirements.

Another area of improvement lies in making literacy services more available to adult learners and helping them to become aware of choices. Learning opportunities must be more available to the adult at home, in the workplace and through a network of accessible learning centres. In all communities, there must be a diverse range of learning formats such as tutoring, independent study, small group and computer-assisted instruction. The development of a Web-based learning resource called Alpha Route will allow learners even greater control over their learning. Once accessibility to the technology is addressed, learners will be able to determine when and what they study, for how long and for what purposes — with greater confidentiality.

Literacy providers must reach out to the workplace. Public awareness and promotional campaigns need to include workplace stakeholders so that they can identify their roles in the effort. Initiatives like WestNet's regional conferences for business and labour help to disseminate the economic impact of literacy. Communication events like these start the dialogue that leads to action. As well, partnerships with local training boards and sector councils help forge connections among business, labour and literacy groups at a local level. People Over Programs, a project of the Metro Toronto Movement for Literacy, identifies this local work as the only way of achieving a fully integrated employment and training service system.

Campaigns promoting literacy to adult workers need to provide clear and helpful information. Personal interest stories, often preferred by the media, can fail to reach large numbers of potential listeners. Like the campaigns to promote workplace literacy to business and labour, the message to individual working adults needs to be delivered through a sensitive media, local unions and company newsletters. Such campaigns could also help workers identify their own needs for upgrading and ways to continually use their new skills. Workers need to know who to talk to about starting a program or how they can access workplace training. Literacy providers need to speak about their services in a language that workers understand so that they feel valued as learners. And finally, employers and union leaders need to continue to foster a workplace environment that supports literacy by developing opportunities for the practice of essential skills on the job.

Directions towards effectiveness and portability

In implementing Ontario's LBS program, the government has created a multi-year strategy called Recognition of Adult Learning (RALS). The strategy is rooted in an outcomes-based approach that focuses on the learner and the learning rather than on the curriculum or the skill. A learning outcomes-based program approach begins with a clear determination of the exit outcome — what the learner will be able to do. The next step is to define the required demonstration — how to know the learning has been achieved. The approach then determines assessment criteria — how the quality and level of learning will be evaluated. At this point, learning activities are designed based on the assessment indicating how the learner needs to be supported. Because learning is always demonstrated against pre-set criteria, the approach exemplifies the integrity of a system, and provides the flexibility necessary for the learner to take control and responsibility of the learning reflecting changing workplace demands.

As part of the new system, literacy practitioners are now developing a common language around adult learning describing the needs and accomplishments of their clients, and devising better ways to assist learners in the identification of their goals and the related learning outcomes. They are examining how to assess the starting point of a learning plan and how to provide measured indicators of progress that are clear to the adult learner and other stakeholders. It is envisioned that this flexible framework will accommodate any adult learning path and be credible enough to document learning in a meaningful way.

Directions towards transferability

Since adults come to literacy programs for a variety of reasons, the end results of their learning should be reflected in both their personal and working lives. Some learners are able to describe the expected differences in their lives because of this training, while others are not. Therefore, adults need a literacy practitioner who can help identify potential skills as well as link the learning to practical tasks reflective of those skills. Often, when learners identify personal or work tasks as goals, they are not aware of how to transfer that learning to other situations. It is hoped that this learning-outcomes approach will assist practitioners in describing the transfer of learning process.

Learning outcomes make it easier to talk about tasks combining skills across different levels, and curriculum can be designed with a focus on contextual applications. Practitioners who can illuminate the range of applications for their learners will instil a sense of empowerment. The new role for service providers will be to help workers see that the acquired knowledge and skills have application in various contexts — in their jobs, in jobs other than their own and in their community, union and family. Helping learners become aware of what they have learned and how it is transferable demonstrates the important quality of respect. Giving adults the tools to describe their abilities also helps them to demonstrate their employability. This metacognitive aspect is now a central component of literacy learning. Although further research is needed on the transfer of learning, we do know from experience that learners who are comfortable with transferring their skills are more likely to be comfortable with change, thus increasing the quality of their personal and work lives.

This new literacy delivery system must also be flexible enough to accommodate economic shifts while addressing the needs of unemployed, underemployed, part-time or vulnerable workers. This means that practitioners need to partner creatively and responsively to take into account the training capacity of workplaces and varying production schedules. The development of the learning-outcomes approach and the implementation of an adult learning recognition strategy will accommodate this flexibility for the individual learner and the changing needs of the workforce.

Directions towards portability

At the core of most learning situations, adults need to be able to do or know something, and then to demonstrate this knowledge or skill. Balancing these twin objectives of competence and recognition has been an ongoing struggle for adult literacy in Canada. Programs that focus entirely on the specific knowing and doing needs of the learner may have difficulty providing recognized accreditation. Programs that only provide learning around standardized requirements may not mesh with the particular needs of a learner. Although modifying a standardized curriculum to better reflect the needs of the adult learner is a solution, it only serves those learners whose needs still fall within the scope of that curriculum. From our experience we are finding that numerous adults wish to explore material beyond a set or required curriculum. So we need to explore ways of recognizing adult learning that transfers to the broader education and training systems and across workplaces. Projects like Promoting Adult Learning to Employers (PALE) provide an opportunity for business, labour and literacy stakeholders to consider ways to address the recognition of learning question.

The paths between literacy learning and the broader education and training system such as apprenticeship, secondary school credit and the General Educational Development (GED) certificate must be made transparent and seamless. Adults need to see that there are paths of learning beyond literacy and that smooth transitions between steps are possible. Workers need to feel assured that upgrading programs are connected to the requirements of further education and other types of training programs, and that efforts in a preparatory course will be recognized in an eventual diploma or certificate program. As well, they need to know that Prior Learning Assessment and Recognition (PLAR) methods can help in this process of transition and recognition.

Working in concert

How the workplace informs literacy programs is an integral part of the system. Business and labour bodies, such as Sector Councils and Local Training Boards, must work with educators to identify the emerging skills of the current and future workforce. In addition, educators must listen to trends in the world of work through task analyses, the macro-organization of operations and the regulatory standards of the industry.

Websites such as Human Resources Development Canada's Essential Skills Profiles (ESP) provide generic definitions of jobs that help make programs more relevant. Projects such as Learning Outcomes and the Workplace (LOW) help to ensure the local applicability of such definitions. LOW is using the ESP as a starting point in working with local employers to determine the actual requirements for entry level positions in local workplaces. In this way, skills defined by employers as appropriate can be used as exit outcomes in literacy learning plans. Other projects that have developed tools, like the Test of Workplace Essential Skills (TOWES) and A Literacy Employment Readiness Test (ALERT), help to assess broad and specific literacy skills of potential workers.

Employers, employee organizations, and individual employees need to work together with literacy practitioners to make workforce training effective. They need to talk about their expectations of new and existing workers, to negotiate common objectives, to provide ongoing support to the educators and to follow through on agreed-upon evaluations. By taking an active role in the reform of adult training programs that upgrade the workforce, business and labour share the responsibility of determining the outcomes of this new system.

Research bodies can also play a key role in bridging the worlds of work and education. For example, the Conference Board of Canada and ABC Canada have numerous reports that deepen our understanding of the workplace. As well, research conducted by the stakeholders them-selves, such as the Canadian Grocery Producers Council, provides cru-cial information on ideas such as return on investment. Information management facilities such as AlphaPlus can help to organize research data, resources, and project developments, making the information accessible to stakeholders and literacy programs striving to improve their services.

Government must continue to refine the map that charts our new course and listen to the changing needs of the adult in the workplace, in the family and in society so that the system can respond more effectively. There must also be sufficient investment to ensure flexibility. Connected to this, adult learners must demonstrate a commitment to learn, and they need to be actively engaged in the learning process from goal setting to assessing progress. Learners also need to devote sufficient time and effort to produce a reasonable and satisfying pace of learning. And they need to demand accountability from all stakeholders in the provision of support needed to make their learning effective. Workplace stakeholders and educators must also continue to work in collaboration through advi-sory groups, conferences, think tanks and development projects that can foster innovative learning approaches.

The education system cannot teach us everything we need to know about work and life just as the workplace cannot provide all the upgrad-ing and learning opportunities needed by adults. Learning must be seen as an ongoing, lifelong process that is supported by employers, unions, government, the community, and educators. By working together and learning from each other, we can develop a literacy system that is flexi-ble and responsive to change as we break into the new millennium.

RESOURCES

ABC Canada
   Address: 333 King St. E., Toronto, ON M5A 4N2
   Phone: (416) 350-6270 or 1-800-303-1004
   E-mail: Abc@corporate.southam.ca
   Website: http://www.abc-canada.org/

ALERT — Preparatory Training Programs of Toronto
   Contact: John McLaughlin
   Address: 5468 Dundas St. W., Suite 330, Toronto, ON M3C 1H9
   Phone: (416) 239-4153
   E-mail: Jrmptp@interlog.com

Alpha Plus Centre/Alpha Route/AlphaPlus Resource
   Address: 21 Park Rd., Toronto, ON M4W 2N1
   Phone: (416) 975-1351 or 1-800-788-1120 or TTY (416) 975-8839
   E-mail: Info@alphaplus.ca
   Website: http://www.alphaplus.ca/

Canadian Grocery Producers Council
   Address: 302-61 International Blvd., Rexdale, ON M9W 6K4
   Phone: (905) 670-3844
   E-mail: info@cgpc.org
   Website: http://www.cgpc.org

Conference Board of Canada
   Address: 255 Smythe Rd., Ottawa, ON K1H 8M7
   Phone: (613) 526-3280
   Website: http://www2.conferenceboard.ca

Human Resources Development Canada, Essential Skills Profiles
   Contact: Debra Mair, Sr. Researcher, Occupational & Career Info. Branch
   Address: 140 Promenade du Portage, Phase IV, 5th fl.,
            Ottawa/Hull, ON K1A 0J9
   Phone: (819) 953-7480
   Website: http://www.hrdc-drhc.gc.ca/hrib/hrp-prh/skills/profiles.shtml

TOWES/Skillplan(BC Construction Industry Skills Improvement Council
   Address: Suite 242, 4299 Canada Way, Burnaby, BC V5G 1H3
   Phone: (604) 436-1126
   E-mail: skilplan@acionet.com
   Website: http://www.towes.com
   Contact: Conrad Murphy, Bow Valley College
   Address: 332-6 Avenue S.E., Calgary, AB T2G 4S6
   Phone: (403) 297-4938
   E-mail: cmurphy@bowvalleyc.ab.ca

LOW Project
Contact: Jane Tuer, The Literacy Group of Waterloo Region Inc.,
Address: 291 Westminster Dr. N., Cambridge, ON N3H 1S3
Phone: (519) 650-3783 or (519) 743-0474
E-mail: jtuer@golden.net

PALE Project
Contact: Cindy Davidson, QUILL Literacy Network
Address: 111 Jackson St. S., 3rd Fl., Walkerton, ON N0G 2V0
Phone: (519) 881-4655
E-mail: Info@quillnet.org
Website: http://www.quillnet.org

People Over Programs Project, Metro Toronto Movement for Literacy
Contact: Colleen D'Souza, MTML
Address: 365 Bloor St. E., Suite 1003, Toronto, ON M4W 3L4
Phone: (416) 961-4013
E-mail: mtml@interlog.com
Website: http://www.nald.ca/province/ont/mtml/poppub/intro.htm

Knowledge Acquisition in the Field of Practice

Nancy Steel

Workplace education providers primarily acquire their knowledge by experiential learning rather than by formalized education in a certified program. This approach to professional growth is in keeping with their assumptions about adult education, consistent with the values they have about learning for themselves and others as workers, and reflective of the experiences they enjoy by working in a variety of dynamic workplaces.

My discussion begins with a narrative describing a crisis of thought situation that challenged my previous assumptions, values and experience of worker assessment. This narrative exemplifies knowledge acquisition in the literacy field and invites critical thinking about how we learn and develop our practice, about how our field experiences are the source of our knowledge and about how this then shapes the future of formalized professional development and certification.

In his earlier chapter, Blunt remarks that "all literacy practitioners and researchers, regardless of where their work is located need to be reflective practitioners." And "My thinking about literacy work is influenced by my prior experiences as a frontline literacy worker ... through these experiences I have constructed my personal understanding of literacy policy and practice." The discussion in this chapter is in some ways a development of those remarks.

KNOWLEDGE THROUGH CRISIS OF THOUGHT

As a practitioner in the workplace education field for several years, I have spent some time considering the issue of worker assessment, the philosophies, tools, and approaches that clothe the issue. Indeed, for many years I conducted diagnostic assessments of workers' reading comprehension skills, and so my need to think about the issue was immediate and real, not mere musing. I also participated in discussions at a national think tank, read ideas put forward in the research, and synthesized what I learned into a set of assumptions and principles that complemented my early roots in community literacy practice. However, this set of assumptions and principles was seriously challenged in the fall of 1998, and the experience has left me convinced that challenge, and even crisis, seed knowledge acquisition for practitioners in the workplace education field.

In the fall of 1998, I was excited to be asked to create a contextualized reading comprehension assessment tool for workers who were entering job training that would lead to their employment. I read the excellent needs assessment report made available to me and talked with the client extensively. I developed a draft test and proceeded to try it out with workers on a one-to-one basis, using it to ascertain their ability to read-to-learn effectively. The client provided me with a project partner, a testing expert, whose expertise would ensure that the test was valid and reliable. Already my education had begun, but soon my assumptions about what constituted effective assessment would be challenged.

Over the months we field-tested this test with several groups of candidates. I found this to be effective because it helped me to distinguish which test questions were sound and which needed to be recast. However, as enjoyable as that learning was, I experienced discomfort. My principle that testing should be conducted one-to-one and be diagnostic in purpose, a vehicle for determining required support and development, was challenged. This test was to screen job recruits who lacked the reading skills to participate in job preparation skill training. While I balked at this purpose, I also had to admit that allowing people to participate in training without the essential skills could propel them towards failure. I presumed that referrals to basic skills programs were offered by the company, and accepted. I could walk away from the contract, or I could re-examine my principles and adjust them to accommodate and influence the situation to allow for best practice in these circumstances.

I was also uncomfortable with the delivery of the test to groups of workers. To ensure consistency of results the verbal instructions I gave for writing the test had to be scripted and were required to be direct and succinct. This clinical approach offended my own principle that testing directly tied to employment must be conducted in a way to diminish testing anxiety, not increase it. I struggled with the requirement for a succinct script, arguing for greater latitude to take an instructional rather than testing approach. My principles were challenged once again, and only with a struggle did I find a way to accommodate both my passion for a non-threatening test environment and the need for a set of test instructions that were uniform and brief.

Conflicting perspectives and understandings can lead to insight

The fundamental issue was that my colleague's perspective and understanding of assessment was contrary to mine, and our approaches were also very different. However, with discussion and compromise both of us could eventually emerge richer and more competent.

Two insights occurred to me afterward. One was that this experience exemplified the nature of partnership. In the workplace education field partnership is considered a linchpin, the primary partnership being between the workers as represented by their union, and the company management. As an educator, I am an invited third party, and while I understand the significance of this partnership, I am outside of it, and so see it as a value without having to experience the struggle. But only by struggling with a partner with differing values, yet who nevertheless had much to offer, did I appreciate how partnerships are often painful, and that the struggle forces the bloom of new ideas and results in professional growth.

The second insight was that this experience also exemplifies the primary learning process for most educators in the field. Most workplace educators have come from elsewhere professionally; we were not trained in a formal way to do this work, and so our professional growth and our knowledge acquisition are seeded by challenge and occasionally by crisis.

A CRITICAL REFLECTION ON HOW WE LEARN

The acquisition of knowledge as the outcome of a challenging experience is not unique to me. Indeed, many of my colleagues have recounted incidents causing them to reconsider their assumptions, to adapt their practice and to shape their learning into a future guiding principle. For example, an experienced adult education consultant in Vancouver describes this event from 1993 that shaped her practice ever after:

" *... the workplace education committee that I was working with was not yet running on all cylinders. It was new. The Needs Assessment report was just finally complete in written form and a time was set up to present it to the managers. I had a phone call from the union representative on the committee and he gave me the time and place for the meeting and said it was to be brief and 'casual.' So I planned a 10-minute presentation on the report, thinking they would have to take it away and read it.*

I arrived about half an hour early — and the HR manager and I sat down for a pre-conference. It became apparent that this is a BIG DEAL — our chance to sell the idea and make a case for support. I made a few overheads and scrambled around, but the meeting fell very flat. I basically dropped the ball and people were left with the Needs Assessment report to take away and read.

Yikes! We called a post mortem for the committee and we learned that the problem was the message on the phone — and the fact that the union representative had never been to a managers' meeting and really did not understand the expectations. We learned, from then on, to communicate between the committee and caucus before every meeting or presentation. But mostly what I learned is that it is not up to me to carry the ball. In the next meeting the committee members each presented the findings, and the HR representative, together with the union representative, presented the plan. I only answered questions about process and costs and things, and wrote on the flipchart.

This agonizing moment changed my practice 25 percent. I was always trying to facilitate and to "share power" and all that, but from this I learned that it is just wrong to carry the ball rather than to teach ball carrying and support learning to carry the ball. I treat committees differently now — they are a community of learners and they are trying to gain competencies and I am there to help. Most people I work with are surprised at how much I want them to do things — but it is the best way.

Afterwards I was really hard on myself so I processed this with everyone (HR representative, union representative, finance representative). It helped the committee see me as a fallible person and we were all the closer for it afterwards. It was what made it everyone's responsibility to get things right. (T. Defoe, personal communication, 1999) "

Other practitioners recount similar experiences with as much passion. In each case, their experiences resulted in more than just incidental learning; these were experiences and critical incidents that deepened their practice and shaped their principles. Another colleague with a wealth of experience in the field told me that a lesson she learned in the early days of her practice was that

> *I should be cautious in what I promise as results from basic skills programs ... literacy is interwoven within the culture of the workplace, and thus is complex rather than simple. I want to see it in all its complexity, rather than its simplest terms. (S. Folinsbee, personal communication, 1999)*

This is not knowledge that she acquired by reading, or by listening to others' ideas, but rather by her front line experience and struggle with issues and problems. What she learned by working now provides her with a firm foundation of principles and values. In this field, this is how we learn.

The acquisition of knowledge in this fashion has been especially necessary because workplace education practitioners have come into this field from elsewhere, not from a formal training experience that prepared them for this work, but rather from related fields. For example, I moved from teaching Business English to community literacy work to workplace education; another colleague moved into this field after undertaking volunteer ESL literacy work while in university, while others have moved from the elementary and secondary school system into the adult education and then workplace education field. Some practitioners have arrived here from other disciplines entirely, for example, from a sociology background, or a communications background.

The point is that presently not even one workplace education practitioner in Canada has been formally trained at a university or college to deliver workplace essential skills education to workers in Canada. However, this does not mean that formal professional development has been ignored, or that the notion of an education path that prepares one for this kind of work has gone unimagined. A series of workshops, think tanks, and conference presentations has contributed to the growth of knowledge in the field. These events are generously sponsored by the National Literacy Secretariat, which clearly sees the professional development of workplace education practitioners as a sound investment. Such activities have served to structure, to collect and to formalize the knowledge that is being shaped by practitioners' experience. In short, our professional development is being shaped by the experience of our peers, who are also our mentors. This grass-roots transference of knowledge says clearly that we learn best by experience and from each other.

The role of experiential learning

The axiom that experience is the best teacher is nothing new. What makes it shine in this case is that it is the perfect example of experiential learning, an approach to education that most workplace educators espouse for their learners, but seldom see as relevant for themselves. Many workplace educators rightfully associate themselves with the work of leaders in the field of adult experiential learning, such as David Kolb and Paulo Freire. Practitioners in workplace education support these leaders' belief that experiential learning is not simply the involvement of the learner in classroom activities so that they "get experience in a hands-on way as they learn." Rather, as defined by Kolb (1984, p. 20), experiential learning "is the process whereby knowledge is created through the transformation of experience." Experiential learning means that learning is rooted in the learner's experience, and so should derive from that place, not from an outside source, defying a more traditional view that individuals are empty pitchers into which teachers pour information and ideas. Workplace educators develop programs shaped around needs articulated by workers in the context of their work and life situation, and these programs may shift as the context shifts and the needs change and develop.

As workplace educators, this is how we learn too, and so our experiential approach to our professional development should be consistent with the approach we take to education for others.

The role of ambient knowledge

Taking an experiential approach to our work means we can also then admit the value of what might be called "ambient knowledge." Some of the knowledge we acquire as we practice and learn contributes directly to our bank of skills and to our principles. Other knowledge that is not central to our practice but which nevertheless enhances our practice is acquired along the way too. For example, critical to our job as workplace education practitioners is the knowledge of how to conduct a needs assessment, how to develop curriculum, how to assess workers for placement and progress, how to evaluate program efficacy, and effective adult teaching strategies. Not critical to the actual doing of the job, but certainly enriching, is an understanding of contextual issues relevant to the workplace — issues relating to health and safety, to current models of management, to union principles, to the Canadian economy. Such acquired ambient knowledge derives from our experience, and sometimes from crisis.

For example, few practitioners in Canada have come from the labour field. Most are new to labour principles the first time they work with a joint management-labour committee exploring the idea of creating an essential skills program. Navigating the waters of labour relations as an outside, unfamiliar, third party is very challenging, and many practitioners have occasionally found themselves in a quandary as they struggled to balance the sometimes conflicting values that labour and business hold regarding workplace education. An experienced practitioner in Manitoba once found herself uncertain as to which of the two parties she was most accountable. On the one hand the union was a full partner at the table, but on the other hand the employer paid her salary. Both were asking different things of her. An understanding and appreciation of both positions was critical, in the end, to her eventual success and the success of the program. Her knowledge acquisition of such ambient issues as business-labour relations was acquired experientially, and became as critical to her practice as her set of how-to skills.

The role of workplace dynamics

The workplace is a complex and changeable stage for teaching, and so for this reason workplace educators may be more likely to learn from experience or crisis than, say, the adult college classroom teacher. Every workplace that the practitioner enters is different. Each has its own culture influencing the nature and dynamics of the program; each has its own vocabulary or jargon that the practitioner must learn and use correctly; each has its own set of economic imperatives influencing the need for a sustainable program; each has its own code of labour practice affecting why, how, and when the program will be offered. Into each workplace the practitioner must bring acquired knowledge about the ambient issues of corporate culture, health and safety, labour practices and economics — and then get ready to learn even more. The practitioner is always the outsider invited in, and so must be prepared to ask about and observe workplace dynamics that are a backdrop for practice.

For example, a practitioner charged with developing a program at a sawmill must quickly understand the general operation of processing lumber for market: removing bark from logs, cutting logs to specifications, grading lumber, producing wood chips, preserving and treating wood. The practitioner must learn about the various occupations or jobs that workers do, which may range from kiln operator, to sawmill equipment operator (of which there are many types), to lumber grader. Understanding the safety hazards confronting the worker, economic impacts affecting the availability and security of work, and the general working conditions will all be important because of their impact on the worker, and therefore the program.

After developing a program at a sawmill, a practitioner may then immediately move into an entirely different workplace, perhaps a bakery, and be confronted again with the necessity to learn. There, the operation would involve food processing with its attendant safety issues, occupational categories, job skill requirements and job security issues. Unlike the classroom teacher, who is stationed in the same place and works under the same conditions each day, the workplace education practitioner is continuously exposed to differing and dynamic environments.

Business and labour trends in Canada are driven by economic trends. Market demands fluctuate and may impact whole industrial sectors. A decline in demand for a product will result in a decline in demand for labour, which, in turn, requires that workers be re-skilled and redeployed into other areas of work. As an example, if the demand for Canadian wood products in Japan diminishes, workers in the sawmills in British Columbia are directly affected by the lack of demand for their labour. Workplace essential skill education is sometimes a part of the response to such a crisis, offering an opportunity for workers to strengthen foundation skills so that they might take on new training that will lead to work in new areas. In this way, workplace education practitioners are affected by the dynamics of business and labour trends in Canada. How we practice, when we practice and why we practice are determined by the need for workers to develop skills in the context of these shifting economic and social imperatives.

The report by Statistics Canada (1995) describing the results of the International Adult Literacy Survey has been an excellent resource for workplace educators to learn about the relationship of literacy skills of workers and employment. While for many years practitioners argued for ongoing worker education and training, they did so on the basis of their observations, their experience, and anecdotal evidence. This report provides facts and statistics and conclusions supporting their experiential knowledge.

LEARNING FROM OUR SITUATIONAL EXPERIENCES

In the same way that the report by Statistics Canada (1995) formalizes and confirms our experiential knowledge as we practice, so too do the workshops, the think tanks and the conferences that we attend to further our professional development. Leading practitioners in the field have given much thought to shaping, developing and articulating what we need in order to develop our skills and knowledge. Belfiore (1998) produced a collection of narratives written by a variety of workplace education practitioners entitled *Chronicling the Learning Curve: Workplace Education Instructors Share Their Stories*. As the title suggests, these writers describe the learning experiences and crises that have provided them with an accumulated knowledge base from which to practice. Folinsbee (1999) interviewed practitioners across Canada to determine how they are continuing to grow, what resources they have, and what resources they now need to further that growth. Her study gives voice to practitioners' collective knowledge. In another discussion Bennett (1997) articulates the skills and attributes required to be an effective workplace instructor and suggests professional development approaches that will ensure good practice.

Questions around what we need to do to provide new instructors with knowledge and skills and experienced instructors with ongoing professional development were addressed directly in a two-day Practitioner Forum held in Winnipeg, March 1999. At that meeting, participants had the opportunity to explore not only practitioner development, but also the more challenging issue of recognition and certification. Several significant points were made.

- Participants believed that professional development efforts should reflect the diversity of the field, responding to different levels of experience, as well as differing needs and interests of practitioners regionally.
- The value of a mix of formal and informal expertise-building, specific training, mentoring and hands-on experience was emphasized.

- There are too many questions about the nature of assessing and measuring practitioners' competencies to as yet address the question of formal recognition or certification. (Roger & Nichol, 1999, p. 4)

Creating nationally consistent approaches to professional development

The latter point leads directly to the question of skills, knowledge and aptitudes that practitioners in our field must possess to fulfil the various roles of a workplace educator, for without identifying the requirements we cannot determine effective development nor assess for certification. So, as a first step practitioners informally brainstormed the knowledge, skills and aptitudes required of them in their various job tasks.

This inventory allowed for a further analysis of the skills, knowledge and aptitudes underlying the job of a workplace educator to understand which of these are critical and should be introduced to new practitioners, and further developed among experienced ones. Such analysis can be the foundation for a more formalized approach or strategy for professional development and competency standards, which can then lead to some consideration of nationally consistent approaches to assessing and certifying practitioners.

There is already much happening in the way of workplace education training at the provincial level for new practitioners, although only a few provinces — Manitoba, for example, have offered multi-level, beginner and advanced practitioner training. The training has always been of a grass-roots nature: experienced practitioners sharing their day-to-day knowledge with those just entering the field. A certificate is always provided at the end of the training, but it must be noted that the certification is not authoritative because it has not been issued by a recognized institution, and so it does little to assure that the practitioner has met a set of professionally determined standards.

However, recognizing that workplace education is an emerging field of endeavour, universities are extending their usual portfolio of academic offerings to include courses that address the education needs of the business community. Currently, these courses address issues of adult teaching theory, management theories, and labour studies. They do not prepare specific workplace skills, but they offer good ambient knowledge. However, several universities are exploring partnerships with literacy organizations that may eventually develop this kind of formal, credentialled training for workplace practitioners.

About professional certification

Certification remains a forefront issue for every province's practitioners because the primary motivation for this is credibility of performance and professionalism. As the demand for workplace essential skill education increases, the clients, employers, and unions want to know that they will receive quality service as a return on their investment, based on reliable standards.

In a report by Kelly (1998) some possible operational directions for delivering a certified, professional development program are provided. "It could be offered through an institution ... delivered via distance education in the form of modules ... It could be offered through a series of workshops" (p. 17).

Regardless of the format chosen, it is clear that an authoritative institution or body must endorse the certification in order to provide the credibility sought. Universities' interest in supporting this kind of professional development may be just the answer.

The value of experiential learning

Given the experiential learning approach assumed by many practitioners, Prior Learning Assessment and Recognition (PLAR) will play a key role in determining entry requirements into such programs and in the development of appropriate assessments for skills and knowledge. PLAR involves the assessment of experience, as well as the learning that has resulted. In this way, experienced practitioners can potentially receive advance placement or advance credits towards certification, as a recognition of the learning acquired experientially during their years of practice.

Aldous Huxley said, "Experience is not what happens to you; it's what you do with what happens to you." But as uncertified and uncredentialled as this learning is, it is not without value and authority. Experiential learning is endorsed by academia and is often the preferred way to learn by many practitioners who don't discount the value of formalized training and certification of training, but who believe that experiential learning is primary: "Experimentation, the ability to be creative, practice-by-trying things out, and working with colleagues ... has contributed to my growth the most, rather than any formal training" (S. Folinsbee, personal communication, October 1999). Indeed, when asked at the March forum what I thought the best professional development might look like I replied: "More work. More work offering me a variety of new challenges and questions to explore on my own and with colleagues across the country is the best teaching possible. It broadens both my skills and ambient knowledge. It forces the bloom."

REFERENCES

Belfiore, M.E. (Ed.). (1998). *Chronicling the learning curve: Workplace education instructors share their stories.* Toronto, ON: ABC Canada.

Bennett, K. (1997). Retaining workplace instructors: Issues of recruitment, training and support. In M. Taylor (Ed.), *Workplace education: The changing landscape.* Toronto, ON: Culture Concepts Inc.

Freire, P. (1993). *Pedagogy of the oppressed.* New York: Continuum.

Kelly, S. (1998). *Determining the road ahead.* Halifax, NS: Author.

Roger, M., & Nicol, L. (1999). *Workplace education practitioner forum summary report.* Winnipeg, MB: Author.

Statistics Canada. (1995). *Literacy, economy, and society: Results of the first International Adult Literacy Survey.* The Organization for Economic and Cooperative Development. Ottawa, ON: Author.

12

SECTION SYNOPSIS

Workplace Literacy
Reflections on Practice as the Bar Keeps Rising

Marilyn T. Samuels

The five chapters in this section present many common themes even though each is written from a different perspective. The authors represent diverse constituents in the field but their messages converge to present a picture of what is happening in the area of workplace literacy and what is needed. A common thread throughout the chapters is that we live in a changing world where literacy is increasingly important. Thorn's contention that only the very literate will prosper in this new information age is cause for concern and raises a second recurring theme — what it means to be literate. The authors also vary in how they define literacy, yet there is general agreement that early definitions of basic literacy as the ability to read and write just don't hold anymore. Definitions keep changing and, as the authors suggest, the educational bar depicting who is literate keeps getting higher and higher. Walton (2000) reported that Ford Motor Company will soon be giving a computer to all 17,000 employees. As this action suggests, the definition of literacy at Ford will certainly change. New definitions suggested in this section and elsewhere (Samuels, 1999) include communication, problem solving, critical thinking and learning how to learn. Computer literacy and other technological literacies are also rapidly being considered basic literacy skills in many workplaces today.

Blunt's chapter presents an overview of "the contested terrains of policy and practice." He discusses the competing paradigms of emancipatory literacy and technical-rational literacy. Minke agrees with Blunt that literacy is a social-political construct manipulated and shaped by each of the stakeholders. While the other authors do not directly address this ideological question, their ideas are grounded in one or the other of these models. All the authors believe that literacy among workers is still a concern today and each presents ways to address this problem. Wiebe, writing from a business perspective, suggests that literacy programs need to focus on the enhancement of employees' performance with the fundamental aim of increasing profits. This view of literacy fits with the model of literacy as a component of human capital. Thorn, writing from a union perspective, argues that literacy for the economy alone will fail us all. He maintains that literacy, learning skills development and life skills must be for the purpose of enhancing the individual's whole life. Minke agrees with this and focuses on how one province is helping learners go beyond literacy training to lifelong learning.

The need for collaboration is yet another recurring theme in these chapters. Collaboration between management, unions, workers, federal and provincial governments and communities is seen as critical to successfully increasing workforce literacy. There is also the issue of programs to address the needs of the whole person. A repeated concern is that government programs have been aimed primarily at corporate and business interests. Minke, a self-described government bureaucrat, argues that workplace literacy must meet the needs of the learner. In general, there is agreement that a broader conceptualization of literacy learning is required to meet the needs of the individual in the workplace, home and community. Literacy programs that go beyond immediate corporate and business interests will benefit all parties.

Steel discusses workplace literacy from the perspective of literacy trainers, indicating that while literacy training has always been somewhat informal and grassroots, it is now becoming more entrenched in universities and other formal programs. Steel makes a case for reflective practice, with reflection based primarily on experience. How literacy instructors could integrate theories and research on adult learning into their practice needs to be addressed. Blunt suggests that both training programs and practice must be grounded in research and theory but raises concerns regarding the philosophical bases of formal training at the post-secondary level.

Definitions of literacy, curriculum content, and best practices clearly vary and, hence, there needs to be a convergence of the different paradigms into a new literacy discourse. Literacy instructors must also be ongoing learners and reflective practitioners and help learners engage in active reflection and effective self-monitoring as evidenced in the literature on adult learning (MacKeracher, 1997; Smith, 1991). Knowledge of both the adult literacy and the adult learning literatures is critical for effective instruction in adult literacy. I believe instructors must also be familiar with the literature on teaching adults with learning difficulties as many individuals in adult literacy programs have encountered problems with learning. Prior learning experiences, both positive and negative, can either enable new learning or become obstacles.

Each author represents a different constituency in the workplace literacy field and I come from yet another one. I am an educational psychologist working with adults encountering learning difficulties. In the adult literacy field, assumptions are often made that if literacy programs are available, individuals will want to access them. This may be the case for some but adults who have long-standing learning difficulties are often hesitant to become involved in workplace literacy programs. The shame, discouragement, and hopelessness that many learners feel often prevents them from attending a literacy program. Some are identified as having an attitude problem because they go to great efforts to hide their learning difficulties. Concerns about adults who have difficulty learning impact on all stakeholders. Clearly, academics and trainers need to ensure that they have an understanding of the diversity of learning needs and the reasons for not engaging in workplace literacy programs.

HELPING LEARNERS WITH DIFFICULTIES

In Alberta, literacy instructors raised concerns about how to teach unsuccessful learners in their programs and with support from the National Literacy Secretariat, a manual, entitled *Asking the Right Questions: Assessment and Program Planning for Adults with Learning Disabilities* (Samuels, Burrows, Scholten & Theunissen, 1995), was written. Training videos (Samuels & Todd, 1995) were also produced. Not only do literacy instructors need to know how to help learners with difficulties but other stakeholders such as union representatives, management, and front-line supervisors need to be aware of these employees (Samuels & Scholten, 1993). Workplace disciplinary measures and other types of actions may relate directly to learning issues.

Several years ago, I was an expert witness in a hearing in which an employee with a learning disability was terminated from the company after 12 years of service. While the issues were complex, the situation might have been handled differently had the employee's supervisors understood the impact of this person's learning disability on performance. To address the needs of employers, a CD-ROM, *Assessing Learning Difficulties in the Workplace* (Samuels & Todd, 1996), was developed. These materials were designed to teach a problem-solving process to better understand when someone is not performing as expected, whether it be in a literacy program or on the shop floor. Success in a workplace literacy program depends on the learner's beliefs and motivation, the approach used to teach literacy and a multitude of other factors discussed in this volume.

Workplace literacy programs, while still grappling with ideological issues, are becoming an accepted practice in business and industry, and must be broadly based and collaborative to address the needs of individual learners. The message that individuals have multiple roles as employee, community member, parent, and family member is one that business and government funding agencies must keep hearing. As the literacy bar continues to rise in this new era, literacy programs will need to evolve to meet the changing demands of both society and the workplace.

REFERENCES

MacKeracher, D. (1997). *Making sense of adult learning.* Toronto, ON: Culture Concepts Inc.

Samuels, M. (1999). Basic literacy: What does it mean in an information rich society? In J. Kelley & G. Stacey (Eds.), *Navigating the information "rich" society* (pp. 7–18). Calgary, AB: The Calgary Institute for the Humanities.

Samuels, M., Burrows, I., Scholten, T., & Theunissen, D. (1995). *Asking the right Question: Assessment and program planning for adults with learning difficulties.* (Rev. ed.). Calgary, AB: The Learning Centre and Alberta Vocational College.

Samuels, M., & Scholten, T. (1993). A model for the assessment of adults encountering learning difficulties. *International Journal of Cognitive Education and Mediated Learning, 3*(3), 135–151.

Samuels, M., & Todd, A.K. (1996). *Assessment of adults in the workplace — CD-ROM.* Calgary, AB: University of Calgary Communications Media.

Samuels, M., & Todd, A.K. (1995). *Assessment of adults with learning difficulties* [Video series]. Calgary, AB: University of Calgary Communications Media.

Smith, R.M. (1991, April). How people become effective learners. *Adult Learning*, 11–13.

Walton, D. (2000, February 4). Ford to give 350,000 workers home PCs. *Globe and Mail.*

SEC**3**ION

Family Literacy

FRAMING CHAPTER

Family Literacy
Issues and Directions for Research and Practice

Adele Thomas

Current concern about low literacy is related to increasing demands and expectations for literacy to meet rapid technological change, yet disparities continue to occur between rich and poor families, regarding access to literacy resources and support for education (Ross, Scott, & Kelly 1996). While poor families struggle to overcome social and economic obstacles in fostering literacy, they also face systematic obstacles to education and training to meet the rising demands of a technological society.

Yet, amid these economic and political inconsistencies, the field of family literacy has matured and identified a solid foundation of research and principles. Family literacy unites research and practice from several fields of study and social service. Because of family literacy's wide scope, it becomes difficult to keep the family in focus for literacy practitioners and the public alike. When literacy program or learner objectives shift back and forth, emphasizing child literacy learning or adult literacy learning, the focus on family literacy may be obscured. Understanding this complexity, family literacy educators continue to clarify misconceptions about family literacy, question assumptions about family literacy intervention, and renew demands for standards of good practice.

An overview of research and theory related to family literacy development is presented to set the stage for critical appraisal of family literacy practice in Canada. Issues related to defining family literacy are fundamental to an understanding of underlying assumptions that drive decision making about program models and instructional practice.

Perspectives on family literacy definition and program development relating to issues of family participation, cultural diversity, and socioeconomic influences will be reviewed. With ideas shared about promoting and sustaining family literacy initiatives, concern is also presented about possible misconceptions regarding the intergenerational nature of literacy development. Common misconceptions about family literacy in the light of standards for appropriate practice and suggestions for future directions in family literacy will be discussed as a focal point for critical reflection on social planning for family literacy development.

WHAT IS FAMILY LITERACY?

In North America during the 1980s, the beginning of the family literacy movement was prompted by concerns about national educational levels and the failure of the education system to address the needs of families identified as low-literate or educationally disadvantaged (Morrow, 1995). At the same time, in Europe and elsewhere, parental involvement approaches were implemented to encourage family support for children's school literacy (Topping & Wolfendale, 1985). While developing countries had no formal family literacy programs, organizations such as Save the Children Foundation included family interventions supporting family learning environments (Puchner, 1997).

In the early days of the family literacy movement, questions about definition addressed observable characteristics of family activities and programs supporting literacy at home — how families engage in literacy at home and what family literacy activities should be included in programs. Based on early ethnographic studies of families in their homes and communities (Heath, 1983; Taylor, 1983; Taylor & Dorsey-Gaines, 1988), family literacy is understood to encompass the ways family members use literacy during the routines of daily living, reflecting their ethnic, racial and cultural heritages (Morrow, Paratore, & Tracey, 1994).

The concept of family literacy continues to be viewed as multifaceted and complex, with no single definition of family literacy in use today. Other related terms receiving attention in the literature (Tracey, 1995) include

- *family literacy programs* — recognizing the influences of the family on literacy development of family members, and trying to have a positive effect on them;

- *intergenerational literacy programs* — where direct literacy instruction is provided to more than one generation of family members (e.g., a mother and her child receive literacy instruction, including exposure to high-quality early literacy experiences);
- *parental involvement programs* — attempting to work with parents to positively influence their ability to support their child's literacy development.

CRITICAL REFLECTION ON FAMILY LITERACY DEFINITION

Throughout the family literacy movement, concerns have been expressed about deficit-driven assumptions of families implicit in definitions of family literacy (Auerbach, 1989, 1995). The impact of such assumptions has simplified research findings on family literacy in a narrow range of recommended, educator-directed instructional strategies for family literacy support. In this process, well-meaning programs give the message that the responsibility for literacy problems lies with families, while ignoring imbedded social conditions. "They paint a picture of family inadequacy and promote the view that only intervention by mainstream professionals will prevent an unending downward spiral of intergenerational illiteracy" (Auerbach, 1995, p. 22). This view of literacy as school-like reading and writing activity within a family context is narrow and does not represent the diverse functions of literacy in the family. As a result, family literacy practices that focus on traditional school learning tasks may be considered inappropriate as the basis for recommended parent literacy strategies because they are limited to criteria for school success.

Accordingly, objections to this transmission of school practices model extend to tasks such as

- assisting parents to promote "good reading habits"
- giving parents guidelines and techniques for helping with homework
- training parents in how to read to children or listen to children read
- providing training in effective parenting
- teaching parents to make and play games to reinforce skills

Some practitioners have objected to the characterization of these common family literacy practices as part of a deficit-driven approach, and the reaction of Edwards (1994) is noteworthy. As an African-American family literacy researcher, Edwards objected to the notion that, because literacy exists in the homes of poor, minority, and immigrant children, it is not important to assist families to build upon their own literacy environments. She reminded other researchers that the most commonly requested assistance by minority families was help in reading *with* children.

Concern about communicating unintentional, implicit deficit messages is part of the critical self-reflection that family literacy practitioners must develop, as they review their programs and relationships with families. Griswold and Ullman (1997) stress that a transmission perspective in learning is so pervasive for both educators and family participants that it can mask the many ways in which families and practitioners learn from each other. They recommend that practitioners develop a reflection process through journals and diaries, among family participants and staff, in order to encourage reflection, dialogue, and collaboration on personal experiences in learning.

GUIDING PRINCIPLES FOR FAMILY LITERACY PROGRAM PRACTICE

While critical appraisals of family literacy practice continue (Gadsen, 1994; Puchner, 1997; Taylor, 1997), there is consensus that programs must respect and celebrate the diversity and uniqueness of families. As well, programs must incorporate collaborative practices in which family participants determine learning goals and real family experiences are part of the curriculum. Taylor (1997) emphasized that literacy programs must, "recognize and honor not only the diversity of literacies that exist with families, but also the communities and cultures of which they are a part. No single, narrow definition of 'family literacy' can do justice to the richness and complexity of families, and the multiple literacies, including often unrecognized local literacies, that are a part of their everyday lives" (p. 4).

Recognizing uniqueness and cultural diversity as the necessary context for family literacy practice, Taylor (1997) proposed a Declaration of Principles for family literacy. The declaration is the result of international consultations with a wide spectrum of family literacy researchers, educators, and participant families. One of the goals of the declaration was the development of policy and practice guidelines for literacy organizations and communities based on recognizing of family knowledge and problem-solving capacity. One hundred and twenty six principles were identified across seven categories: (1) family; (2) language and literacy; (3) research and program development; (4) ethics in family literacy; (5) pedagogy; (6) assessment of family literacy programs; and (7) guidelines for educators, policy makers, and funding agencies.

Research and practitioner discussions about family literacy will continue to establish new dimensions for family literacy standards. Attention to family diversity, collaboration, and reciprocity with families and local communities gives rise to a wide range of literacy options and new questions will emerge as practitioners continue to wrestle with the complexities of developing programs.

TWO DOMINANT THEORETICAL PERSPECTIVES IN FAMILY LITERACY RESEARCH

A solid foundation in theory and research supports many of the developments in family literacy practice. Emergent literacy and sociocultural theories of learning have been the foundation for intervention strategies developed to support literacy development in families.

The essence of the emergent literacy perspective is the view that literacy learning begins in home and community contexts, well before formal schooling, as a natural occurrence of daily life (Holdaway, 1979; Taylor, 1983; Purcell-Gates, 1996). Emergent literacy research affirms that the child constructs meaning from early literacy experiences and recognizes the reciprocal influence of the child and the parent on the literacy environment of the home. Emergent literacy places the family at the centre of literacy development and recognizes that within family communication, children also make a significant contribution to the dialogue about literacy and the literacy learning of adults. Emergent literacy research (Wells, 1986; Teale & Sulzby, 1986) has focused attention on parent-child interaction in the early years and given support to the conclusions that early, oral and written literacy activities in the home have a significant effect on later development. Young children using language and print in natural interaction with parents learn about

a) print-speech relationships,
b) different ways written language is used and the different forms it takes (signs, lists, sentences in a letters, stories in a book), and
c) specific cultural views about how written language is used and valued.

The sociocultural view (Heath, 1983; Langer, 1987; Purcell-Gates, 1995) provides insight into the nature of literacy learning and has become a dominant perspective in adult education. In this view, everyday social interactions are the basis for learning and using oral and written language. At the same time, social experiences around language reflect individual family and community norms and uses. From a sociocultural perspective, then, family socioeconomic status, ethnicity, gender and cultural heritage all provide a context and filter for processing and interpreting the world through oral and written communication. Researchers (Purcell-Gates, L'Allier, & Smith, 1995; Taylor & Dorsey-Gaines, 1988; Varenne, Hamid-Buglione, McDermott, & Morison, 1982) have documented within-class variation in literacy practices among families. Thus, some families, regardless of social status, read avidly themselves, are actively involved in their children's play and school activities, and routinely read with their children. On the other hand, some families rarely engage in sustained conversation with children, do not model reading or provide children with easy access to print materials.

From a sociocultural perspective, traditional education systems are inadequate to bridge the social gulf that exists in effective collaboration with families. Changes in school cultures are needed to address inequalities in relationships between school and home. Researchers stress that schools must transform their ways of communicating with families to emphasize family-centred rather than teacher-centred instructional practices to support families in bridging the distance between home and school literacy.

Family influences in literacy development

Numerous studies of parents and children (Scarborough & Dobrich, 1994; Snow, Barnes, Chandler, Goodman, & Hemphill, 1991) attest to the importance of parent-child interaction, book-reading experiences, parental language and parental reading models for child literacy development. This research points out that literacy is a developmental process beginning at birth, in which parents have a profound influence. Early literacy develops from the many parent-child interactions around everyday experiences, such as noting signs when shopping or travelling together, making informal parent commentary on what is happening throughout the day, and listening to stories.

It has been suggested (Scarborough & Dobrich, 1994) that since there is a weak association between parent-child shared book reading and the development of later written literacy skills, family literacy influence on literacy development and later school achievement is minimal. But this conclusion has been criticized by others (Dunning, Mason, & Stewart, 1994), noting methodological problems in research designs that combine strong and weak studies and give equal weighting to them. More fundamentally, even if parent-child shared reading accounted for only a small portion of total literacy achievement, it is one of the few factors that families can control and has been consistently identified as exerting a direct positive effect on children's literacy.

Parents who provide multiple opportunities for parent-child conversation, who read themselves and who read frequently with their young children are teaching specific things about oral language use and print, even though this learning occurs incidentally and naturally. Their children come to school well prepared to read, compared to youngsters in homes where parent-child reading is infrequent and parents themselves engage in little or no reading or writing activity. At the same time, results from parental involvement programs (Dickinson, 1994; Morrow & Young, 1997) confirm the benefits of supporting parents to engage more frequently in shared reading and writing activities. Thus, early home literacy activities that prepare children for school literacy include

- a view of reading and writing as enjoyable
- a sense for how print is useful
- knowledge of the structure of stories in books
- general thinking and questioning skills related to dialogue about books
- letter and word knowledge

Nevertheless, this type of cause/effect reasoning has been considered restrictive, perhaps ignoring other complex relationships in families that affect their literacy development (Auerbach, 1989; Neuman, et al., 1995; Puchner, 1997). A different question may be asked. Within the complex dynamics of family interaction, are there other important aspects of the home setting contributing to children's literacy development? Researchers (Fuligni, 1997; Goldenberg, et al., 1992; Lareau, 1989; Snow et al., 1991) suggest that significant family influences include

- *the literacy environment of the home* — parents' own interest in reading, and the provision of literacy materials in the home;

- *parental teaching* — frequency of interactions with children and a positive, supportive manner to child schoolwork, whether reading with them or participating in homework;
- *parental education* — educational attainment levels of the parents;
- *opportunities to learn* — ways parents promote children's learning by increasing access to other people and activities, using extended family members, exercising control over leisure time, and having a variety of personal interests;
- *parental expectations* — positively stated expectations for children's school success.

In summary, child-focused family literacy research has identified significant family influences that include a constellation of positive attitudes and supports for child achievement, positive family communication patterns, parent investment in their own learning and personal development, as well as specific reading-related parent-child interactions.

In translating research to practice, family literacy educators have reaffirmed the success of collaborative programs that offer opportunities and support for parents to engage in school-like reading and writing activities at home. It has become clear to practitioners that these literacy activities must be experienced as comfortable and meaningful within individual family cultures. As a first step, programs must establish reciprocal and collaborative relationships with families that enable families to set their own learning goals, based on respect for individual family attitudes and views about literacy. Developing home-school collaborations for child literacy usually means that schools must "do things differently" in taking steps to understand the legitimate literacy perspectives of minority and poor families. Examples of school change for family involvement have been documented by the Center on Families, Communities, Schools, and Children's Learning (Johnson, 1994).

FAMILY FOCUS IN ADULT LITERACY DEVELOPMENT

Relatively little research has been devoted to intergenerational influences in the literacy development of adults. Adult literacy has been studied in relation to the workplace, literacy education and training needs of adults, but not in the context of the family. For the most part, adult literacy surveys have ignored the family as a context for adult literacy practices (Smith, 1995; Statistics Canada, 1992, 1996). When the family context of adult literacy has been noted, research has been conducted: (a) within the context of family literacy program participation; (b) in studies of parent perceptions and practices which affect children's literacy achievement; and (c) in research on cultural and social practices of families. These studies give a more detailed picture of how the adult role of parent and parental responsibility for child education affect adult literacy plans and self-concept.

With respect to research findings on parent perceptions and attitudes related to children's literacy and school achievement (Goldenberg, et al., 1992; Neuman, et al., 1995), it has been found that ethnic minority families may have limited English proficiency and may be living in poverty. Nevertheless, they hold optimistic views about their children's capabilities, have high expectations for their children's academic success, and are willing to engage in a wide range of support activities on behalf of their children's literacy. This positive picture of support for child literacy among low-income, disadvantaged families contrasts with findings that many children of disadvantaged, minority families continue to struggle with literacy in school.

Some explanations for this contradiction have centred on the negative effects of poverty and ineffective schooling on literacy achievement. Other explanations for this contradiction have been found in investigations of differential relationships and communication patterns between family cultures and traditional norms and expectations of school cultures (Heath, 1983; Puchner, 1997; Purcell-Gates, 1995; Taylor & Dorsey-Gaines, 1988). These latter studies document positive adult motivation, aspirations, and problem solving in families where literacy use is related to distinct cultural and class traditions. Heath's (1983) research about underlying social forces shaping the patterns of adult literacy use in different communities concluded that local, cultural patterns of social interaction and communication greatly affect how families will react to traditional expectations of school.

Heath (1983) and Lareau (1989) contend that while culturally and economically diverse families hold positive educational values and high aspirations for their children, personal dispositions towards school may not match the learning dispositions required by traditional school cultures. Thus, Lareau (1989) observed that working class parents believed that it was important for schools to teach children manners and basic skills, while parents should not intervene in the school program. Child respect for teachers and adults often meant passive compliance rather than asking questions, or engaging in verbal interchange and negotiation with adults. A study of teenage mothers with children in daycare (Neuman, et al., 1995) found that many parents believed in the importance of teaching children through drill, practice and recitation. Beliefs about child learning emphasized discrete skills. Nevertheless, other parental beliefs about teaching and learning were highly compatible with school learning goals. Some of these are outlined below.

- Schools should teach practical life skills (how to deal socially with others) and academically oriented skills (letter names, numbers, listening skills).
- Children should be in a safe environment. School should be a place where children learn cooperation and independence.
- Respect is a critical component in establishing and maintaining family/school relations. Teachers who are nurturing, maintain order, and teach skills receive parent respect. Teachers who show children's skill development through reports, portfolios, and conversation earn respect from parents. Teachers show respect for parents through sharing information and communicating informally.
- Parents must be positive role models for their children. This is a central belief motivating parents to become involved in home-school collaboration.

Neuman and her colleagues (1995) found that although disadvantaged parents held constructive and empowering attitudes related to child learning and education, these parents also believed that they lacked skills and resources to help their children become successful. Neuman demonstrated that when parents were able to express their beliefs about education and learning, and teachers responded with respect and reciprocity, strong collaborative relationships developed between families and educators. Creating such collaborative relationships requires curriculum adaptations which incorporate activities that match parental educational beliefs and expectations, while requesting modifications to their parent-child practices.

It is clear from the research reviewed that adults face external obstacles in communicating with schools as they try to develop literacy skills in the context of their commitment to their parenting role and their desire to secure a positive adjustment to school for their children. Family literacy practitioners have to be prepared not only to listen to parental views and values about literacy, but also to make accommodations through collaborative problem solving. At the same time, communicating expectations and beliefs occurs subtly and unconsciously. Are practitioners and families taking time to engage in dialogue on implicit beliefs about literacy and schooling? How are practitioners ensuring self-reflection regarding transmission approaches? At present, there is no literature on critical reflection in family literacy practice, although concerns about deficit views and transmission perspectives are a fundamental to developing standards for appropriate practice.

FAMILY LITERACY PROGRAM CLASSIFICATION

As the number of family literacy programs has increased along with demands for program evaluation and competition for limited program funding resources, practitioners have sought to further specify criteria for determining what constitutes a family literacy program. Family literacy programs have been depicted as a hodge-podge of models and approaches with varying degrees of evidence to support claims of effectiveness and with few theoretical frameworks (Gadsen, 1994). Nevertheless, the variety in approaches to family literacy reflects the diversity of local initiatives and community partnerships and exemplifies the multi-faceted character of family literacy services. Many programs involve parents to strengthen home support for the school success of children. Others attempt to restructure adult literacy education in light of meaningful adult experiences as parents.

A trend has been noted to identify family literacy programs in terms of the distinctions between family literacy services and other literacy services offered separately to adults or to children. For example, the family literacy approach in the United Kingdom is noteworthy because it specifically identifies the intergenerational link between parent and child achievement in literacy as an essential element in family literacy program delivery (Poulson, et al., 1997).

Probably the most widely known framework for categorizing family literacy programs was developed by Nickse (1991), who identified four types of learner participation. As family literacy programs have increased to meet a diversity of local needs, an expanded version of the

Nickse schema has been developed by the National Adult Literacy Database to identify seven types of family literacy initiative in a Canadian directory of family literacy projects. Projects may be identified as

1. **Intergenerational** — Literacy instruction is offered to both parent and child and both are seen to be the primary beneficiaries of the program.
2. **Focus on parent or primary caregiver** — Adults are the primary participants in training that includes ways for parents to develop children's literacy at home. Children are assumed to receive indirect benefits. Childcare may be provided while caregivers attend sessions.
3. **Parental involvement** — The focus is on increasing parental involvement in child literacy development through joint caregiver-child sessions that engage both in literacy-related activities.
4. **Family literacy activity for the general public** — The focus is on public awareness or informal participation for literacy enjoyment.
5. **Projects for family literacy resources** — Materials and resources are made available to support family literacy.
6. **Family literacy professional training and resources** — These are directed to practitioners, either for preparing prospective practitioners, or providing continuing education.
7. **Resources for the general public** — There is a focus on public awareness or informal participation in literacy activity for literacy enjoyment.

In addition to the types listed above, services contributed to family literacy programs by other organizations are also identified. Family support services include transportation, childcare allowances, and parental support, provided by agencies or organizations that do not offer direct family literacy services.

TRENDS IN CANADIAN FAMILY LITERACY PRACTICE

A current listing of family literacy projects on the National Adult Literacy Database Website shows an increase in program development across all provinces, since 1998 (Thomas, Skage, & Jackson, 1998). This increase has been due to greater provincial coordination of disparate, local family literacy efforts by literacy networks as well as new partner-ships with private corporations and other family service organizations. Provincial literacy groups, including Literacy BC, Literacy Partners of Manitoba, Prospects Literacy Association of Alberta, and the Saskatchewan Literacy Network, have adopted new family literacy strategies to reach a broad audience and identify new funding sources. For example, the Centre for Family Literacy was established by the Prospects Literacy Association to better coordinate program develop-ment, funding, and research efforts across Alberta, with provincial fund-ing for family literacy from Alberta Learning and the Children's Service Authority. A notable feature in all provincial organizational efforts is the use of Web pages to highlight activities and the formation of e-mail net-works of family literacy practitioners.

The 1998 Directory of Family Literacy Projects Across Canada (Thomas, Skage, & Jackson, 1998) identified a range of family literacy initiatives across seven types of program. These program types are described below.

Intergenerational projects

In Canada, intergenerational programs have developed locally and offer program activities averaging about five hours a week. This contrasts with national mandates and extensive funding support by the Basic Skills Agency in the UK and Even Start in the US.

Three Canadian programs are representative of intergenerational lit-eracy initiatives, since they have specific program components that involve sustained parent-child literacy interaction. Families in Motion operates once a week in Chilliwack, British Columbia, sponsored by a coalition of community organizations in collaboration with the Skwah First Nations Band. The Family Learning program in Niagara Falls, Ontario, supported by private foundation grants in partnership with a local school board, offers a program of 15 hours weekly over six months or longer (Thomas, Fazio, & Stiefelmeyer, 1999). The Parenting and Family Literacy Centres of the Toronto District School Board operate over 30 program sites from a family resource centre approach to meet the literacy needs of families.

Finally, there is some controversy about whether the Parent-Child Mother Goose Program is an intergenerational or parental involvement program. The Parent-Child Mother Goose Program is unique in that it is based on oral language, encouraging families of diverse cultures and languages to share family folktales and nursery rhymes for parent-child literacy interaction. While this program has an informal drop-in format, there is an intent to focus on developing language for parents as well as children.

Focus on parent or primary caregiver

Canadian programs that focus on literacy instruction for parents include Come Read with Me programs throughout Saskatchewan, Book Mates and Book Bridges in Manitoba, the Learning Together Program of the Nova Scotia Department of Education and Culture, and the Literacy and Parenting Skills (LAPS) program across Canada. While quite distinct in workshop content, these programs are similar in providing parents with ways to support home literacy and to foster reading with children. In addition to literacy workshops for parents, provision is also made throughout these provinces for training to conduct these workshops.

Parental involvement

A focus on child's literacy development, with adults enlisted to provide program support, is characteristic of family resource programs such as the Fun and Learning Centre in Newfoundland, some school-based book bag programs, home-based tutoring programs such as Learning with My Child in Quebec, and Reading Circles programs of Frontier College. As examples of parental involvement, these programs maintain communication with parents beyond distributing family literacy materials and support parent-child literacy interaction in play activities and/or reading books together.

Family literacy activity for the general public

Little or no direct literacy instruction is provided in this family literacy initiative, where both adults and children, as part of the general public, are invited to participate in literacy activities for enjoyment. Family literacy initiatives that raise awareness of literacy in everyday life include local "celebrate literacy" and "literacy tent" activities for general participation. Frontier College is prominent across Canada in organizing family literacy activities for the general public.

Projects for family literacy resources

Family literacy materials are created by volunteers and distributed to families for home literacy use. In this type of project, there is no ongoing contact with recipient families to support the use of the literacy resources in the home. Projects include hospital- and school-based Books for Babies programs. The success of these programs is based on carefully selecting books that match the cultural experiences of Native families, establishing community partnerships to maintain continuity and funding support, and conducting follow-up discussion with health professionals when parents bring babies for immunizations.

Family literacy professional training and resources

As previously noted, practitioner training is available across Canada to conduct a variety of "focus on caregiver" workshops. The Toronto-based Parent-Child Mother Goose Program, Come Read with Me in Saskatchewan and Literacy and Parenting Skills (LAPS) offer training for program leaders in almost every province and territory.

A valuable source of professional development for family literacy practitioners is the National Adult Literacy Database, which is a clearinghouse for family literacy resources, a communication network for literacy professionals and an updated directory of family literacy initiatives across Canada. A newsletter also informs practitioners on current practices, research, events, and conferences of interest to literacy learners as well as professionals.

Resources for the general public

National/international commemorative stamps, family literacy days, television programs, public brochures and family books, and special interest articles in magazines and newspapers (Calamai, 1999) are examples of public awareness activities to foster interest in developing literacy activities in the home. Canada Post and ABC Canada have been prominent in sponsoring such public awareness activities. Project sponsorship for public awareness activities by corporations such as Honda and Starbucks is also on the increase for national and provincial family literacy initiatives.

COLLABORATIVE PROGRAMS FOR THE FUTURE

Continued strong interest in family literacy, a developing theoretical framework and research base, and rapid program development in communities around the world have set family literacy firmly in future social policy and planning considerations. In exploring ways to make adult literacy programs more responsive and useful to adult participants, a variety of family literacy approaches have taken hold across Canada. Family literacy programs appear most successful when they address the practical concerns of families from diverse cultures and linguistic backgrounds, and are accessible and open to shared ownership for program operation and planning. Family literacy programs are complex undertakings because concerns about adequate health care, nutrition, and housing are also family literacy issues and may be barriers to program access. Many family literacy participants are single mothers who face obstacles to program participation from lack of support, isolation, low income, and inadequate childcare. Programs that work collaboratively with families and with other community organizations seem to be most successful because such programs support parents in dealing with these obstacles in the context of literacy as an enabling experience.

Canadian family literacy has been characterized by relatively short-term, low intensity programs. Central government support and consistent funding is associated with development of family literacy models that provide a full range of literacy services for parents and children. Policy discussions regarding literacy development have frequently identified a model of coordinated or integrated social services as an optimal system for ensuring more intensive literacy opportunities for families (Benjamin & Lord, 1996; Crowson & Boyd, 1993; McCain, Mustard, & Hamilton, 1999). Coordination of services for family literacy within provinces, together with federal and provincial cooperation, will be required in order to implement integrated programs for children and families where literacy is a key component.

Integration of community and educational services is consistently recommended to support family literacy program development, because parental involvement in child literacy is linked to many aspects of child and family well-being. In order to engage parents more actively in aspects of decision making about child and family education and welfare, it helps to simplify and improve access to related services for families. Families should be able to access social and educational services in a holistic, com-

munity context. Integration of family services is a way to make community resources more responsive to family needs. In this context, increased
interagency collaboration and partnership activity will require significant
investment of time and effort by family literacy practitioners.

We know that coordinated services models for families are most successful when adult literacy needs are also recognized and where adult
family members have access to a full range of adult educational opportunities in the community. Family literacy practitioners who work with
adults know that parental confidence, esteem and "parenting" are affected by the sense of competence and achievement that adult family members experience in accomplishing their learning goals. If there is to be a
literacy future for children and families, it must include true access to
adult literacy opportunities for parents with young children. This means
that opportunities to pursue family literacy aims must be available as a
legitimate program alternative to other choices in employment training
or basic skills upgrading.

REFERENCES

Auerbach, E. (1989). Toward a socio-contextual approach to family literacy.
    Harvard Educational Review, 59, 165–181.

Auerbach, E. (1995). Which way for family literacy: Intervention or empower-
    ment? In L.M. Morrow (Ed.), *Family literacy: Connections in schools and commu-
    nities* (pp. 11–27). Newark, DE: International Reading Association.

Benjamin, A., & Lord, J. (Eds.). (1996). *Family literacy: Directions in research and
    implications for practice*. Washington, DC: U.S. Government Printing Office.

Calamai, P. (September, 1999). Literacy matters: Can we close our literacy gap?
    Saturday Night, 1–15.

Crowson, R., & Boyd, W. (1993). Coordinated services for children: Design arks
    for storms and seas unknown. *American Journal of Education, 101*, 140–179.

Dickinson, D. (Ed.). (1994). *Bridges to literacy: Children, families, and schools*.
    Cambridge, MA: Blackwell Publishers.

Dunning, D., Mason, J., & Stewart, J. (1994). Reading to preschoolers: A
    response to Scarborough and Dobrich (1994) and recommendations for
    future research. *Developmental Review, 14*, 324–339.

Edwards, P. (1994). Responses of teachers and African-American mothers to a book-reading intervention program. In D. Dickinson (Ed.), *Bridges to literacy: Children, families, and schools* (pp. 175–208). Cambridge, MA: Blackwell Publishers.

Fingeret, A., & Jurmo, P. (Eds.). (1989). *Participatory literacy education.* San Francisco, CA: Jossey-Bass.

Fuligni, A. (1997). The academic achievement of adolescents from immigrant families: The roles of family background, attitudes, and behavior. *Child Development, 68*(2), 351–363.

Gadsen, V. (1994). *Understanding family literacy: Conceptual issues facing the field* (Technical Report TR94-02). Philadelphia, PA: University of Pennsylvania National Center on Adult Literacy.

Goldenberg, C., Reese, L., & Gallimore, R. (1992). Effects of literacy materials from school on Latino children's home experiences and early reading achievement. *American Journal of Education, 100*(4), 497–535.

Griswold, K., & Ullman, C. (1997). Not a one-way street: The power of reciprocity in family literacy programs. New York: Herbert H. Lehman College Institute for Literacy Studies. (ERIC ED 413 420)

Heath, S.B. (1983). *Ways with words: Language, life, and work in communities and classrooms.* New York: Cambridge University Press.

Holdaway, D. (1979). *The foundations of literacy.* Sidney, AU: Ashton Scholastics.

Johnson, V. (1994). *Parent centers in urban schools: Four case studies* (Report No. 23 of the Center on Families, Communities, Schools and Children's Learning). Boston, MA: Boston University Institute for Responsive Education.

Langer, J.A. (1987). A sociocognitive perspective on literacy. In J.A. Langer (Ed.), *Language, literacy and culture: Issues of society and schooling* (pp. 1–19). Norwood, NJ: Ablex.

Lareau, A. (1989). *Home advantage: Social class and parental intervention in elementary education.* New York: Falmer.

McCain, M., Mustard, F., & Hamilton, C. (Eds.). (1999). *Early years study: Reversing the real brain drain.* Final report to the Ontario Legislature. Toronto, ON: Ontario Government Printing Office.

Morrow, L.M. (Ed.). (1995). *Family literacy: Connections in schools and communities.* Newark, DE: International Reading Association.

Morrow, L.M., Paratore, J., & Tracey, D. (1994). *Family literacy: New perspectives, new opportunities.* [Brochure]. Newark, DE: International Reading Association.

Morrow, L.M., & Young, J. (1997). A family literacy program connecting school and home: Effects on attitude, motivation, and literacy achievement. *Journal of Educational Psychology, 89(4)*, 726–742.

Neuman, S., Hagedorn, T., Celano, D., & Daly, P. (1995). Toward a collaborative approach to parent involvement in early education: A study of teenage mothers in an African-American community. *American Educational Research Journal, 32(4)*, 801–827.

Nickse, R. (1991). *A typology of family and intergenerational literacy programs: Implications for evaluation.* Paper presented at the American Educational Research Association Annual Meeting, Chicago, IL. (ERIC ED 333 166)

Poulson, L., Macleod, F., Bennett, N., & Wray, D. (1997). *Family literacy practice in local programmes.* London, UK: Basic Skills Agency.

Puchner, L. (1997). *Family literacy in cultural context: Lessons from two case studies.* Philadelphia, PA: National Center on Adult Literacy. (ERIC ED 412 376)

Purcell-Gates, V. (1995). *Other people's words: The cycle of low literacy.* Cambridge, MA: Harvard University Press.

Purcell-Gates, V. (1996). Stories, coupons, and the TV Guide: Relationships between home literacy experiences and emergent literacy knowledge. *Reading Research Quarterly, 31,* 406–428.

Purcell-Gates, V., L'Allier, S., & Smith, D. (1995). Literacy at the Harts' and the Larsons': Diversity among poor, inner city families. *The Reading Teacher, 48(7)*, 572–578.

Ross, D., Scott, K., & Kelly, M. (1996). Overview: Children in Canada in the 1990s. In Human Resources Development Canada & Statistics Canada (Eds.), *Growing up in Canada: National Longitudinal Survey of Children and Youth* (pp. 15–45). Ottawa, ON: Statistics Canada.

Scarborough, H., & Dobrich, W. (1994). On the efficacy of reading to preschoolers. *Developmental Review, 14,* 245–302.

Snow, C., Barnes, W., Chandler, J., Goodman, I., & Hemphill, L. (1991). *Unfulfilled expectations: Home and school influences on literacy.* Cambridge, MA: Harvard University Press.

Statistics Canada. (1992). *Adult literacy in Canada: Results of a national study.* Ottawa, ON: Author.

Statistics Canada. (1996). *Reading the future: A portrait of literacy in Canada.* Ottawa, ON: Author.

Street, B. (1997). *Adult literacy in the United Kingdom: A history of research and practice.* Report to the National Center on Adult Literacy, University of Pennsylvania. Lancaster, UK: The Research and Practice in Adult Literacy Group (RAPAL).

Taylor, D. (1983). *Family literacy: Young children learning to read and write.* Portsmouth, NH: Heinemann.

Taylor, D. (Ed.). (1997). *Many families, many literacies: An international declaration of principles.* Portsmouth, NH: Heinemann.

Taylor, D., & Dorsey-Gaines, C. (1988). *Growing up literate: Learning from inner-city families.* Portsmouth, NH: Heinemann.

Teale, W., & Sulzby, E. (1986). *Emergent literacy: Writing and reading.* Norwood, NJ: Ablex.

Thomas, A., Fazio, L., & Stiefelmeyer. (1999). *Families at school: A guide for educators.* Newark, DE: International Reading Association.

Thomas, A., Skage, S., & Jackson, R. (1998). *Family connections: 1998 directory of family literacy projects across Canada.* Welland, ON: Soleil Publishing.

Topping, K., & Wolfendale, S. (Eds.). (1985). *Parents and their children's reading.* Kent, UK: Croom, Helm, Beckenham.

Tracey, D. (1995). Family literacy: Research synthesis. In D. Leu & C.K. Kinzer (Eds.), *Perspectives on literacy research and practice.* Forty-fourth Yearbook of the National Reading Conference. Chicago, IL: National Reading Conference.

Varenne, H., Hamid-Buglione, V., McDermott, R., & Morison, A. (1982). "I teach him everything he learns in school": The acquisition of literacy for learning in working class families. New York: Columbia University Teachers College. (ED 227 452)

Wells, G. (1986). *The meaning makers.* Portsmouth, NH: Heinemann.

WEBSITES

ABC Canada. www.abc-canada.org

Frontier College. www.frontiercollege.ca

Literacy BC. www.nald.ca/lbc.htm

Literacy Partners of Manitoba. www.nald.ca/litpman.htm

National Adult Literacy Database. www.nald.ca

Prospects Literacy Association of Alberta. www.nald.ca/pla.htm

Saskatchewan Literacy Network. www.nald.ca/sklitnet.htm

Critical Reflection on Family Needs and Literacy Skills of Adult ESL Learners

Hilary Craig

In this chapter I will examine two experiences that were superficially very different, but which radically affected my point of view with respect to family literacy. I hope to

- suggest that our concept of family literacy is often rather limited and fails to address urgent family needs;
- challenge educators in a variety of settings to address the urgent everyday literacy needs of families, rather than just to follow a predetermined curriculum;
- validate and build upon learning that takes place outside the classroom;
- encourage connections between adult programs and schools that would help parents and children to build on and connect with each others' learning;
- promote adult education by placing family needs and support on an equal basis with employment-related skills; and
- develop training and support infrastructures for family literacy workers.

I hope to accomplish this by drawing on my own experience to examine what Adele Thomas describes as the "cultural lenses" — the worldview and expectation of both students and educators.

A CHASM OF DIFFERENCE IN LIFE EXPERIENCES

My decision to work as an ESL teacher was informed by a number of my life experiences. As an English-speaking immigrant and as a person who chose to live as an exile during the civil war that raged in Zimbabwe during the 1970s, I could relate to the experiences of other immigrants. As a white person from southern Africa who vehemently opposed the racism that had been perpetrated in my country of origin, I wanted to work in an area that allowed me to find positive solutions to racism in Canada. In the context of southern Ontario (where I lived from 1965 to 1980), I observed that it was non-white immigrants who most often faced racism.

During that time I read widely in areas pertinent to my work. This included an exploration of popular education theory, starting with the work of Paulo Freire. In the mid-1970s, when I started working with adults, I also had opportunities to attend workshops and read works by educators such as Elsa Auerbach, Deborah Barndt and Ira Shor.

Over time I consciously developed a number of principles that informed my work. I may not have had these written down, but I believe that the following statements accurately represent my beliefs.

I tried to facilitate learning by

- being respectful of the people I worked with, by acknowledging and honouring their wisdom and experience and by helping them to tell authentic stories about themselves and their lives;
- providing them with tools for coping as well as possible with daily life in a new country;
- providing opportunities and occasions allowing people to name, to discuss and to come to terms with their experiences as immigrants and refugees;
- providing a positive classroom environment for people to discuss and evaluate how their lives in Canada were similar to or different from the lives they had led before they came here;
- encouraging people to understand how their experiences fitted into the larger scheme of things and to take appropriate action where possible; and
- encouraging them to build and celebrate community.

Originally I came to Canada as a foreign student intending to return home when I finished my degree. The experience of settling in a foreign country — even another English-speaking Commonwealth country — was much more difficult than I had anticipated. However, the dislocation and alienation I felt at that time paled in comparison with my subsequent experience of returning to Zimbabwe after Independence. There were two factors contributing to the stress of this latter experience. First of all, I returned with my Canadian husband and two school-age children. Secondly, the whole country was undergoing substantial political and social change as a result of the outcome of the elections leading to black majority rule.

I had been raised in a middle-class, white, urban environment. The household I grew up in was highly literate and cultural activities were a normal part of everyday life. I knew, of course, that the lives of black people, especially those living in the countryside, were very different from mine. But limited social contact left me with only theoretical knowledge of these differences.

However, when I returned to Zimbabwe in 1981 both my paid work and volunteer neighbourhood involvement enabled me to get to know many local black women who had experienced this very different reality. It was then that I realized the depth and width of the chasm of life experience separating us.

My first job in Zimbabwe was with the Girl Guides. My task was to write a series of high-interest/low vocabulary booklets that would be used with young rural women. The booklets were intended to help these women retain their literacy skills in English. The topics included "Using Knitting Patterns," "Working with Playgroups," and "Working with the Disabled."

Although the booklets were intended for rural women, there was not enough money to finance travel to rural areas to test the materials. My employers suggested that I recruit local women to help with this stage in the project. So this was how I became known to a group of women, some domestic workers and others the wives of domestic workers, who asked me to help them organize a neighbourhood self-help group and later a small sewing cooperative and literacy classes.

As I worked with these women I learned about their lives, their strengths, and their struggles. About a third of the group could speak, read and write in both their own language and English. The schools that they attended had been rural, probably poorly equipped, with large classes taught by inadequately trained teachers. Most of them could knit and crochet although they did not all know how to use written patterns. Most of them probably read the newspaper daily and could read recipes and other household reading material. Their main concern was the fact that they were stuck in dead-end domestic work and poverty.

Another third spoke a little English and had minimal literacy skills. The remainder, most of whom were the wives of domestic workers, spoke no English and had had little or no schooling. They struggled with almost anything they did in the group. For example, activities demanding small motor skills (e.g., cutting and sewing) were particularly challenging for them.

The women who were the most educated were mostly widows and divorcees. They had a strong sense of responsibility for the needs of those who had had even fewer opportunities than they for education and skill development. They were also very aware of the complex issues that faced these women, not the least of which was domestic violence. It was they who advocated for literacy instruction, and one of them agreed to be trained and subsequently to work as a literacy instructor.

While working with these women I tried to learn their language. I quickly discovered that learning a Bantu language — as opposed to a European language — stretched me to the limits. In particular I was baffled by cultural concepts embedded in the language. For example, I never quite figured out which of the several greetings should be used at a given time of day. I was profoundly humbled by my lack of success in this endeavour.

As I worked with these women I learned to appreciate their culture and was fascinated by their way of life, still primarily oral. Storytelling remained an integral part of personal and cultural expression and singing and dancing were seamlessly woven into all aspects of life. Games were enjoyed by people of all ages. Rituals were lively and healing. Participation was far more important than performance. I felt enriched by this experience, and not a little envious of the way in which they enjoyed life in spite of continuous and severe economic hardship.

In Zimbabwe in the 1980s books and print materials were scarce — valuable commodities available only to city people who could afford them. While the civic infrastructure was generally quite sophisticated, some services that we take for granted in Canada (for example, public library services) were minimal. Foreign currency restrictions meant that foreign newspapers and magazines were rarely obtainable.

Despite the lack of materials and services, there was, however, a tremendous demand for and interest in reading material. Entrepreneurs sold old magazines on street corners and second-hand bookstores were everywhere. It was common to see people reading in public places. Even among the white, middle-class population books were prized and shared as they rarely are in Canada.

Many of the print items that North Americans take for granted in daily life were either unnecessary or did not exist outside of urban areas. If there are no phones, there are no phone books. If there is one bus a day, there is no bus schedule. If most people walk within a limited area, there are no street names or maps.

Middle-class, urban people certainly used newspapers to look for jobs and accommodation, to read the news, obituaries and book reviews. However, people living in the high density suburbs or the rural areas relied primarily on word of mouth to get or share information.

LIVING AS A CONTEXT FOR LEARNING

Upon returning to Canada from Zimbabwe, I got a job in a community college ESL program in Regina, Saskatchewan. From the start my awareness and approaches to teaching had definitely been modified as a result of the African experience. However, the extent and significance of the changes became very clear when I worked with one particular class of people whose life experiences and literacy levels were closer to those of the least educated Zimbabwean women than to many of the other ESL students with whom I had worked. This group was labeled a "literacy" class because most of the participants spoke languages with different alphabets, or had had little formal education. They came from countries as different as Laos, Eritrea, El Salvador, Iran, China and Vietnam.

Learning from daily life

At the beginning of the five-month-long class I made a choice not to use the published materials that were normally used by other instructors because I considered them to have little relevance to the daily lives of the students. Instead, I developed my own materials designed to meet the expressed needs of the class at the same time as giving them opportunities to learn and practice immediately useful structures and vocabulary.

There were a number of regular activities that we engaged in. Every day we had a "check in." This included taking attendance by noting verbally and in writing who was present, absent or sick. We also named the day of the week and the date and took note of the temperature, weather and any unusual events. Special personal or school news was shared, and past and planned activities were described. Concerns were often raised. Notes from school or other pieces of information were brought to class for interpretation and action.

On chart paper I took down all that was talked about. The class then copied the text into their exercise books. Subsequently I devised exercises that provided practice with vocabulary, conversational items, grammar, phonics and spelling. In the course of these mundane, but important activities I made sure that everyone learned how to engage in activities such as using a calendar, reading a thermometer, using bus schedules, following and giving directions, making simple street maps, making a personal dictionary, and making lists. Several of the group with school-age children learned how to write a very simple note to school about a child's absence. This was something they really took pride in doing.

Sometimes issues raised led us to further discussion and activities. A sick child might provide the opportunity for naming symptoms and suggesting remedies. A seasonal event like Hallowe'en led to related activities. Sometimes we named and talked about feelings like homesickness and confusion. We explored words and concepts like "polite," "acceptable," and "normal" as we investigated the terrain of cross-cultural communication.

In the first couple of months our "news" was fairly structured and repetitive. By the end of the five months each person was capable of writing a short, but uniquely personal journal entry which was usually shared with the class.

More confidence and more complexity

As the students acquired some vocabulary and became more confident, we explored more complex topics. Whenever possible personal stories were used as a way of increasing vocabulary. For example, each class member drew a picture, or series of pictures, depicting departure from their country. I was particularly moved by pictures of jail-like Hong Kong refugee camps and boats filled with refugees. Each picture included written information that the artist considered important, such as the number of people in the refugee camp or on the boat. I was impressed by the fact that each one knew and could write the date of their arrival in Canada.

Just as pictures were used to describe houses and journeys, so they were points of departure for narratives about daily activities. The students often drew pictures to show their routines (using the present tense) or their family's activities over the previous weekend (using the past tense). These pictures enabled me to provide the necessary vocabulary. Subsequently I developed a variety of exercises to provide practice and reinforce learning.

Initially many of the daily activities were fairly structured; however, by the end of five months there was much more spontaneity. I particularly remember the last day when one of the class made a very moving tribute to the only man (a gentleman in his '60s) whom she described as "our father."

A special unit about housing

Early on in the class I found out that three members of the group were not happy with their living arrangements. So I decided to do a unit on housing. Since this was a class of beginners with very limited literacy skills it seemed sensible to begin at the very beginning: with the word "house." It was from there that we embarked on a journey that probably stretched my knowledge and worldview as much as it stretched theirs.

Given the limited language skills of the group, we started with floor plans of the homes we had lived in before leaving our original countries. I wanted to give a clear message that nobody was expected to be an artist and that it was acceptable to depict a reality that might be quite different from the Canadian reality. I also felt strongly that I should affirm that each family is unique. So I drew a diagram of a rural Zimbabwean homestead. It included huts for two wives, indoor and outdoor cooking areas, a pit latrine and a river for water. The diagrams gave us a chance to name the spaces and their features. We then proceeded to draw floor plans of our homes here in Canada. Once we had some basic vocabulary about different parts of a family living space, furniture, etc., I thought it might be useful to visit some homes. Three of the class eagerly extended invitations.

On a pleasant fall afternoon we set out on our trip. Within a few minutes of entering the somewhat seedy neighbourhood there was much to

talk about. We watched a couple of men involved in some kind of trans-
action. I assumed they were dealing drugs. The class wanted to know
how to describe this event in English. A little further on we passed a
scantily clad young woman clearly on display. We watched as men in cars
cruised by slowly, and as a young fellow observed what went on. Once
again I was asked for vocabulary. There was no point, I thought, in giving them euphemisms when they were confronting this reality daily.
One of the women became very animated as she communicated her fear
and distress because she and her 10-year-old daughter dealt with this situation daily. This incident later led to a discussion about what to do
when being harassed on the street and how to ask for help. This was
functional English at its most basic!

The first home we visited was so awful that nobody said anything,
except the woman whose family lived there. She made it clear that she
thought it was horrible. We could only agree. It was dirty and depress-
ing and it stank. The second home, the upper floor of a house that had
been subdivided into two apartments, was not too bad. However, as the
occupant led us up the stairs she signaled her embarrassment about the
state of the extremely ugly and rather dirty 60's-style shag rug. This
prompted an animated response from several other class members. The
words they uttered were "garage sale" and "vacuum cleaner." There was
much nodding.

Each room gave opportunities for the group to use vocabulary words
they had learned. However, there were also many questions and comments. Students commented on items that they liked, made suggestions
about where to get other items, asked questions. I could see that a huge
amount of communication and peer learning was occurring. I also realized that I was unprepared for the amount of vocabulary and the complexity of utterances that the students struggled to make.

The third home was relatively pleasant, although small for the number
of people living in it. There was, however, an undercurrent. We all knew
that the woman who lived here was in a very abusive relationship. Nobody
said anything, but I sensed that the group was pondering the situation.
Which was the superior choice: a nicer place or freedom from abuse?

Each of us went home without returning to the classroom. My head
was filled with the enormity of this Pandora's box I had opened. I was
immensely excited about the unexpected learning that had obviously
taken place. However, I was quite overwhelmed. First of all, I knew I

could not leave the matter here, especially since I was aware that there were better housing alternatives available in the community. I felt obligated to make these options known to the group. I was also aware of the enormity of the task that lay before me.

Within the next few weeks I arranged two additional outings. On the first trip we visited a municipal social housing unit and on the second we went to a unit in a private, non-profit social housing project. Between the first set of visits and the second set the students spent a great deal of time learning and using vocabulary and grammatical structures geared towards our task. For example, they worked hard practicing different kinds of questions needed to elicit information about rental conditions. These included the following: "How much is the rent?" "Is there a damage deposit?" "Are the appliances included?"

The occupants of the units we visited were present and available to answer questions. I was impressed by how much better the members of the group were able to express themselves and I was excited at how much their language skills had improved. I was also encouraged by the fact that several of them were keen to apply for units and insisted that we obtain application forms.

There were some significant long-term outcomes to these early activities — outcomes that made a difference to the lives of all the students and their families.

Significant outcomes from routine activities

First, several members of the class went on to obtain low-rental units either with the city or with the private foundation. Second, I spent a considerable time developing materials and resources on housing that could be used with a variety of different groups, both ESL and English speaking.

Another significant outcome of this series of activities was a social one. Now that the class knew where three of them lived, they started to visit each other and to do things together. They went to garage sales, prepared food, and developed friendships that outlived the existence of the class and provided them with ongoing occasions for using the English they had learned.

DEVELOPING A NEW CONSCIOUSNESS
ABOUT CULTURE AND LIFE

Looking back on these two experiences I am able to see how living and working in Zimbabwe made me conscious of the probable life experiences of people from other poor countries. And both experiences made me aware of the tremendous challenges, including literacy challenges, that face people who have little education and who are poor and powerless.

The importance of cultural issues

In spite of the fact that I grew up in Africa it was not until I returned and did literacy and development work that I began to appreciate the gap between the lives of white middle-class Canadian teachers and students who come from countries like Laos and El Salvador. I learned in a very practical way about how culture and life experiences shape the way we see and respond to the world. Many of the issues that arose in Zimbabwe were similar to those faced by students in Canada. I would like to mention some examples of cultural issues that confronted me in the two situations.

- Rural Zimbabwean women will often leave children as young as six to babysit infants. I have also had Asian students who expected the same of their kids.
- The teenage daughters of one of my students were expected to do all the cooking for the family. They were not necessarily expected to spend much time on schoolwork.
- Both Asians and black Zimbabweans have practices and rituals involving the veneration of ancestors. Also, elders are respected and treated well.
- Polygamy is common in rural Africa and was certainly well known to some of my students.
- In Zimbabwe women without partners are much less pitied than women without children.
- For the people in my class and the women in Zimbabwe, sharing is much more important than having more possessions than others have.
- Each culture has a different way of using domestic space. For example, for many of these people the mother would share bedroom space with the young children while the father would have his own room.

The often misunderstood concerns of immigrants

At least I had some awareness of what it is like to be an immigrant. I remember how overwhelmed I felt in my first few months when there was so much to learn. For example, I knew nothing about heating, thermostats, insulation, storm windows, winter boots, or warm underwear. In spite of my literacy skills I felt totally out of my depth. And my own task was considerably easier than that of my students because I was a single person. Going to Zimbabwe with my children gave me some appreciation of a whole new range of immigrant concerns: safety, schooling, social life, recreation, different norms, etc.

With this perspective I look at the most common type of family literacy programming — encouraging adults and children to read together — and I realize that it would have been simply irrelevant to the needs of the people I had in my class at that stage in their lives. What they needed most was information, language, and guidance about how to navigate their way in a society radically different from the one they came from.

We need to remember that many of these people were also suffering from multiple losses: loss of their country, loss of their homes, loss of family members, loss of status, to name a few. Many had also been through harrowing journeys and experiences while escaping from past situations.

The students in my class indicated that what they needed most was to have safe time and safe space in which to regain their equilibrium, to get some personal support, to learn what would help them to settle in and become self-reliant as soon as possible. They also made it clear that they wanted to have some fun together while doing these things.

The importance of mutual understanding within the community

Something that I learned from this group of people was how important it was to venture out of the classroom and into the community in an intentional way. The outings during which we visited different residences were also incredibly important for my own learning. They provided an opportunity for students to raise and discuss issues that would never have come to the surface had we only stayed in the classroom (e.g., worries about prostitution in the neighbourhood). They also informed me about other issues: the information that they had already acquired (e.g., garage sales); vocabulary, grammatical structures and concerns that I had not thought of.

Some lessons I learned

From my present perspective as a family literacy coordinator I am conscious of some of the things that I did not do with this class but which I would probably do now. I would certainly make contact with elementary schools in order to do the following:

- Establish ongoing contact with staff in order to promote mutual understanding between parents and teachers.
- Organize one or more opportunities for parents to see what happened in their kids' classrooms.
- Identify particular areas of concern/interest.
- Suggest ways in which the learning of both groups could be maximized through coordination.
- Identify activities and practices that might be beneficial to both groups.

With reference to the last point, I would like to comment on the importance of people telling their stories. I noticed that, each time I asked students to share information about themselves and their lives, they threw themselves into the project with tremendous enthusiasm, whether the task was using family photographs and family trees in order to describe their relationships or drawing pictures and floor plans of their homes. If I were to work with another group like this I would encourage the participants to develop a portfolio that would serve two purposes. First of all, it would document their progress at the same time as providing material that could later be shared with others, especially with younger family members. Second, I would also consider suggesting that some of this information be shared with their children both in their mother tongue as well as in English.

My own isolation and loneliness

As I reflected on both the Zimbabwe group and the ESL group I realized that there was one unpleasant emotion I experienced in both situations: a sense of isolation and loneliness. In both cases I felt as if I were out on a limb without any support. In Zimbabwe I connected with all the organizations I could, but there was not a coherent support infrastructure, and contact was sporadic. In Regina I felt isolated by the fact that colleagues were not particularly supportive of my choice to follow the needs of the students rather than a set curriculum or set of materials.

Isolation is also an issue for many family literacy practitioners, especially those in smaller centres. While they might have colleagues, they often are the only ones with training and experience in family literacy. They are handicapped by the fact that few of them have had a chance to see how their work relates to the "big picture." Also, there are few opportunities for meeting and sharing experiences with others doing similar work. Short-term project funding stands in the way of long-term planning, and limited training options make it difficult to become more knowledgeable.

It is quite obvious that the needs of families, whether for appropriate literacy skills or for other types of support, are not yet recognized.

Although I have written about my experiences with a specific ESL class with low literacy skills, I believe that there are also many English-speaking families who face hurdles which to them are quite as daunting. In fact, what sustains most immigrant families is hope — a belief that their children will have it better than they did. For poor Canadians, especially those who come from a culture of poverty, the future may not look as bright.

In talking about Zimbabwe I commented on the preciousness of print. A friend who used to work in child protection put the local situation in perspective when she said: "You know, I never went into a house assuming that there would be a pencil and paper there." Just because the urban middle class is drowning in paper and print does not mean that all households have books, pencils, paper, calendars or any of the many tools of literacy that we take for granted.

WE STILL HAVE A LONG WAY TO GO

I would like to offer some suggestions about what needs to happen to move family literacy from being a disposable, luxury item to a critical part of support systems for all families.

- We need to develop an overview of family literacy that includes a wide variety of program possibilities responsive to the particular circumstances and needs of the participants.
- We need programs that are community-based and have long-term funding.
- We need well-trained personnel who have the capacity to move beyond limited curricula and to tailor programs to meet the needs of the particular participants and the specific communities.

- We need to encourage and facilitate connections between adult programs, early childhood programs and school programs. In particular, we need more and better intergenerational programs.
- We need programs that recognize that many families need support in coming to grips with raising healthy, competent children in a challenging and rapidly changing world.
- We need opportunities for family literacy practitioners to meet and exchange experiences and information.
- We need training and accreditation for facilitators who are knowledgeable about adult education, child development, cross-cultural communication and community development.
- We need to recognize that what is probably the biggest challenge of our lives is the one for which we get little formal preparation: raising healthy, literate children with the capacity to think critically. That must change!

15

Getting to the Heart of the Matter
Low-Income Women Break the Silence

Rhonda Rubin

> *"And what is as important as knowledge?" asked the Mind.*
> *"Caring and seeing with the heart," answered the Soul.*
>
> Author unknown

The importance of literacy, the ability to read and write, permeates the lives of all people. The traditional view of family literacy was based on a deficit model that aimed to transmit the cultural values and practices of a privileged class to those who were believed to lack them. Paradoxically, as Thomas points out in the opening chapter of this section, poor families face many barriers to accessing programs that were originally designed to help them overcome their social and economic difficulties.

The purpose of this chapter is to highlight the views of women from low-income situations whose voices are commonly shut out and whose literacy is often shut down by those in a position of power (Key, 1998). The discussion opens with a statement of four guiding assumptions about literacy and low-income families that challenge some of the dominant myths about literacy.

It was the experience of over a decade of challenging work in the public school system combined with my life experiences that propelled me to further formal education. As I study specific problems in educational practices, I have grappled with a more sophisticated understanding of the education system. The interviews that follow were conducted as part of my doctoral research. For illustrative purposes, I allow the insightful voices of Anna, Andrea, Beth, Michelle, Julie, Lynne and Natalie (not their real names) to be heard expressing poignant examples from their daily life experiences. These will be interspersed with my interpretations of their statements.

In the next section, you are invited to reflect on current popular conceptions of family literacy and to identify some of the pitfalls. This is followed by a framework in which the definition of literacy is extended to recognize and to validate the everyday learning occurring as families struggle to meet their daily needs. Through this lens, literacy can be seen as a catalyst for social change.

WOMEN'S VOICES ARE OFTEN NOT HEARD

Women are silenced by power politics (Giroux, 1988). Not only are there class-based distinctions for women living in poverty, but also gender issues. Anna, who was an abused and substance-dependent woman, has rebuilt her life. She is now a single parent raising four young children and trying to cope with the school system, but becomes confused and frustrated by the unwritten rules of conduct. As Nagle (1999) points out, she did not know how to access what she needed and felt helpless when she was silenced by her child's teacher. "I approached the teacher last year suspecting a learning disability and she just blew me off ... I didn't know what to do." Julie, a mother raising three children alone, related a story about her son's precocious activity, and she noted that his own teacher was skeptical: "Like the teacher was stunned. She couldn't believe it."

Andrea appears to be an astute and perceptive woman. She lives with three of her four children and a manipulative, abusive husband. He can neither read nor write, suffers from a serious gambling addiction, and so her best friend safeguards Andrea's cashed cheques. Andrea is cautious to meet with me only when her husband is out. On one occasion when he arrived unexpectedly, Andrea signalled to me to leave immediately. It was apparent that her husband did not trust strangers in the home with her alone. As I left, I overheard Andrea trying to explain my presence to him, "What? She's just a student doing a project."

The silence and intimidation suffered by Andrea and other women may not be openly expressed, but we can understand the barriers they face in enhancing their literacy development. For Andrea, it is a struggle with day-to-day survival issues; money is always on her mind. When she had eggs thrown at her house, she was not concerned with the mess, but more with the waste, "Who the hell has the money to throw a dozen eggs at a house?"

Family strengths and needs are ignored

Presently, although there is a heavy emphasis on the literacy practices of the school, there is a concomitant failure to acknowledge how literacy is used in families. Because many women are directly engaged in literacy activities to conduct their tasks, they are also at the centre of family literacy practices. For example, Andrea offers her neighbours a home-based catalogue sales business; Beth works closely with a friend to help a candidate on a political campaign; and Michelle studies at home and faithfully completes the home assignments for her alcoholism addiction program.

Children can learn much about reading and writing in the context of family-based interactions within the constant flurry of activities in most homes. But families need support to encourage these. Often though, family members do not recognize that they have a powerful influence on their children's literacy development and they fail to maximize incidental learning opportunities

Multiple realities exist

Most educators were socialized to follow white middle-class values and may be less familiar with other cultural realities (Nagle, 1999). They often fail to recognize how language and literacy are inextricably linked to the family experiences forming the essence of their reality and influencing their learning. Contrary to frequently accepted stereotypes, disadvantaged families do offer support for literacy learning in their homes. Like most parents, they want their children to have more than they had as children and they often hold high aspirations for them. Andrea dreams of her daughter becoming a doctor, while Lynne and her partner arrange to work opposite shifts, so they can reduce babysitting expenses and buy a computer for their daughter with the savings. When the family is together, they play educational games such as Yahtzee and Scrabble or go on long walks in the woods, offering many experiences to develop literacy skills outside of the institution of school. Often after the walks, the family will go home and read and talk about nature topics, thereby increasing learning opportunities.

Low-income families recognize that poverty has cast a dark and ominous shadow over them, setting them apart even as they struggle to blend in. They seek highly visible signs of the middle class and may spend much of their disposable income on middle-class consumer goods to help them feel that they fit in, when more of this money could be spent on learning materials. Although they may have a strong commitment to learning, some, like Andrea, express a fear of teaching their children too much or having their children get "too far ahead." Further, Michelle articulates a rather troublesome belief, unheard of in middle-class circles, about teachers "becoming upset with me" if their children should know more than their classmates. They fail to recognize the variation in knowledge and achievement in all classrooms and may speak only of their child passing rather than excelling.

Literacy may provide opportunities

Becoming literate can be empowering and self-fulfilling for low-income mothers. Parenthood was the catalyst that sparked the desire and need for both Julie and Michelle to pursue educational upgrading in spite of their childhood struggles with the public school system. These mothers aim to complete their high school equivalent and by advancing their own education, feel that they will be able to inspire and help their children with homework and to feel more comfortable in their dealings with the teachers.

For others, literacy will offer them some control over their lives through increased financial independence. Julie aspires to be a child counsellor and feels her own background experiences with various childcare workers will be valuable. Similarly, Natalie enrolls in a variety of short courses to meet her needs for self-fulfillment while persisting in her struggle for financial assistance to pay the tuition required for a training program to work with seniors or mentally challenged individuals. Understandably, Natalie is reluctant to bear the burden of a student loan. She has two young children under her care, no savings, and she fears the consequences of being unable to secure employment upon completion of her program.

RETHINKING LITERACY

Widely held assumptions about literacy are frequently simplistic and even harmful in their unyielding effort to retain the status quo. Those with economic and social power have a vested interest in keeping it (Stuckey, 1991). They benefit from maintaining their dominant position in the class structure by controlling the knowledge that reflects their interests. According to Nagle (1999), failing to account for the full range of literacy experiences in people's lives results in positioning people as either academic successes or failures based simply upon their acquisition of school literacy. There are many ways that children may be socialized in literacies. Key (1998) acknowledged that some family literacy activities may not directly involve reading or writing, but may make subtle or indirect uses of literacy skills and "what these acts make possible" (p. xi). However, in the popular view, promotion of the single school-based literacy places schools in a position of control and power to function as agents for social, cultural and economic regulation.

CRITICAL REFLECTION TOWARDS A CONCEPTUAL FRAMEWORK IN FAMILY LITERACY

Literacy is seen as a human invention. It is often viewed as being at the centre of education with literacy standards serving to maintain privilege (Stuckey, 1991). Stuckey adds that current approaches to literacy education can prevent freedom and limit opportunity. As discussed, many models of family literacy are deficit-based. They stress attainment of a single school-based literacy and marginalize those from working class communities whose literacies may not be valued equally with that of the dominant middle class (Tett & Crowther, 1998). Thus, many children may unwittingly be slotted by teachers into an outsider position when they enter public school and labelled as not ready for school literacy.

We must recognize the existence of multiple literacies, which are the socially constructed practices occurring within the context of language and culture and linked to notions of social justice. As Nagle (1999) maintains, critical theory seeks to understand the unfair power distribution between individuals and institutions, and strives to control it by giving voice to the silenced. Key (1998) claims that those in power, consciously or not, "often drive others to silence as they shut them out of their worlds" (p. 1); with limited exposure to other life circumstances many middle-class teachers cannot relate to the issues that disadvantaged families face.

To understand any literacy, one must consider the political, historical and sociocultural context in which it appears and how it positions people within power structures (Nagle, 1999). For example, literacy education is a political process that can limit participation for those "that do not have full access to the dominant code" (Tett & Crowther, 1998, p. 455). Heath (1983), and later Nagle (1999), claimed that young children who have not had experience with a literacy that parallels school literacy will be marginalized. In contrast, those who have had exposure to the mainstream literacy will know what is valued, may have mastered some of the basics, and will find school literacy more accessible.

Taylor and Dorsey-Gaines (1988) argue forcefully that it is the lack of social, political and economic support that places families at risk, not the family's purported failure to adopt mainstream literacy practices. In Auerbach's (1995) socio-contextual views of family literacy, the whole family is positioned at the centre of the educational intervention and the members act in relationship to an environment. It is this environment that must be recognized and its voices encouraged to be heard.

EMERGENT THEMES FROM THE RESEARCH WITH LOW-INCOME FAMILIES

A number of themes considered to be important in influencing educational achievement and literacy emerged from my interviews with the mothers. Each theme will be introduced individually as it relates to family literacy in low-income homes.

Lack of basic educational materials

The family's financial situation determines the amount of money that can be spent on educational resources. Since there is little disposable income in poor families, planning and saving for even a small purchase is common practice. Andrea enjoys reading escapist romance novels and keeps a collection in her bedroom that she has proudly purchased at reduced rates.

I have 75 romance books up in my room I haven't read yet ...Well I can buy them ...There is a place ...you can get them three for a quarter ...And some of the books are worth $2.99 and $3.99! So usually what I do is when I get two or three dollars, I'll go up and buy them and put them away.

When Andrea began talking about her desire to read a hard cover book on Princess Diana, she had not yet saved enough money, but was "itching to get [her] hands on one."

Likewise, Lynne rarely spends money purchasing reading material for herself. Instead, she collects newspapers and magazines that have been cast off by others at her place of employment and frequently reads them during her breaks. "People leave them in their room and they're no good ... We bring them on dinner times and we have a chance to look at it (sic)."

Andrea's and Beth's children like writing and drawing pictures, but scrap paper or drawing paper is scarce in these homes. Andrea explains her compromise for the lack of paper. "What they do is use up all my envelopes."

Parental practices

A variety of parenting practices that correlate with positive learning outcomes in students have been identified. Desimone (1999) explained that parental involvement patterns may vary according to the economic situation of the family. For example, parents from both low- and middle-income families may hold different beliefs about their role in the education process. Those parents from lower socioeconomic status groups are not as likely as those from middle-income groups to volunteer at school. Schools should be cautious about assuming that all parents are available to help their children with schoolwork. Some parents are so consumed with their own business and social life that there is very little time or energy remaining to help their children with schoolwork or to volunteer at school.

Julie attends therapeutic counselling sessions on a regular basis and is on medication for a psychiatric disorder. Generally she functions well in her daily routine, but any stressful situation can disrupt her and result in a sudden personality shift. She lives with deep emotional scars from a disrupted childhood during which she was abused physically, sexually and psychologically. She and her siblings were split in pairs and sent to spend their impressionable years in foster homes. Julie had no contact with most of her family for many years.

> Do you know what it's like to arrive at a foster home with only the clothes you are wearing and all your possessions in a garbage bag? It's like they're telling you you're garbage ... I never had much of a background. I never had much of ahhh ... upbringing there. It was a struggle. So I'm just starting ... I'm just learning now. I find it's like at times there it can be very hectic and overwhelming.

Julie's comments resonate with the writings of Tett and Crowther (1998). They state how negative views are internalized "and this has consequences for how people see themselves" (p. 455). Julie also turns to her spiritual side in an effort to help herself, "I am starting to see a little bit with Christ beside me ... He's the biggy — the main one in my life."

Julie encourages her son with his homework. She describes the process:

> I'd say, You never even gave yourself a chance ... I know you know how to do it ... And then there'll be an example to show him how to do it ... especially his math. There would be an example. It says right here. Oh ... there it is. Just look at it.

This example illustrates the parental interest and value placed on school-work and the sincere efforts made to support and encourage the child.

Similarly, Natalie wholeheartedly promotes reading with her son.

> You don't know how to read? Oh yes you do! You're learning to read. Oh yeah. It takes time ... Remember what I said practice and practice and practice and it gets better every time you practice ... Their education is very important because I don't have mine and I can see today you need that and if you don't have that — And grade 12 is nothing. Grade 12 today is like having grade 6.

The Lack of crisis resources

The structural composition of the family is important for family functioning. Many women living in low-income circumstances are without a partner to offer them financial and emotional support and they often lack assistance with homemaking and child rearing tasks. Some, like Natalie, deal with the stress, instability and confusion from a broken marriage.

> *And then uh — there is so much racket goin' on with their father and I that I moved to see some peace … I wanted to get as far as I could — But you know I needed to be away from it so I could have time to sort things through …*

A recurrent theme among low-income mothers was that they suffered a lack of time. Roscigno and Ainsworth-Darnell (1999) point out that the number of siblings affects family functioning and they emphasize that each additional member reduces the amount of time available from the parent. The greatest impact is felt on children in single-parent homes.

Impact of health problems

The prevalence of physical and mental health problems in low-income homes is staggering. The management of chronic physical health problems, such as asthma or poor mental health, can be demanding and impact on family functioning. Sometimes, the sudden illness of a family member or close friend could set the family into complete turmoil. Beth pointed out her own fear following some inconclusive test results that her son might have cancer. When she planned the train trip to see the specialist with her son, this required a considerable amount of organization on her part.

> *I had to call [our MLA] to speed it up so I could get my voucher. Then there was the shopping for underwear and pajamas for both of us … I had to buy a couple of new T-shirts. And he wanted a toy to take, so we had to go to another store …*

The lack of provisions for outings and acquisition of cultural capital

Key (1998, p.101) discusses how poor children do not get exposed to "other worlds of possibility" — the cultural capital. One factor for low-income families is transportation restrictions. They may lack a personal vehicle and the public transportation system may be limited. Natalie talks about the hassle she has in taking the bus to a volunteer job that will give her the valuable work experience that she requires.

> *I walk the kids to school and then I race back to grab the bus for downtown. I wait about a half hour at the mall and then I have to transfer. There is really no time, because I have to rush back before the kids are out of school or what would happen? It doesn't work well for people with small kids, but I have no other choice. I don't have a car and a taxi is just too expensive.*

Without ready access to a vehicle or an accessible public transportation system, it is difficult to explore the world beyond their neighbourhood. The families rely on their children being able to attend events sponsored by the church or the Boys and Girls Club because these groups offer transportation from their neighbourhood. Julie describes a restricted number and variety of excursions offered to her children, and these were only in the summer months. "That's when they do the outings. They go to [water theme park], they take them bowling, or they have car washes." These low-income mothers can offer little in the way of input in other agencies' choice or schedule for outings and they lack the means to supplement these events with their own family excursions.

Insufficient finances also limits access to modern technology, such as purchasing a home computer or other household educational resources including books and newspapers (Roscigno & Ainsworth-Darnell, 1999). These items would help the children to experience "other worlds of possibility" (Key, 1998, p. 101), at least vicariously. In addition, Roscigno and Ainsworth-Darnell (1999) stress their importance for "shaping orientations to school" (p. 159). These are the educational tools that are commonplace in schools. Children from low-income homes may have only limited access to these items outside of the school, and no experience with them before entering school.

Roscigno and Ainsworth-Darnell (1999) describe how parents from lower socioeconomic backgrounds are less able than those from middle and upper classes to access or provide the equivalent cultural experiences. Bourdieu and Passeron (1979) elaborate upon the interaction between culture and education. They state that cultural capital, or one's familiarity with high culture, contributes to social reproduction in education. Thus they offer an explanatory link between social circumstances and behaviour. Roscigno and Ainsworth-Darnell (1999) add that these cultural attributes and practices, such as trips to museums, music classes and dance lessons, are highly valued in our society and are considered important for enhancing academic skills.

VISIONS FOR THE FUTURE

Partnerships with parents

In all socioeconomic classes, parents are their children's first and most influential teachers and serve as important role models. Snow (1993) refers to the notion of the "family-as-educator" (p. 21). Other researchers also have shown how the home environment is an important site for learning and the development of young children's literacy knowledge and attitudes about reading and writing (Heath, 1983; Taylor, 1983; Taylor & Dorsey-Gaines, 1988). We need progressive and adaptable teachers who can recognize the value of a variety of diverse literacies and accept that all families have rich resources to bring to the learning process. An obvious implication for teacher education programs is to ensure that teachers are fully prepared to work with students from diverse cultural backgrounds (Burant, 1999), and are sufficiently trained and at ease working with the families of the students. Key (1998) recommends that teacher education programs "include courses that focus on teacher attitudes and arrogant perceptions" (p. 91).

As Taylor (1997) purports, it is important to avoid deficit models that promote a single school-based literacy that "embodies the language of power" (Tett & Crowther, 1998, p. 456). Educators must also learn to identify and promote the multiple ways that families can engage in literacy outside of the school (Taylor, 1983). By privileging the silent voices of the disadvantaged families, educators may gain an understanding of the diversity in their thought and language patterns and the meaning that these people attach to their lives (Tett & Crowther, 1998).

Educators must be open-minded to gain a deeper understanding of the various social conditions under which these families, from backgrounds dissimilar to their own, live (Auerbach, 1995; Burant, 1999). How parents view their role in helping their children is largely shaped by the challenges, barriers and other circumstances they face, and these conditions must be understood and accepted as valid for their situation. Then, educators may proceed to build strategies for improving parent involvement and forging effective partnerships between schools and homes, teachers and parents.

In developing this networking, we cannot overlook the unbalanced power relations that pervade the education system. The power structures are easily recognized at the school level in the form of social control mechanisms for promoting conformity in practice and in implementing curriculum policy. These mechanisms must be studied and adjusted to become purposeful for less privileged families before linkages can be established and strengthened. Parents will then learn how to share power and responsibility with the teachers in what could be labelled as a counter hegemonic practice.

Reworking public policy

Social policy makers also need to drop their cultural arrogance about the "rightness of their philosophical views" (Key, 1998, p. 104) and recognize the "intimidating power of literacy" (Key, 1998, p. 104). The deficit view only serves to perpetuate a division between classes and marginalize those from the non-dominant class. Social policy makers must understand the underlying connections between knowledge and power in order to make more informed decisions about public initiatives. Further, they must recognize how education is intertwined with political, cultural and socioeconomic factors.

Natalie's case, cited earlier, offers a powerful example of some of the barriers that low-income families face in trying to change their life circumstances. Existing public policies in Canada serve to discourage families from leaving their unemployed position where they have been receiving housing subsidies and health benefits, to an employed position where they must cover their transportation costs to and from work, babysitting expenses, health costs and rent. Since they often do not hold a high school diploma, they are usually unable to obtain a high paying job that would keep them in the same financial position despite the additional demands.

Practitioners in the field of family literacy should define the pertinent issues facing those living in low-income situations. They, rather than our politicians, need to outline the future direction for social policy because they work in this context. Inclusion of a socio-cultural perspective in family literacy will serve to mitigate current practices of stereotyping disadvantaged populations as illiterate and will offer a new philosophy to underlie policy and practice decisions.

A serious shortcoming of our education system involves the promotion of one form of literacy and the failure to adequately acknowledge the value of other vernacular literacies. This results in schools unwittingly perpetuating a distancing and reproducing social relationships that maintain the dominant structure in society. Low-income families, as has been shown, are as interested as the dominant class in supporting their children's schooling and academic progress. They attempt to provide whatever support they can offer, given the various limitations they face (Roscigno & Ainsworth-Darnell, 1999).

School personnel must be more open to cultural diversity and networking with families to better understand their needs as Burant (1999) has argued. Those people who have been "shut out" (Key, 1998, p.100) and silenced need to be heard. These are the voices that have been overlooked and neglected for too long in family literacy research. We must establish close connections with these people and encourage them to share their perceptions that will take us to the very heart of the matter.

REFERENCES

Auerbach, E. (1995). Deconstructing the discourse of strengths in family literacy. *Journal of Reading Behavior, 27*(4), 643–661.

Bourdieu, P., & Passeron, J. (1977). *Reproduction in education, society, and culture.* London, UK: Sage Publications.

Burant, T.J. (1999). Finding, using, and losing voice: A preservice teacher's experiences in an urban educative practicum. *Journal of Teacher Education, 50*(3), 209–219.

Desimone, L. (1999). Linking parent involvement with student achievement: Do race and income matter? *The Journal of Educational Research, 93*(1), 11–30.

Giroux, H. (1988). *Teachers as intellectuals: A critical pedagogy for practical learning.* South Hadley, MA: Bergin & Garvey.

Heath, S. (1983). *Ways with words.* Cambridge, MA: Cambridge University Press.

Key, D. (1998). *Literacy shutdown: Stories of six American women.* Newark, DE: International Reading Association.

Nagle, J. (1999). Histories of success and failure: Working class students' literacy experiences. *Journal of Adolescent and Adult Literacy, 43*(2), 172–185.

Roscigno, V., & Ainsworth-Darnell, J. (1999). Race, cultural capital, and educational resources: Persistent inequalities and achievement returns. *Sociology of Education, 72,* 158–178.

Snow, C.E. (1993). Families as social contexts for literacy development. *New Directions for Child Development, 61,* 11–24.

Stein, D. (1998). *Situated learning in adult education*. Columbus, OH: ERIC Clearinghouse on Adult, Career and Vocational Education, Center on Education and Training for Employment, Ohio State University.

Stuckey, J. (1991). *The violence of literacy*. Portsmouth, NH: Boynton/Cook.

Taylor, D. (1983). *Family literacy: Young children learning to read and write*. Exeter, NH: Heinemann Educational Books.

Taylor, D. (1997). *Many families, many literacies: An international declaration of principles*. Portsmouth, NH: Heinemann Trade.

Taylor, D., & Dorsey-Gaines, C. (1988). *Growing up literate: Learning from inner-city families*. Portsmouth, NH: Heinemann Educational Books.

Tett, L., & Crowther, J. (1998). Families at a disadvantage: Class, culture and literacies. *British Educational Research Journal, 24*(4), 449–460.

Evaluation in Family Literacy
Consequence, Challenge, and Choice

Sharon Skage

In the earlier chapter by Thomas, the evaluations of two intergenerational models of family literacy are summarized and compared. One of these evaluations, conducted by the National Foundation for Educational Research (NFER) on the Basic Skills Agency programs in the UK, has had a significant impact on family literacy here in Canada. The findings of the evaluation are causing heightened interest in this approach to literacy development, and show the importance of effective, credible program evaluation in Canada to "make a case" for family literacy.

> *After the NFER study, I had something that piqued the interest of both my colleagues as well as senior officials in government in possible benefits of family literacy programming ... It provided well-researched and well-documented longitudinal information about real, concrete, everyday benefits that resulted for all who participated, both parents and children ... The other important impact for me was knowing that family literacy programming could be very accountable ... It showed me that I could make a strong case in government for funding for family literacy that was not based upon emotional appeal or hunches but upon solid evidence of worth — both for what individuals and their families achieve but also for cost-effectiveness in the broad social context. (Keith Anderson, senior literacy consultant, Alberta Learning, e-mail, September 9, 1999)*

> *From the time I first initiated family literacy programs at Prospects about seven years ago, I have been concerned about being able to demonstrate the value of these programs ... So, from the start, we made sure that evaluation was part of every program we offered ... However, minimal resources for program evaluation meant that it was difficult to go beyond fairly limited, short-term evaluation of programs.*
>
> *When I first read* Family Literacy Works, *I was intrigued not only by the concept of the program itself ... but also by the idea of longer-term evaluation. I knew that I would jump at the chance to try such a program and to build on the relationship already established with researchers at the University of Alberta to replicate the research study. I felt that this would provide an opportunity to demonstrate the value of at least one type of family literacy program and thus set the scene for more sustainable funding of programs. I also felt that it might open the door for similar research and evaluation of many of the smaller family literacy initiatives now being offered in the province. (Maureen Sanders, executive director, Prospects Literacy Association, e-mail, November 14, 1999)*

There are many factors, in addition to the impact of success stories like the one from the UK, that are contributing to the growth of family literacy in Canada. Tireless efforts on the part of literacy programs and coalitions, an increasing awareness in related sectors of the importance of literacy, and large-scale promotional events undertaken with corporate support have all added to the approach's credibility and increased numbers of programs. There are also new opportunities for networking and communication, both regionally and nationally. Although stable, adequate funding is still an issue, there has been an increase in the sources of support for programs, with new government funding available in some provinces. However, as the field develops and the number of programs increases, the need — and expectation — for appropriate and effective evaluation also increases.

This chapter begins with a critical reflection on evaluation in family literacy. We'll then look at evaluation as an element of consequence in family literacy practice, and examine the primary purposes of evaluation. This is followed by a description of some of the challenges and issues relating to evaluating family literacy programs. The chapter closes with suggestions regarding the choices practitioners have available to them for evaluating their programs, and with a look ahead to what the future might hold. Although parts of this chapter reflect the Alberta experience, broad applications can be made across the country.

A CRITICAL REFLECTION ON FAMILY LITERACY EVALUATION

> *Trying to identify the assumptions that underlie the ideas, beliefs, values, and actions that we (and others) take for granted is central to critical thinking (Brookfield, 1988, p. 7).*

Critical reflection is important in examining our practice, and to establish a context for this chapter. Here is a summary of the elements that have shaped my point of view on evaluation.

I have worked in the field of literacy since 1989, and in the field of family literacy since 1994. In the many projects that have filled this period of time, three, in particular, relate to evaluation and assessment. The first of these was to research and develop a manual on family literacy program evaluation for the Family Literacy Action Group (FLAG) of Alberta. The second was to develop good practice statements, standards, and an evaluation process for volunteer literacy programs for the Association of Literacy Coordinators of Alberta. Finally, I am coordinating a project to adapt the Basic Skills Agency's family literacy demonstration programs for use in Alberta. In all of these endeavours, priority was placed on developing practical approaches that result in useful information.

The values that underlie the views expressed in this chapter are framed by the knowledge that I am very much a learner in this field, and I feel that it is essential to continuously work towards gaining new knowledge and improving my skills and expertise. This is done by working with and learning from other practitioners, and with the people who take part in our programs.

I acknowledge a number of assumptions in the area of family literacy program evaluation, including these:

1. Evaluation is an essential element of any program for a number of reasons, and meets a number of needs, both within and external to the program.

2. A systematic, ongoing evaluation process and a participatory, flexible approach to program delivery are not mutually exclusive concepts.
3. Many family literacy programs have appropriate, effective evaluation methods in place, but there are also many programs that are evaluated only informally and inadequately in relation to their own and their partners' needs for information.
4. There are still very few resources and training materials specific to evaluation in family literacy programs.
5. There is largely a lack of expertise among practitioners in involving families in program planning and evaluation.

Having stated these experiences, values, and assumptions, it's important to place them within the theme of this book. The idea of "coming of age" applies not only to literacy in Canada in general terms, but to the understanding held by individual practitioners, individual family literacy programs, and the larger family literacy community regarding program evaluation. As the field matures — most programs in Canada began in the last decade — we must be careful that we are not only addressing the increasing demand for information and accountability. We need to avoid the easy solutions and ensure that as evaluation systems develop, they are thoughtfully conceived, and are consistent with and integrated into other aspects of practice as these are refined.

Some of the issues relating to evaluation will be identified later in this chapter, but one area of debate serves to illustrate the growing pains being experienced in family literacy program evaluation. The National Center for Family Literacy (NCFL) in Louisville, Kentucky, has operated as a nonprofit educational organization since its inception in 1989, with its mission being the advancement and support of family literacy services for families across the United States through programming, training, research, advocacy, and dissemination of information. Among the resources NCFL has produced are a number of materials relating to participant assessment and program evaluation. According to NCFL (1996), programs need several kinds of assessment tools to support the varied purposes of assessment. They describe the advantages and disadvantages of standardized tests, materials- and curriculum-based tests, and alternative assessments. Their description of "alternative" assessments, however, hints at the highly charged debate taking place over appropriate assessment and evaluation: "But, alternative to what?

While much of the criticism of these tests ... and advocacy for 'an alternative' is well-intended, it also is generally ill-informed" (p. 11). The authors go on to say that while critics may be right in seeing a need for concern and change, they are misguided in placing the blame on standardized tests.

In contrast, Murphy (1997) writes that although NCFL "lets itself off the hook" by cautioning users of standardized tests to establish their appropriateness for clients, practitioners often uncritically accept the tests as appropriate. Furthermore, she sees that agency's expectation that programs will use standardized tests as a bias against the very people their projects are intended to serve, given its own statements on the likelihood of poverty in those families.

Debate over the appropriateness of standardized tests and their broader implications for how we view participants is nothing new. Part of our growth in the family literacy field must be to examine all sides of such debates, and to ferret out what really works, considering all other aspects of family literacy practice. As for the questions about program evaluation methods, the approach taken by the NFER, combining some standardized tests with the use of qualitative data to capture the broader range of program impacts, seems the most appropriate and the most likely to address the wide range of program stakeholders' information needs. Holt (1994) advocates such a balanced approach, saying that successful evaluation and assessment depends on using a variety of approaches, including both standardized and alternative methods. This variety will provide staff with the in-depth information necessary to make decisions about the program.

EVALUATION AS AN ELEMENT OF CONSEQUENCE

Why is evaluation important? Many people associate evaluation with accountability, and think of it as a way of summing up what impact the program has had so as to justify its funding. But evaluation can have far broader applications, and can be seen as serving three primary purposes: to develop effective, relevant programs, to determine the impact of the program, and to demonstrate the program's value and success.

To develop effective, relevant programs

An effective evaluation design provides learners and staff members with accurate and useful information for designing, modifying, and improving their project (Holt, 1994, p.5).

Evaluation serves many purposes, the most important being to support the development of effective, relevant programs. Family literacy programs should include a continuous cycle of planning and evaluation so as to allow for continuous monitoring of program activities. Such a process supports program development, revealing what works well and what, if anything, needs to be changed for future program delivery. Thomas and Fisher (1996) describe evaluation as a problem-solving or decision-making process, one that works best when practitioners can work collaboratively to identify areas of program effectiveness, review current practices, and set new goals based on chosen instructional approaches.

To determine the impact of the program

Evaluation is also important in enabling us to determine the overall impact on participants, and — depending on the type of program and scope of the evaluation — the impact on the broader community. Are learners meeting their goals? How do families use literacy and language after participating in a program, compared to before? What other effects has the program had on families?

If evaluation is to include the program's impact on the broader community, areas might include, depending on the type of program and its objectives, use of library services, change in local employment statistics, enrollment in other adult education programs, preschool/kindergarten statistics related to school readiness, and parental involvement in the schools.

To demonstrate value and success

This is an exciting time of unprecedented growth and development in family literacy. Evaluation will play a key role in sustaining that growth and increasing support for family literacy. As new programs and approaches are launched, we need to use evaluation to assess their effectiveness. We need to look at not only how effective new programs are, but also how effective different types of programs are with different types of participants, in different settings, and at different times (Weiss and Jacobs, 1988). As family literacy gains a higher visibility amongst other professions and with the general public, there will be a correspondingly increased demand for information and demonstrated effectiveness.

Increasing emphasis on accountability and performance measurement in literacy and education generally mean that funders and program partners need to see their support justified by positive program results:

> Gathering only subjective impressions [of the Basic Skills Agency programs], though necessary to understand how any gains were achieved, would not have been sufficient to convince funders that the aims had been met (Brooks, Gorman, Harman, Hutchinson, & Wilkin, 1996, p.20).

Evaluation allows us to demonstrate the value and success of family literacy programs. With solid evaluation results, we can address the demand for information from fellow practitioners, people in related fields, potential participants, and the general public. How else can we answer questions like these: Why should literacy programs take on these projects? Why should the community support it? Why should I attend? Why should it be funded?

CHALLENGES AND ISSUES IN EVALUATION

Practitioners face many challenges and issues when it comes to evaluating family literacy programs. Dealing with the diversity of programs and their participants, isolating evaluation from program operations, meeting the needs of different audiences, gaining access to suitable training and resources, sorting through trends in evaluation, and forming different definitions of success are just some of these challenges. Because of their significance during this time of growth and development, let's briefly examine these latter three issues.

Training and resources

Program evaluation requires adequate knowledge and training on the part of practitioners, and appropriate tools as well. During a presentation on program evaluation at the Family Literacy Information Day held in Alberta in 1998, participants were asked to raise their hands if they had taken training in any model of family literacy. Approximately 20 hands were raised. They were then asked how many had received information on program evaluation as part of that training, and none raised their hands. After a moment, three or four people seated at a table reconsidered. While a systematic survey would certainly yield more conclusive results, the incident seems to support the view that evaluation has largely been left out of program development and practitioner training.

Another resource consideration is that time for evaluation is often a challenge for practitioners, who are often working many extra hours already. Many if not most family literacy programs have scarce human and financial resources, and little may be available for program evaluation, even when training is available to staff. Evaluation and its costs should be seen as part of the program itself, not as an "add on." Paid staff time for evaluation-related activities and resource materials should be built into the program's budget.

While not abundant, there have been some very useful resources published in Canada to address evaluation in family literacy, and studies currently underway promise future support in this area. For example, the Saskatchewan Literacy Network's three-year research project Value of Family Literacy will examine the impact of family literacy programs on parents and children and the factors needed for sustainable family literacy programs.

Trends in evaluation

There is a great deal of interest today, particularly from program funders, in evaluation that measures program outcomes. While it is essential to look at program results, it's also important to realize that every evaluation method, including outcome measures, has limitations that can only be overcome by using a combination of methods. Thomas and Fisher (1996, p. 4) cite as one of the field's key evaluation principles that "No single measure can adequately evaluate the complex literacy interactions in family literacy." In addition, evaluation should be recognized as an integral part of programming, part of a cycle of planning and evaluation that leads to continuous improvement; Weiss and Jacobs (1988) argue that we need to be collecting information across programs that comes from examining practice as well as program outcomes, in order to improve the way we design and implement programs. This includes information on "staff recruitment, training, and supervision; outreach strategies; staff turnover and burnout; the use of volunteers; and meshing evaluation and service delivery needs" (pp. 8–9).

Definitions of success

It is a challenge to try to reconcile the different expectations held by different stakeholders in a family literacy program. The funder, community partners, program staff, and program participants can often have very different ideas of what the program will accomplish, and what constitutes "success." Such differences have direct implications on what aspects of the program get evaluated, and how.

In a recent electronic discussion, Isserlis (NIFL-FL listserv, June 3, 1999) stated that the important thing in evaluating family literacy programs is to look at what learners' stated goals are at the beginning of the program, and then look at progress towards those goals. The rest, she says, is a matter of translating that progress for different audiences. In contrast, predetermined outcomes are being considered by many funders, and performance indicators have become de rigueur. The United States Congress, for example, has enacted legislation requiring results-based educational performance measures for children participating in Head Start programs. The *Reading Excellence Act*, passed by the United States Senate in 1998, specifies that states must develop indicators of quality outputs, both for adults and children, for use in monitoring, evaluating, and improving programs.

The authors of the national evaluation of the Even Start Family Literacy program suggest that government interest in measuring quality outputs makes it possible to set performance goals for Even Start programs in that country. The report gives the following suggested examples of outputs for children enrolled in Even Start:

> *Fifty percent of all Even Start children who are entering kindergarten will score at or above the 50th percentile on PPVT. This percentage will increase by 2 percentage points per year over each of the next 10 years (U.S. Department of Education, Planning, and Evaluation Service, 1998).*

For adults in the program, the report suggests the following example of outputs:

> *After one year in Even Start, 50 percent of all adults who are in ABE will score at or above the 50th percentile on either the TABE [Test of Adult Basic Education] or CASAS [Comprehensive Adult Student Assessment System] reading test. This percentage will increase by 2 percentage points per year over each of the next 10 years (same as above).*

CHOICES IN FAMILY LITERACY EVALUATION

As we examine our practice and seek to refine the way we evaluate our programs, it may be useful to develop criteria for choosing evaluation methods and tools. The following suggested criteria have been adapted from those developed for Alberta's volunteer literacy programs (Skage & Schaetti, 1999). Other examples of key principles in family literacy evaluation can be found in Thomas and Fisher (1996) and Taylor (1997).

Methods used in family literacy program evaluation must be

Useful
- meets ongoing internal needs for program information
- meets external accountability needs
- is meaningful and significant in each program's particular context

Ethical
- respects participants' rights
- is consistent with the program's values statements

Integrated
- is designed to build evaluation into program operations

Collaborative
- encourages program partners to share responsibility and have input

Realistic
- is both methodologically and economically feasible
- includes strategies for use

Flexible
- offers a variety of evaluation methods
- goals and context of each program form the basis of the evaluation

Accurate
- uses sound research methods
- is believable (has face validity)

Holistic
- considers both program processes and outcomes
- considers the whole of the program as well as the parts

Identifying existing resources

Whether family literacy programs have evaluation processes in place, or whether they have yet to be developed, learning about the experiences of other programs is worthwhile and can aid in making choices about evaluation. Speaking to other practitioners and finding published accounts of evaluation can be helpful. (Specific references can be found in the Resources section at the end of this chapter.)

Other practitioners can be an invaluable source of information about evaluation. Contact programs you are familiar with; they will likely be happy to share their experiences. Use directories of programs, electronic conferencing services, and listservs to find other programs similar to yours. Attending conference sessions and presentations on family literacy programs and asking questions about evaluation can be another useful way of collecting information first-hand.

The provincial literacy coalitions are often a good source of information about evaluation-related publications and resource people. Some provincial coalitions have published bibliographies of family literacy–related materials. These and other documents are available on the National Adult Literacy Database Website, which has great networking information, lists of publications, and some full-text documents on-line.

Lists of projects funded by the National Literacy Secretariat of Human Resources Development Canada are available from that agency, and include contact information and a brief description that can be used to identify evaluation-related projects.

There is an obvious relationship between evaluation in family literacy and good practice statements and standards for the field. Several provinces, including British Columbia, Alberta, and Saskatchewan, have already developed or are developing good practice guidelines. Program evaluation should be grounded in recognized good practice statements endorsed by the family literacy community.

Choosing appropriate tools and methods

Weiss and Jacobs (1988) warned us to beware the allure of measurement and the neglect of context in evaluating family programs, while at the same time warning us of the serious problem of inadequate child measures and lack of adequate and culturally sensitive parental/family functioning measures (p. 6). Ten years later, the debate over quantitative and standardized methods versus qualitative and alternative approaches is still going on. Concerns over the lack of assessment tools specific to families are still with us as well.

The selection of assessment tools and evaluation methods cannot take place in isolation; they must be chosen or developed within the context of a clear understanding of the nature of family literacy, the dimensions of family literacy learning, the importance of using a framework for evaluation, and clear and common definitions of success and progress. There are examples of tools to consider in the References and Resources sections, but they must be weighed and adapted based on the needs of individual programs.

It is heartening to see an increased interest in and support for research in literacy generally and family literacy in particular. This should result in an increase in the number of relevant and effective tools. Practitioners should make policy makers and funding agencies aware of the need for continued and additional work in this area.

LOOKING AHEAD

What do we see when we look ahead to envision the future of family literacy, and the role that evaluation will play in that work? Some of the issues identified in this chapter suggest future developments. For example, evaluation tools and strategies will be viewed as an integral part of family literacy programming, and will be part of program design and practitioner training. Work will continue at the provincial and territorial level to develop guidelines and standards for good practice in family literacy, and that work will inform the development of — and expectations for — evaluation methods and results. There is already interest in a national discussion on good practice in family literacy, and that discussion will have important policy implications.

In the coming years, it will be important for family literacy practitioners to learn from the work being done in the adult literacy community regarding learner participation in programming. Advances in participatory approaches (Auerbach, 1992, 1996; Draper & Taylor, 1992; Fingeret & Jurmo, 1989; Norton, 1997) can help us to ensure that families have input into program planning, delivery, and evaluation, resulting in more effective, relevant, and meaningful programs.

In the introduction to this chapter, Sanders spoke of the important partnership between her literacy program and the University of Alberta, and the role that has played in the evaluation of Prospects' programs. The author's six years of observing family literacy development provincially and nationally suggest that partnerships of this nature, and evaluation to this extent, are rare indeed in family literacy. In the future, family literacy programs will benefit from similar partnerships as a way of accessing expertise and resources that support program evaluation. The differences between rural and urban programs need to be considered in the development of such partnerships, but advances in electronic forms of communication and collaboration present opportunities not available in the past.

Finally, as we look ahead to family literacy in the 21st century, we see a need for an evaluation framework that works for all of the diverse types of activities and services operating under the umbrella of "family literacy." Such a framework would outline a basic process that programs could use, and would encompass all the elements that we have touched on in this chapter: philosophical principles endorsed by the family literacy community, collections of appropriate and effective tools, potential roles for stakeholders, and so forth. Such a framework would need to be flexible enough to accommodate a wide range of activities, and also allow for programs at different stages of development.

The "five tiered approach to program evaluation" developed by Weiss and Jacobs (1988) could provide a model for just such a framework. It organizes evaluation activities at five levels or tiers, "each requiring greater efforts at data collection and tabulation, increased precision in program definition, and a greater commitment to the evaluation process" (p. 50). Researchers such as Nickse (1993) and Ryan (1991) have further developed this five-tiered approach. In Canada, Weiss and Jacob's framework was used by Thomas and Fisher (1995) and Skage (1997) in developing a framework for family literacy evaluation in Ontario and as the basis for a guide to evaluation in family literacy in Alberta. This framework, or other appropriate tools, will be used in the future to develop holistic evaluation plans conceived as an integrated element of family literacy programming. Such "big picture" thinking will be possible as family literacy practitioners continue to broaden their skills and expertise, supported by the resources and funding that they require to bring family literacy into the new millennium.

REFERENCES

Auerbach, E. (1992). *Making meaning, making change: Participatory curriculum development for adult ESL literacy.* Washington, DC: National Clearinghouse for ESL Literacy Education.

Auerbach, E. (1996). *Adult ESL/literacy: From the community to the community. A guidebook for participatory literacy training.* Mahwah, NJ: Lawrence Erlbaum Associates.

Brookfield, S.D. (1988). *Developing critical thinkers: Challenging adults to explore alternative ways of thinking and acting.* San Francisco, CA: Jossey-Bass.

Brooks, G., Gorman, T., Harman, J., Hutchinson, D., & Wilkin, A. (1996). *Family literacy works: The NFER evaluation of the Basic Skills Agency's demonstration programmes.* London, UK: The Basic Skills Agency.

Draper, J,. & Taylor, M. (Eds.). (1992). *Voices from the literacy field.* Toronto, ON: Culture Concepts Inc.

Fingeret, A., & Jurmo, P. (Eds.). (1989). *Participatory literacy education.* San Francisco, CA: Jossey-Bass.

Holt, D. (Ed.). (1994). *Assessing success in family literacy projects: Alternative approaches to assessment and evaluation.* Washington, DC: Center for Applied Linguistics and Delta Systems Co., Inc. (ERIC Document Reproduction Service No. ED 375 688)

Murphy, S. (1997). Who's reading whose reading? The National Center for Family Literacy evaluation process. In D. Taylor (Ed.), *Many families, many literacies: An international declaration of principles.* Portsmouth, NH: Heinemann Trade.

National Center for Family Literacy. (1996). *Outcomes and measures in family literacy programs.* Louisville, KY: National Center for Family Literacy.

Nickse, R. (1993). A typology of family and intergenerational literacy programmes: Implications for evaluation. *Viewpoints: A Series of Occasional Papers on Basic Education, 15,* 6–8.

Norton, M. (1997). *Getting our own education: Peer tutoring and participatory education in an adult literacy centre.* Edmonton, AB: The Learning Centre Literacy Association.

Ryan, K., and others. (1991, April). *An evaluation framework for family literacy programs.* Paper presented at the Annual Meeting of the American Educational Research Association, Chicago, IL. (ERIC Document Reproduction Service No. ED 331 029)

Skage, S. (1997). *Guide to evaluation for family literacy projects in Alberta.* Brooks, AB: Family Literacy Action Group of Alberta.

Skage, S., & Schaetti, M. (1999). *Setting the compass: A program development and evaluation tool for volunteer literacy programs in Alberta.* Calgary, AB: The Association of Literacy Coordinators of Alberta.

Taylor, D. (Ed.). (1997). *Many families, many literacies: An international declaration of principles.* Portsmouth, NH: Heinemann Trade.

Thomas, A., & Fisher, B. (1995). *Developing a framework for program based family literacy evaluation: Final report to the National Literacy Secretariat.* Ottawa, ON: National Literacy Secretariat.

Thomas, A., & Fisher, B. (1996). *Assessment and evaluation strategies in family literacy program development.* Ottawa, ON: Bonanza Press.

US Department of Education, Planning and Evaluation Service. (1998). *Even Start: Evidence from the past and a look to the future.* Washington, DC: US Department of Education, Planning and Evaluation Service. [On-line] Available: http://www.ed.gov.

Weiss, H., & Jacobs, F. (Eds.). (1988). *Evaluating family programs.* New York: Aldine De Gruyter.

RESOURCES

The following is a brief list of resources that may be useful. For more extensive listings, consult one of the bibliographies listed below.

Directories and networking

Thomas, A., Skage, S. & Jackson, R. (Eds.). (1998). *Family connections: 1998 directory of family literacy projects across Canada.* Welland, ON: Soleil Publishing Inc.

Family Literacy Canada listserv. (Visit the National Adult Literacy Database Website for information on how to subscribe.)

National Adult Literacy Database (http://www.nald.ca)

National Institute for Literacy — Family Literacy listserv. (Visit the NIFL Website — http://www.novel.nifl.gov — for information on how to subscribe.)

Bibliographies

Family literacy: Annotated list of selected materials. (1997). Vancouver, BC: Literacy BC. [On-line]. Available: http://www.nald.ca/lbc.htm

Moar, T. (1998). *Family literacy: Annotated bibliography of resources.* Winnipeg, MB: Literacy Partners of Manitoba.

Standards and good practice

Morrow, L.M., Paratore, J., & Tracey, D. (n.d.) *Family literacy: New perspectives, new opportunities* [Brochure]. Newark, DE: International Reading Association Family Literacy Commission.

Saskatchewan Literacy Network. (1999). *Family literacy standards* [Draft]. Saskatoon, SK: Saskatchewan Literacy Network.

Taylor, D. (Ed.). (1997). *Many families, many literacies: An international declaration of principles.* Portsmouth, NH: Heinemann Trade.

The Influence of Significant Males on Boys' Literacy Levels

Jan Greer

Responsibility for the development of literacy and language skills in young children usually is undertaken by women. But it is just as important for fathers and other significant males to support and promote literacy, especially at home and especially with boys. Research shows that boys are doing poorly in literacy-based activities and the primary reason is a lack of men as reading role models. Literacy and education was a male-dominated field until the last century, yet reading currently is viewed primarily as a female activity. This has to change if we are going to transform the way boys view language-based activities. Men must become equal partners in developing and supporting literacy skills in children, especially boys. This chapter will illustrate the ways fathers, or other significant males, have contributed to the literacy development of boys and the impact these contributions have had on their lives.

There are high profile men encouraging others to participate in literacy activities in their families by publicly stating that reading is important. While this public platform is important, more far-reaching efforts are needed. For example, there is a program in Australia that actively involves men reading to boys, and a unique school reading program designed for boys, a model currently working in England. Making men aware of what their literacy contributions are and can be is a goal of this chapter. Understanding the importance of their contributions may motivate men to elevate and celebrate their investment in raising boys' literacy levels.

LITERACY — A WOMAN'S WORLD

You've been there. It's a literacy conference. The meeting rooms and workshops are filled and what do you hear? The voices of women. There may be a few men but let's face it, literacy is a field clearly dominated by the female gender. The majority of practitioners are women and the majority of volunteers are women. Literacy, however, is not or at least should not be primarily a women's issue. There is a valid concern about boys' lack of interest in books and their inferior reading ability in comparison to the skills of girls. Most agree that a major reason is an absence of male reading role models. Men are desperately needed in the literacy field in many capacities but most importantly they are needed as role models to provide early literacy experiences for children, especially boys, at home and within early childhood teaching systems. A boy who sees a man reading and talking about the value of stories and books will in all likelihood follow his lead. With more involvement from men there could be a rise in the interest level and reading ability of boys.

Wragg (1998) states that "boys start down and stay down" and his work in primary school literacy improvement shows that 75 percent of children aged five to seven were read to regularly by their mothers, but only half from their fathers. He also notes that boys need role models in reading as in everything else. From one of Wragg's case studies, a young boy's reading scores improved sharply once the significant males in his life started reading to him.

THE LACK OF INTEREST IN FAMILY LITERACY

I worked with a handful of dedicated women representing the areas of social work and education to organize a family literacy conference that was held in April 1999, in Fredericton. Designed for parents and caregivers of pre-school and elementary school-aged children, about 100 people attended and of those, perhaps three were men. I was astonished that so few men showed up. In my view, this translates into a lack of interest in family literacy. There was no reason to stay away. It was free, held on a Friday night and Saturday, in good weather, at a local community school and there was plenty of good food available. The conference workshops were dynamic and interesting with many fun literacy activities for parents to engage in with their children.

Where were the fathers, grandfathers, uncles and stepfathers? Where were the men involved in Scouting, the Y and Big Brothers? Do they feel that they have little or nothing to contribute to raising literacy skills of children, especially boys? Is there a general feeling among men that they don't have a role to play in the education of children until they don skates, pick up a hockey stick or are old enough to drive?

THE MALE LITERACY TRADITION

Whether it's the practitioner in the classroom, the tutor in the volunteer movement, or the participant at conferences, the field of literacy is clearly a female domain. Historically this was not so. Frontier College celebrated its 100th anniversary in 1999. The celebrations across the country were filled with memories and stories about a volunteer literacy movement made up primarily of men. Young university students, sons from elite families, headed out into the untamed frontiers of Canada to work side-by-side with laborers during the day and teach literacy at night. Called labourer-teachers, these young well-to-dos toiled in lumber camps, built the railway and sweated it out on farms. The movement and the frontiers have changed with the majority of tutors being young university women taking literacy to people on the street, in prisons and in community centres.

Two influential people also noticed that men were missing from the literacy conference that I helped to coordinate. The first was Ron Buck, a well respected educator in New Brunswick, who told his personal story of the main literacy influence in his life. It was a man. This man had such an influence on him that Ron pursued a career in education and hopes that, in return, his involvement as well as his being a reading role model has influenced boys in his school to love books and reading.

> *I didn't get a chance to say thank you to the most important literacy role model in my life. Gordon was a labourer on the farm in Sussex where I grew up. Of all the people I knew in my young life, he was the smartest! He could read! When we went into town to the country store, he could read the seed catalogues. He could put machinery together because he could read the instructions. Everybody came to him for help and looked up to him because he could read. And I wanted to be just like him. (R. Buck, personal communication, April 23, 1999)*

The second person to note that the conference was made up primarily of women was the lieutenant governor of New Brunswick. The Honourable Marilyn Trenholme Counsell is an avid supporter of family literacy. She participates in hundreds of literacy functions and is concerned about male participation in literacy especially since too many boys lag behind girls in literacy skills. At the conference closing, she remarked about the need to get more men involved in reading to their sons, and in being reading role models for boys.

A few days later, a colleague, Bob Stranach, dropped into my office. We shared the ways our fathers influenced our literacy development as children.

I recalled my father reading aloud, not from books, but from the newspaper and the dinner table discussions about the trucking industry and the family's home-run business, along with stories about fishing, hunting and family foibles.

Bob had discussed this topic with a number of his friends who also remembered their fathers as the primary literacy influences in their lives. If our fathers actively participated in literacy activities with their children, then what has happened to our generation? There may be many explanations, but the challenge is to get men to take responsibility now in the development of literacy skills within their families and by doing so, raise the interest levels of boys in becoming avid readers.

A CRITICAL REFLECTION ON MEN AND LITERACY

There are men who do read to their children, talk to them and play with them. I've witnessed it inside and outside of my family. However, those of us who work within the literacy movement recognize that many more women are involved in literacy activities than men. The field would like to see a greater gender balance in the literacy movement.

Most people assume that mothers, or other significant women, are the primary educators of children. When I ask colleagues what family literacy is or what they mean by domestic literacy, they admit that they visualize a woman providing the literacy interactions. We have either forgotten or neglected the significant impact that men have in supporting literacy development within the family, especially on boys.

Bob Stranach thinks that in order to involve more men in this endeavour, we need to broaden our definition of literacy and expand our sense of ability. In doing so he believes that men would be more comfortable and more apt to participate; men would understand that talking with a child and showing him how things work is important. There is a language around male activities as there is one around female activities and this language needs to be learned and understood. A boy will follow the lead of his male hero. Let me illustrate.

Neil Griffiths, director of the National Storysack Project, of the UK Basic Skills Agency, visited our program. He led a number of workshops on the Storysack Project which involves families in literacy activities at home. He begins each workshop by reading a child's story. He uses suspense, focuses on interesting words, uses prediction and pacing, along with many other strategies that hold the attention of the audience. The adults at the workshops respond to the story just like children. They sit quietly, wide-eyed and open-mouthed. Where did Neil learn to give such a theatrical performance when reading a book aloud? From his father who raised two sons as a single parent and who took time to make books a special event every day.

> Boy, could he read a story well," says Griffiths. "He never started a story until I knew it was something special! He would hold the book tightly in his arms, or hide it behind his back. He'd tease me by saying guess which one I have tonight, or, do you know what I have in my arms right this minute? My favourite book in the whole wide world! He'd have me in a frenzy before he even opened the cover! (N. Griffiths, personal communication, May 1999)

Griffiths believes that if more men were simply seen reading at home, and were involved in children's reading experiences, there would be an increase in boys' interest in books.

Purcell-Gates (1995) describes a very different experience of role modelling with her story about a father, big Donny, his lack of interest in words and books, his inability to read and his lack of respect for education, all of which negatively impacts on his son, little Donny.

"No, no! No words for me!" are the agitated words of the frustrated little boy, who, in Grade Two, follows the lead of his non-reading father (p. 12). This example illustrates what can happen when a father conveys a negative response to books and reading.

It is assumed that literacy is education and therefore best left to women. Not so. Sharing ideas, conversation, games and storytelling all contribute to the development of literacy within the family and men have many valuable contributions to make. Looking back on the literacy contributions my father made in his family, he likely did not consciously realize that he was instilling a love for knowledge, a curious nature, or great animation or interpersonal skills in his children. Like my father, Griffiths' father, and big Donny, men may not be aware that they are impacting the lives of the children around them by their actions as well as their words.

ONE FATHER'S CONTRIBUTION

Bob Stranach's father likely didn't consciously realize it either. Bob, now in his 40s, grew up in a family of three siblings, all close in age. They were a military family and his dad was away from home for extended periods of time. Some people think that literacy activities are only available to the affluent. Bob disagrees, "You don't have to go out and buy things, just use your imagination." His family was not well off. The Second World War played a role in his parents coming from poor backgrounds and disrupted homes. Bob's family moved every few years but his parents were determined to keep their family together and to build a sense of community within the home. They used communication and literacy to sustain a family bond.

> My parents made a conscious choice to not let the Donny scenario happen to us. It could have. It was set up to happen, but my parents, especially my father made sure that literacy and learning were highly important elements in our lives. (B. Stranach, personal communication, October 1999)

Bob fondly looked back on the literacy activities his father engaged the family in, both while he was away and when he was at home. They maintained a close bond through letter writing when Dad was away and when Dad came home, he read to the children — a lot. His father's love for books taught him that books are important. These early literacy experiences provided Bob with a vocabulary that was well developed as early as four years.

Even in play, literacy activities were involved. Bob remembered his father taking a milk carton and making it hollow so that it became the hull of a ship. They built a rigging and put the ship into a tub filled with water, then created a story around the activity. This father was ingenious at using resources at hand. They went on hikes and discussed nature. They collected clay from a deposit on a river bank and built things and then let them dry in the sun. There was a map on the wall near the dinner table and each person in the family had to bring a newspaper clipping of a current event to discuss at dinner and they would put pins in the countries or cities in which the events took place. Look at the rich language experiences this father created. Is it any wonder that Bob wanted to be a teacher?

When Bob made a small desk for himself from a tea chest, his parents scrimped and saved and bought him a real desk. "The message was that education is good," says Bob. "I lived in a supportive environment."

An important part of this ongoing support was Bob's father acting as mentor. When Bob signed up for different organizations, his dad signed up too.

> *It is so important for boys to have even just one male role model who will form a warm bond with them and encourage learning and reading. For instance, the drop-out who hangs out at the garage ... if he can connect with someone in the community who will help guide him in lifelong learning then he'll come out the better for it. (B. Stranach, personal communication, October 1999)*

Bob speculates that if a father or another significant male is not involved in a boy's literacy development, then there is a long period of time before the boy meets up with a strong reading role model as there are not a lot of male teachers or volunteers in the early grades. As boys enter school they are generally met with a female teaching figure. Bob didn't meet up with a male teacher until Grade Five. Fortunately this man really liked to read and introduced students to authors like C.S. Lewis and classics like Tolkein's *Lord of the Rings.* "This man was a positive and encouraging person in my life and I owe a lot to him."

Ron Buck, an educator and principal for 34 years, agrees that more men are needed in kindergarten and elementary grades. Throughout his career he has noted that, in fairly stable families with steady incomes and where both parents have strong literacy levels, men are taking more interest in their children's education. For those families in the lower socioeconomic scale with less education, fathers are not as involved. He is concerned that boys, especially boys living in mother-led homes, often don't get a male reading role model until later when they meet up with a male teacher and by then it's often too late to instill a desire for reading.

Buck was raised by an aunt and uncle and says he was fortunate to have three significant male reading role models in his life. As well as Gordon, there was an uncle who had fought in the Second World War and loved to read war and history novels, sharing these and other personal stories with him. The third was his Grade Nine teacher and rugby coach who always had stacks of books on his desk, all of them bookmarked with excerpts that he read aloud to the class. To Buck, this meant two things; the words in the book were important and he was important because his teacher shared these words with him.

The role model is vital in ensuring that a boy becomes a good reader. Stranach wishes that every child could have an adult who introduces them to

> the colour, poetry and song that we call literacy; that each child has a mentor who, in their eyes, loves learning and passes that love on to them. For boys, that person needs to come in the shape of another male. (B. Stranach, personal communication, October 1999)

SOCIETY CAN'T TAKE THE PLACE OF FAMILY WHEN IT COMES TO LITERACY

Upon being sworn in as lieutenant governor of New Brunswick in 1997, Her Honour, Marilyn Trenholme Counsell, chose the issue of literacy, especially literacy for children, as a priority. Her duties take her to hundreds of events across the province each year where she notices a disproportionate representation between women and men attending literacy events.

One literacy event was an exception. It was held at the Saint John Learning Exchange, an organization that actively encourages, targets and involves fathers in its family literacy activities. The Saint John Learning Exchange encourages male staff and board members, and husbands of female staff and board members, as well as male role models within the community, to participate in family literacy activities. It also times events so that more dads can participate. Hiring a male children's activity coordinator at the local family resource centre has also upped the number of participating dads by 25 percent.

As the Hon. Marilyn Trenholme Counsell travels the province promoting literacy, she urges more men, especially fathers and grandfathers, to be involved in literacy activities at home. She, too, feels that boys need more male role models showing a keen interest in books and reading. Generally, however, males are less attracted to books and more attracted to technology and electronic games and traditionally are more active in sports or other types of activities.

The Superior Council on Education, a government appointed body that advises the Quebec education minister, recognizes this and urges schools to use new technologies appealing to boys to encourage them to read and write and also to use extracurricular activities for teaching reading and writing (p. 12).

Another important element in the development of early literacy is dialogue. "Talking around the dinner table is missing in too many homes," says Trenholme Counsell. She points out that there is a different way of expression for men and women and recommends that we engage in a common dialogue. "One must see the gap narrow if our boys and girls are to grow with a love of conversation and story telling."

Her vision for family literacy is for families to continue to make an effort to read together and share stories about the present and the past. She encourages men (and women) to engage in the full gamut of literacy; reading books, sharing both printed and oral stories, magazine articles, writing and numeracy. Another area where men could make a huge difference is through volunteering in literacy program activities. The literacy community needs to get the message out to the corporate world and labour unions that more visible men are needed in the literacy movement.

LITERACY — THE FEMALE CONNECTION

"Image may have something to do with lack of male participation in literacy," says Bob Stranach. The Superior Council on Education report states that reading and writing are perceived as feminine and that boys, under peer pressure, try to avoid being associated with these feminine areas of learning (p. 6).

"We need to get into a new proudness of being male," Bob adds. "We don't all have to be Marlboro Men." Buck's world embodied both; maleness in farmers, war heroes and sports enthusiasts coupled with the love of books, stories and reading.

> *Gordon could role a 'makins' (hand-rolled cigarette) with one hand. He had attended agricultural college. He castrated bulls! But, he read at every opportunity. And he would read every word on every page of every newspaper or book he had in his hands. (R. Buck, personal communication, December 9, 1999)*

LEADERS IN LITERACY FOR BOYS

Some men are trying to change the female brand put on literacy activities. The visibility of male literacy involvement is beginning to emerge in New Brunswick. For instance, hockey teams promote reading. The involvement of the Flames in Saint John and the Wild Cats in Moncton gives boys the message that you can combine reading and sports. When boys see men like Wayne Gretzky supporting reading, it goes a long way to get them into books.

New Brunswickers such as Premier Bernard Lord; Peter Sawyer, current president of Laubach Literacy New Brunswick, and Frank McKenna, former premier, all make statements publicly about literacy and learning in forums where men are present. The lieutenant governor of New Brunswick stresses that it is important for public figures to share their passion for participating in literacy activities in their homes. When Premier Bernard Lord states publicly that he tries to be home at night to read to his children at bedtime it gives the message to other men that this is an important activity. The Legion has embraced literacy and its members are involved in reading to children in many areas of the province. Trenholme Counsell says that it is particularly good for boys to see grown men enjoying reading and sharing books with them.

She says, however, "Society can never take the place of family when it comes to literacy." She urges fathers especially to understand that books are to be enjoyed, that reading to young children makes a real difference.

> *We have to make men aware that too many boys are lagging behind in reading and loving books and this impacts their lifelong direction. Rather than criticizing men, show them that literacy can be part of what they do with their family whether it's sports, business or farming and validate them in their role. (Marilyn Trenholme Counsell, personal communication, November 2, 1999)*

Recommendations from the Superior Council on Education include making fathers aware of the impact of the socialization process on their children's academic achievement, providing them with information on appropriate parental practices (p. 12) and also providing boys, especially those from disadvantaged areas, access to high-quality school libraries (p. 13).

NEEDED: GREATER EFFORT TO PROMOTE READING

People agree that one of the reasons why boys lag behind in their reading skills is the lack of males as reading role models, yet, little is being done to change it, at least in Canada. The literacy movement recognizes the challenge, yet is ill equipped to do much about it. In New Brunswick, literacy groups show men reading in their promotions and use the male voice in advertisements. It helps to have male role models such as sports heroes and other prominent males in public forums reading with children and urging dads and other significant males to read to the boys in their lives. However, there is no large-scale concerted effort to get men reading to boys.

The Canadian School Achievement Indicators Program *Report on Reading and Writing* (1998) once again shows the obvious — boys are behind in reading and writing. Forty-six thousand 13-year-old and 16-year-old students were tested across the country. Females in both age groups performed better in reading competency levels ranging from one to five: Level One being an elementary level response to reading and Level Five being a sophisticated and complex response. Sixteen-year-old girls performed significantly better in higher levels of reading competency than boys, with a 22.6 percent gap in Level Four and a 9.3 percent gap in Level Five (p. 24).

A Globe and Mail editorial (1999), "Boys and literacy: We can do better," which refers to the 1998 report, states that this phenomenon appears to be nearly universal. This editorial makes an interesting point by comparing the "girls and math issue" to the "boys and literacy issue." When girls' math and science scores were lower than boys', society reacted only after interventions from women. Science and math classes were made "girl-friendly." Female heroes promoted girls' involvement in science and math. And, guess what? Things improved. Other countries are doing something about boys' literacy problems. The Australians are actively involving fathers in reading to their sons while in England sports teams are being used in boys' reading promotions.

There is also a school-based initiative in Birmingham, England. This initiative involves Directed Activities Related to Text (DART), activities designed to prompt an interrogative approach to reading. Examples include reading a passage followed by groups or pairs of students filling in targeted or random gaps in text. Then the group discusses what words might fill in the gaps. This exercise could initiate other discussions about writing styles for instance. Other DART activities include colour coding, underlining, placing subheadings in margins, sequencing, transforming passages of text into diagrams and flow charts, re-writing text for different audiences, extracting key sentences, summary activities and so on. The initiative also involves Everyone Reads in Class (ERIC) which provides time for silent reading. These activities are accompanied by a Reading Award Scheme. Boys like the element of page 16 competitiveness that an award system brings and enjoy getting a certificate. Students are also taught a research technique called SQ3R: Survey, Question, Read, Review, Recite.

The effects of these activities were monitored using the *National Foundation for Educational Research* (NFER) *Group Reading Test*. It was found that students had improved, on average, by one and a half years. Some students had improved by three years, some by four and five years. Importantly, there was no longer a discrepancy between the reading levels of boys and girls. The boys had caught up and all students' reading abilities had improved overall (Barclay, 1998, pp. 18–20).

ETHAN'S STORY

Ethan, my nephew, was born in 1992. Ethan is one of those fortunate little boys who has a number of strong, significant male role models: his grandfather, his father and his uncles on both sides of his family.

I sat in amazement one afternoon at my parent's home when Ethan, his father and grandfather were sitting together on the back porch. Ethan was six years old at the time and the men were discussing the differences between the diesel motor of his father's logging truck and the gas driven motor of a regular-size pick up truck. The discussion fully included Ethan and was filled with detail about the intricate workings of how each type of fuel reacted with each motor and what the differences were in order to make these two types of motors work.

It became clear to me that my youngest brother was following my father's example of 81 years in sharing language as my oldest brother had with his son. I wished at that very moment that every little boy and girl could have the type of language support Ethan has. His life is rich in language experience extending far beyond this example. He listens to generational stories, is involved in sports, has a number of interesting pets, his parents take him on trips, he helps out on a nearby farm. He has been read to from birth and has an overflowing book-case containing his own books.

I often ask him if he has read any good books lately, and he always has an answer. When he learned to read, I telephoned him long distance and he read to me over the phone.

It is my vision that as more information comes forward about boys' low literacy levels, men will participate in vital literacy development within their homes and in their communities.

It will be a start if the literacy community can convince men in predominately male organizations to read with boys and to be positive reading role models for boys. But this isn't enough and the literacy community alone cannot make a significant impact. It will take all the fathers, grandfathers, uncles, stepfathers and other significant males in the lives of boys to consciously be reading role models for boys. Often, all it takes is one significant individual to introduce a boy to a book or to share a spoken story and support him in the joy of reading literature and hearing words.

REFERENCES

Barclay, I. Improving boys' literacy. *Basic Skills*, Summer 1999, pp. 18–20.

Boys and literacy: We can do better. (1999, March 18). *Globe and Mail*, p. A14.

Council of Ministers of Education, Canada. (1999). *Reading and writing School Achievement Indicators Program*. Toronto, ON: Author.

Superior Council on Education. (1999, October). *Improving boy's and girls' academic achievement summary*. Sainte-Foy, PQ: Author.

Purcell-Gates, V. (1995). *Other peoples' words: The cycle of low literacy*. Cambridge, MA: Harvard University Press.

Wragg, E., Wragg, C., Haynes, G., & Chamberlin, R. (1998). *Improving literacy in the primary school*. London, UK: Routledge.

SECTION SYNOPSIS

Nurturing Success in Family Literacy

Ruth Hayden and Maureen Sanders

The chapters in this section point to three issues critical to the continued development, expansion and success of family literacy programming. We address each of these issues — partnerships, training, and advocacy — within the context of programs firmly rooted in community.

PARTNERSHIPS

The relatively new approach of working with other related agencies to deliver programs in a collaborative and integrated way has been very timely for the rise of the family literacy movement. Whereas an adult literacy program can operate reasonably well in isolation from other community educational efforts, it is almost impossible for family literacy programs to function successfully alone. These programs depend on the collaboration and synergy created by like-minded people, from a variety of sectors within the community, each with its own knowledge, insights, experience and resources to reach a common goal — providing opportunities for individuals and families to learn, grow, develop and prosper.

To put this concept of interagency collaboration into practical terms, a Mother Goose program might be run in the following way: the family literacy program provides trained, paid facilitators; a shopping mall contributes free storefront space that is appropriately equipped; local social services staff recruit teen parents and supply transportation to the program; a health network contributes food for a cooked meal at the end of each session of the program. Within such a framework of community partnerships, literacy gains recognition as an element of community development, thereby becoming a community responsibility rather than just the responsibility of the local literacy group.

Such partnership efforts require a tremendous amount of time, effort, open communication and goodwill to ensure that the philosophies and goals of our agency partners are in harmony with our own. Roles and responsibilities need to be clearly laid out so that misunderstandings about expectations do not lead to unsuccessful program delivery. Once established, partnerships need regular nurturing to keep them flexible, fruitful and of continued benefit to families.

TRAINING

The topic of training — or perhaps we should say education — for family literacy practitioners is one that has received little consideration in the literature to date. Yet there are increasing numbers of people with a range of backgrounds, knowledge and experience taking on the role of administering or facilitating family literacy programs in their communities. If family literacy practitioners are to gain credibility and respect for their work, and thus for the movement as a whole, it is crucial that they have the knowledge and expertise to do the job well.

Program leaders now need a much wider range of knowledge in such areas as emergent literacy, child development, community development, building partnerships, and cultural diversity, if family literacy is to sustain itself over the next ten years. As Skage points out, it is essential that they also have a good understanding of the role of evaluation in program development and knowledge of a variety of evaluation tools if they are to demonstrate the value of their programs. Generally, however, the proliferation of new family literacy programs across the country outstrips efforts to ensure adequate training to run these programs. While many provinces are working diligently to establish principles of good practice and design training programs, we need to work collaboratively at the inter-provincial level, and build on each other's work to get solid education and training programs in place as quickly as possible. We also need to answer tough questions about how much training is required, in what areas, and for whom, and to establish accreditation procedures to give validity to this field of learning, negotiate with universities and colleges to provide still more options for education in family literacy, and ultimately to bring this area of work more into the mainstream.

ADVOCACY

If we do not want family literacy programs to fall to the same fate as adult literacy programs — the poor sisters of the lifelong learning process — we have to broadcast effectively the importance of our work by advocating and promoting literacy as an integral component of community development. No matter how busy we are running programs for families, we must also find time to run literacy awareness programs for the community at large. The community needs to know the issues so that it can know how to help. Family literacy organizations must become literacy resources for their communities, and must have the knowledge and expertise in literacy development to provide a professional service to the community. It is by creating literacy friendly and literacy rich communities that everyone in the community will recognize the importance of literacy to the healthy development of individuals, families and communities. By everyone, we mean nurses, teachers, physicians, social workers, police officers, business people, professors, accountants, store workers, lawyers, politicians, bureaucrats, artists, day care workers, and stay-at-home parents among a host of others.

Many community members frequently maintain traditional perspectives on how literacy is learned, perspectives repeatedly reported in the media. These views generally do not reflect the socio-cultural and client empowerment perspectives suggested by Auerbach (1989) and others like Rubin in this volume. It is incumbent on the local family literacy group to provide leadership in promoting, and generally "sensitizing" community members to current research about literacy development in general and early literacy development in particular. In short, we have to educate each community to think with a literacy mind-set.

Interestingly, such educative efforts often encourage community members to generate ideas for literacy programming that prove to be novel and exciting. The PROTECTS program (Hayden, 1997) is one example where, after hearing about our work on the radio, police officers initiated a program of reading to kindergarten children as part of their community service work. Publicly promoting our programs may increase the number of men involved in family literacy whose absence has been noted by Greer in an earlier chapter.

In addition, we have found that publishing the results of our work in pro-fessional educational journals helps to sway the opinions of politicians and senior bureaucrats (Metcalfe & Hayden, 1998; Hayden & Sanders, 1998; Hayden & Wahl, 1996). They are sensitive and responsive to the fact that Albertan family literacy programs are being read about, and perhaps even emulated, beyond provincial and even national boundaries.

OTHER DISCOURSES AND LITERACIES

An underlying theme presented by Thomas, Rubin and Craig in earlier chapters is the need to continue to focus our programs around the cul-tural values of the families we serve. However, it is also important to remember that many of our participants want to learn the discourses and literacy of mainstream society so that their children will have equal opportunities as their more fortunate peers. While Gee (1988) suggests that such discourse acquisition is not possible, Delphit (1992) contends that non-mainstream learners can add other discourses to their repertoires while retaining their own language and literacies. We need to maintain a delicate balance between the desires of our participants to access the power of mainstream society and our genuine efforts, as literacy workers, to work within their sociocultural constructs. To do otherwise is to mar-ginalize further those whom we purport to assist. As one aboriginal par-ent commented during a BOOKS program that included several native content texts: "Enough of the feathers, already. Show me how to teach my kid how to be as good (successful) as white kids."

Family literacy in Canada is well established. However, there is still a great deal of work to be done. Addressing the issues we have presented above will offer greater possibilities for nurturing the continued success of family literacy in the future.

REFERENCES

Auerbach, E. (1989). Toward a social contextual approach to family literacy. *Harvard Educational Review, 59*, 165–187.

Delphit, L. (1992). Acquisition of literate discourse: Bowing before the master? *Theory into Practice, 31*(4), 296–302.

Gee, J. (1988). Literacy, discourse, and linguistics: Introduction. *Journal of Education, 17*(1), 5–17.

Hayden, R. (1997). PROTECTS: Police reading outloud to educate children through stories. *Alberta English, 32*(2), 8–13.

Hayden, R., & Sanders, M. (1988). Community service providers as literacy facilitators: A pilot project. *Alberta Journal of Educational Research, 44*(2), 135–148.

Hayden, R., & Wahl, L. (1966). Who's who in family literacy?: A portrait of two women. *Australian Journal of Language and Literacy, 19*(3), 211–220.

Metcalfe, P., & Hayden, R. (1998). Family literacy: Two programs of interest. *Early Childhood Education, 31*(1), 22–27.

S E C T I O N 4

School-Based Literacy

FRAMING CHAPTER

Literacy as Decoding, Thinking, and Integration
Setting the Debate Within School Contexts

Yvonne Hébert and Christine Racicot

Canadian society is almost entirely constituted of immigration, occurring over the last 400 years and continuing into our day. Currently, a global migration pattern feeds a flow of peoples to Canada, unseen since the turn of the century when the Prairies' population increased by 400 percent (Isajiw, 1999). Open to receive refugees and selected immigrants, Canada relies upon educational institutions and community programs to teach one of the two official languages. Such programs are the first step towards integration and participation in Canadian society. With increased foreign-born population, Canada relies on the success of all students for its economic future. Success in "schooled literacy" is still a firm requirement for success in wider socioeconomic life (Wray & Medwell, 1999, p. 3). Literacy, then, must meet the complexities of the technological chameleon that is the global village.

Within educational contexts, ways of teaching and learning languages are constantly being reconsidered and questioned anew, in order to increase the efficacy of school-based literacy efforts. Without a sufficient and reasonable mastery of at least one of the official languages, it may be expected that children who are rooted in this migration will be largely unable to participate fully in society, to contribute productively in the labour market, or to assume the full range of citizenship rights and responsibilities.

THE DIFFERING VIEWS OF LITERACY

What then is meant by literacy? What is sufficient? What does this renewed questioning mean for literacy practices and research? Of particular interest to the re-examination of literacy practices and research bases are three views of literacy:

1. **Literacy as decoding** — a skills-based approach, assumed by many reading specialists
2. **Literacy as thinking** — a common view among adult literacy educators, focusing on cognitive and especially metacognitive development
3. **Literacy as integration** — seen as a means of empowerment, production and citizenship within a society marred by inequities and competing groups

Set within the context of child and adolescent literacy in schools, we explore the tensions between these three views of literacy as their nature and functions are commonly ascribed to literacy development. Data will be drawn from recent studies of second language acquisition dealing with language learning strategies of immigrant youth; educators' views of the relationship between language and citizenship; as well as schools as contested sites of discourse and of citizenship. We propose that distinctions between these three conceptions of literacy are nonproductive and that all are needed, intertwined, in order to respond adequately to learners' needs.

These three different views are influential in the field and yet cannot explain the high dropout rates for English as a Second Language (ESL) students reported in Western Canada (Watt & Roessingh, 1994). ESL students are not attaining the level of academic literacy needed to succeed in secondary school programs and to access post-secondary education. Questioning the assumptions, nature, and impact of the theoretical and practical tensions between the three concepts of literacy is important to be able to assess their pedagogical value and ability to promote the high level of literacy necessary to the school success of learners and hence, their future socioeconomic success as citizens.

The literacy research reviewed here pertains to levels of emergent, child and adolescent literacy in the fields of first and second language study. Emergent literacy is defined as the young child's experiences to "interpret and communicate using symbols" be these print, drawings or scribbles (Dixon-Krauss, 1996, p. 18), in a continuous process throughout the child's early development before formal instruction when the child is first exposed to literacy as a cultural and social activity. We consider child and adolescent literacy as learning occurring in formal schooled contexts throughout a progression of elementary to high school years. We note, however, that formal school environments paint only a limited picture of the literacy learning events and activities that contribute to the individual's development. Research into literacies of children and adolescents in the contexts of the home, community and other social settings shed light on how literacy is used and functions in their lives. Here, however, we focus on the literacy of schooling, involving instruction and assessment, because students' success in this process determines their level of official literacy attainment, and thus impacts on opportunities for further education, social mobility, and occupational status.

Sketching the three views of literacy

LITERACY AS DECODING

A skills approach to literacy instruction focuses on developing the ability to decode and make meaning from the symbols of text (Baker, 1996, p. 296). The decoding, or bottom-up, approach to literacy often takes on primary importance in school literacy programs through phonics instruction, especially with learners who already speak the language in question. In many child literacy programs, attention is given to the segmentation of text using sound-word drills, or cutting up words into smaller units of meaningful sound (Collins, 1986, p. 123). For beginning readers of a language in which they are fluent, this approach may work well because it focuses on the intricacies of the code and minute differences carrying significance. For advanced readers, decoding includes morphological analysis, that is, the identification of word stems and affixes, especially as linked in word families. The mastering of codes for decoding text is based upon a belief that, as skills become more automatic, the more advanced will become the learner's level of reading comprehension.

LITERACY AS THINKING

Giving much attention to cognitive and metacognitive development for thinking, this view of literacy equates thinking with cognition that is viewed as "manipulating symbols that represent information" (Winne, 1989, p. 91) and includes perceptual, linguistic and conceptual operations. Focusing upon concepts within texts as well as upon concepts of language, the literacy as thinking approach stems from cognitive psychological models of learning, which claim that new concepts are best learned by building upon those already in place. Rather than considering the learner as entering the school environment with no prior knowledge, ready to receive information, cognitive perspectives on learning consider "that what we understand of something is a function of our past experiences, our background knowledge, or what are sometimes more technically called our *schemata*" (Coady, 1993, p. 10). Reading is thus viewed as an interactive process integrating textual information with information-in-memory. The aim of research from this perspective is to discover "how humans structure their knowledge and how we process or 'manipulate' those knowledge structures to create new concepts" (Hedley, Houtz & Baratta, 1990, p. 1).

LITERACY AS INTEGRATION

Sometimes termed "literacy as saving grace," literacy as integration refers to the link between literacy attainment and the successful integration and engagement of learners into society. Definitions of literacy favoured in policy and curriculum development often stress the importance of literacy for effective participation and citizenship in the given community. Other well-known definitions from an integrationist perspective (Freire & Macedo, 1987) stress the role of literacy as empowerment and emancipation through critical literacy, developing consciousness and eventually influence over the socially and politically imposed knowledge, ideologies and institutions.

The view of literacy as integration is a powerful one, motivating many community-level initiatives and many adult literacy workers because the participants are frequently among the poor, the down-trodden, the isolated, and the marginalized. For adult immigrants, literacy classes in an official language are key to participation in the labour market and in post-secondary education, to their socioeconomic success and to their engagement in Canadian society as first class citizens. In curricular content however, these initiatives tend to focus on language functions, tasks and situations (on short-term literacy goals) to provide training for the first stages of settlement in a new country. The advanced literacy training necessary for intellectual discourse, for citizen engagement and for social mobility is largely lacking except possibly in large urban areas (Derwing, Gibson, Borisenko, & San Sy, 1998).

Informing school-based literacy programs in either first or second languages, this view of literacy as integration exists within a tension between the broad goals of schooling: the reproduction of society, the development of students to their fullest potential, and the preparation for work and for an unknown future. All are linked to the major issue underlying the integrationist view of literacy, that is, the nature of civic and social participation that is crucial to how democracy works (Hébert, 1998).

Tensionality between decoding and thinking

The tensions between decoding versus thinking as views of literacy revolve around the functions of the former and the strategic significance of the latter. Akin to the broader theoretical shift from functionality to strategic transformation as tools for the construction of knowledge, the literacy debate focuses upon skills and strategies, asking which set of tools is most likely to lead to reader efficacy. Of critical relevance to this renewed debate is the teaching and learning of vocabulary as the key ingredient in language studies (cf., Haynes, 1993 vs. Stoller & Grabe, 1993). In this way, the vocabulary debate encapsulates the tensionality between decoding and thinking.

DECODING

Baker (1996) notes that "Reading is about saying the words on the page and writing about being able to spell correctly, and write in correct grammatical sentences" (p. 296). This skills approach to literacy often leads to the learner acquiring the necessary knowledge and skills to function in a given community in a "collaborative, constructive and non-critical manner to the smooth running of the local community," a competence termed *functional literacy* (Baker, 1996, p. 296). Programs based on such approaches assume that native speakers have intuitions about what constitutes a word. For second language learners, however, these programs pose difficulties as the students' experiences with their first language may not coincide with those of the target language.

Approaches that focus on reading as decoding are critiqued for several reasons. The focus on form rather than meaning is considered to be misguided by some researchers who believe that these skills are best acquired when they are placed in a meaningful context (Simons & Murphy, 1986, p. 203). Moreover, stressing the learning of language forms, such as vocabulary words, be it from a specific list, by multiple exposure, and/or with explicit morphological analysis, virtually ignores the students' cultural experiences. While reading is more than the mastery of decoding skills, proficient processing of text is not possible without them (Farr & Carey, 1986).

THINKING

Viewed as steps that students take to enhance their own learning, learning strategies provide learners with the means to solve problems when faced with new information. These problem-solving strategies have been categorized as metacognitive, cognitive and social/affective. Considered to be higher order executive skills "used to oversee, regulate, or self-direct language-learning" (Rubin, 1987, p. 25), *metacognitive strategies* refer to knowledge, manipulation or self-management of cognitive processes, including selective attention, planning, monitoring and evaluating. *Cognitive strategies* refer to steps or operations used in learning or problem-solving requiring direct analysis, transformation or synthesis of learning materials. They include rehearsal, organization, inferencing, summarizing, deducing, imagery, transfer and elaboration. And finally, allowing learners to engage in and contribute to conversation, *socio-affective strategies* involve interaction with others, or ideational control over affect, and include cooperation, questioning for clarification and self-talk. From this perspective, providing students with training in strategy use is considered critical for effective second language literacy development so as to provide students with the "ability to review their progress, accomplishments and future learning directions" (O'Malley et al., 1983, p. 6).

Leading to differing results and ongoing debates, numerous studies have researched the strategies that successful first and second language students actually use to understand the meanings of words (Chamot & O'Malley, 1994). According to this view of literacy, strong first and second language learners are able, to some extent, to draw from the contextual information available in a text to figure out meanings of unfamiliar words instead of resorting to the more technical skill of referring to dictionaries in search of word meanings as part of decoding (Coady, 1997). Frequently cited, the cognitive strategy of guessing on the basis of contextual information is widely encouraged and yet still debated. Guessing is considered to be desirable as it allows the learner to continue in the reading process rather than leaving the text at several moments to search for outside help, thus possibly hindering comprehension and engagement in the literacy activity. Guessing strategies are not always successful, however, because factors such as the nature of the learner's first language and transfer effects may override the ability to use context to infer meanings and thus sidetrack the learners completely (Haynes, 1993).

Shifts in understanding

Two shifts in understanding literacy have occurred in recent years. There is a shift in emphasis from a view of literacy as isolated skills to "the conception of literacy as thinking that deliberately makes use of language, whether spoken or written, as an instrument for its own development" (Chang & Wells, 1990, p. 209). Literacy and cognitive development have traditionally been treated as separate goals in schooling, the former considered the responsibility of the language arts curriculum and the latter the focus of academic areas (Gambell, 1989, p. 269). However, considering that "as language mediates cognition, cognition is transformed and concepts are reorganized" (Gambell, 1989, p. 270), the ways in which language learning, literacy, and cognitive development are intertwined necessitate a similar merging of academic and literacy goals in formal schooling. This merger occurred in the language across the curriculum programs and later on, in language awareness work, both of which emerged from British school experiences and spread to America (Donmall, 1985; Hawkins, 1984).

Such an analysis is based upon an implicit interrelationship between the three conceptions of literacy. Taking two conceptions in a first merger, we can see that one cannot occur without the other, that is, decoding does not occur without thinking! In fact, morphological analysis involves metacognitive approaches to language; and recto-verso thinking involves technical dimensions. Thus, both literacy as decoding and literacy as thinking draw upon metacognitive processes and skills development. Moreover, the mastery of symbolic forms requires meta-level thinking and reflection, thus bringing together conceptions of literacy as thinking and as decoding, known as the interactive approach to literacy (Coady, 1993).

A recent study clearly establishes links between literacy as decoding and as thinking. Making use of both qualitative and quantitative data, gathered from 300 immigrant youth in a western Canadian city, Parel (1999) finds that reading comprehension is influenced by both receptive vocabulary knowledge and reasoning ability (ie., inferencing), with the latter being the most powerful. Moreover, the ability of second language learners to guess meanings in context, that is, inferencing in combination with morphological analysis, is heavily influenced by reasoning ability rather than receptive vocabulary knowledge. Crucial to the shift from decoding to thinking, Parel demonstrates that proficiency in reading involves both decoding skills (e.g., morphological analysis) and inferencing strategies (contextualized guessing), thus uniting two conceptions of literacy.

Furthering this perspective, literacy contributes to thinking by providing individuals with a "metalanguage for talking about text, for forming text, for developing commentaries, for quoting and paraphrasing and otherwise characterizing the talk, writing, and thought of others" (Olson, 1989, p. 13). Readers bring an amount of background knowledge and their own meanings to text depending "on their culture, personal experiences and histories, personal understandings of the themes and tone of text, and the particular social context where reading occurs" (Baker, 1996, p. 297). The background knowledge presumed in this view of literacy may differ depending on the learner's past experiences with text, since the knowledge brought to literacy activities varies across cultures, over time and space (Street, 1989, p. 65).

Viewed more broadly, then, literacy encodes the symbols used by a particular cultural group and society to represent their world, thus literacy acquisition means gaining a mastery of cultural symbols to enable the manipulation of those symbols (Chambers & Walker, 1991). This symbolic perspective focuses on the transmission and access to symbolic knowledge with language being the primary vehicle. Such a perspective points towards the unification of literacy as thinking, integration, production and citizenship.

A critical reflection on the integration of three views of literacy: Discourse, power and ethnicity

Recent research in a western Canadian city reports a grim picture of school success and high dropout rates among secondary immigrant ESL students (Watt & Roessingh, 1994). However, moving beyond this study, its methodological shortcomings and sense of alarm, other studies indicate the complexity and nuance the picture within that city and elsewhere. The view of literacy as integration opens for consideration aspects of schooling in which labelling, resistance, and social hierarchies may be more influential than instructional and content learning approaches (Wotherspoon, 1998, p. 78–103).

A CANADIAN EXAMPLE

Within a more recent study of immigration in a middle-sized Canadian city (Hébert, 1997), interviews were carried out with teachers of ESL and Social Studies and with school administrators regarding a number of issues including the nature of the ESL program offered in the secondary schools, and the relationship between language and citizenship. In both districts, English is the language of instruction and communication among the secondary schools studied and integrating new students into the majority English-speaking Canadian society is the goal. The study found that the ESL programs in both districts were remarkably similar and that the ESL teachers were equally devoted to their students' learning (Hébert, 1997). There was a noticeable difference, however, in interactions, status and scope of the programs in the two districts.

In District A, the ESL programs are situated in obscure locations within the schools, without benefit of a sign unlike other school subject areas. Students of ethnic origin, including those born in Canada, are labelled "ESL kids," a pejorative from which they cannot escape as it sticks throughout the years of schooling. The ESL programs tend to be extensive, keeping the students as long as possible, so as to enhance the language instruction with specialized courses, such as ESL Science and ESL Social Studies.

Students are also encouraged to spend their spare time in the ESL spaces, making friends, socializing, and doing their homework. When placed in regular classes, students are not encouraged to seek additional help as needed.

The academic placement of students was determined solely on the basis of their proficiency in English. Consequently, students find themselves in non-academic programs which negatively affect their abilities and opportunities for post-secondary studies and inevitably for economic success. Pejorative labelling, a protective approach, and delayed entry into the regular stream of classes as unofficial streaming contribute to the marginalizing message that they are second-class citizens and thus, to the high dropout rate previously reported for this district.

District B ESL programs focus somewhat more on thinking and writing than in the other district. The ESL students are encouraged to go forth, hang out elsewhere in the school, participate in school activities and make friends with other students. Students are enrolled in regular classes as soon as possible and when language difficulties are encountered, the teachers encourage the students to return to the ESL teacher for assistance as needed. A language-learning approach more closely aligned to the fundamental principles of immersion programs which integrate academic content with language learning seems to yield more positive results.

In both districts, the educators' views of the relationship between language and citizenship ranged along a continuum between passivity to activity, considering citizenship as obedience, as positive contributions, as an individual construction of self, as ties to the country, as pride and values, or as acceptance of diversity (Hébert, 1997). These findings reveal a wide disparity between educators' views, ranging from strongly assimilatory and narrow positions to broader views, accepting and even welcoming diversity. Although it is human to be inconsistent, such findings suggest that schools may not necessarily be successful in facilitating integration of citizens through current means, including language learning, social studies and administrative approaches. For second language learners, the ongoing development of literacy competencies along with academic content in the target language is a necessity, as is a positive, integrative, and supportive environment. Teachers of academic courses need to be aware of adolescent second language learners' literacy development and be prepared to respond to them, rather than considering this to be the sole responsibility of the ESL or language arts teachers.

AN AMERICAN EXAMPLE

This is not an isolated study, nor do the findings occur only in Canadian schools. Another study, conducted by MacKay and Wong (1996) in the United States, explored the interplay of discourse and power in the secondary school setting in which Chinese immigrant students are learning ESL and academic subjects in a West Coast city. The study highlights the complexities of learning a new language, interacting with peers, teachers and parents while facing the pressures and the expectations of succeeding academically. Findings highlight the large number of discourses encountered at schools among peers and teachers on a daily basis: among these are the Amerocentric, Chinese Nationalist, social, academic and gendered discourses. Of particular interest is the Chinese students' agency in engaging in a powerful counter discourse as a strategy of resisting dominant discourses, thus repositioning themselves in relation to these (MacKay & Wong, 1996, p. 603).

AN EXAMPLE FROM FRANCE

In yet another example, drawn from a study of local dialects spoken among students in secondary schools in other large urban settings in France (Kasbarian, 1997), treatment in disparaging ways by teachers mandated to teach the standard dialect contributes to a creeping discouragement with school and eventual dropping out. The teachers are in a difficult situation, having to select between discourses, official and non-official, whereas the students are, in effect, choosing between participation in the middle class or within their local lower class community, again a difficult choice. In making such decisions, these French students, largely of immigrant heritage (as well as the immigrant students in California), are involved in *partial* participation as their choices constitute a form of resistance to the dominant social order. This form of resistance, through agency and counter discourses, allows them to participate more fully in the local, peer-driven order; however, the long-term consequences of their decisions contribute to low levels of school attainment and lifelong lower socioeconomic status.

IMPACT OF BIASED PRACTICES

Practices that stream immigrant and racial-minority students in low tracks reflect a system of assessment and placement practices riddled with racial, cultural, and linguistic biases (Cummins, 1988). Parents of such students have complained and rebelled at the placement of their offspring in the lower rungs of the socio-academic ladder, leading to later participation at the bottom of the socioeconomic ladder, and students resist this disparaging solution by dropping out (MacKay & Wong, 1996; Watt & Roessingh, 1994). Power and status relations between majority and minority students exert a strong influence on school performance (Cummins, 1988, 1992). Disempowered by labelling, streaming and social hierarchies, as a direct result of their interactions with educators at school, immigrant students are subject to practices insidiously reinforcing or systematically producing patterns of inequality (Wotherspoon, 1998).

In these ways, second language students are subject to strong contextual complexities and discourses that are in themselves powerful determinants of language learning, completion rates and future socioeconomic success, moving far beyond the particular pedagogical and ideological underlying approaches to literacy, as either decoding or thinking. The social position and status associated with literacy programs also carry meaning for students, particularly poignant for learners who are not yet adults or not yet members of the Canadian club. The result of discouraging, hurtful, and marginalizing experiences is to reduce the likelihood of school completion, civic participation, successful educational development and capacity to earn a decent living — a very high price for the individual but also for Canadian society to pay.

THE COMPLEXITY OF LITERACY ACQUISITION WITHIN A DIVERSITY OF CULTURES

Just as recent models of cultural acquisition stress the role of participants in creating culture intersubjectively, through interpersonal negotiation of intersystemic cultural elements, literacy acquisition set within the diversity characterizing contemporary Canadian society is far more complex than either decoding or thinking. Schools as learning environments sometimes marginalize language learners, in spite of the good intentions and fine work of individual teachers. In doing so, schools work against the integrationist assumptions linked to academic literacy as well as against individual immigrants' personal projects of integration into Canadian society.

For literacy attainment to be successful, it is necessary to critically intertwine all three approaches, decoding, thinking and integration, for the betterment of learners and of society. Moreover, although there are notable differences, first and second language learners tend to approach languages in similar ways, use similar strategies and aspire to a better situation. Recommendations include more training of literacy workers and language teachers with respect to the ways that students learn first and second languages, cultural sensitivity and competencies as well as the ways that citizenship is conceptualized and enacted.

Furthermore, federal and educational policies need to clarify the level of language necessary for school success, entry into the labour market at higher echelons, as well as for citizenship to reflect the social expectations of active citizenship (Hébert, 1998).

Just as there is limited success in the provision of ESL services at the secondary level, there is very little evidence of the power of adult literacy programs to enable better employment. The assumed links between literacy, economic development and citizenship engagement underlying these programs need to be revisited. Consideration needs to be given to the goals of school-based ESL and adult literacy programs as well as what would count as realistic objectives. Making a link between literacy, greater economic and citizenship participation may well necessitate a longer period of time and differential experiences. If adult literacy programs were viewed as a form of personal development rather than assuming a manpower orientation, changes would be needed in the course content, materials, pedagogy, government policies and teacher training. Similarly, if school-based second language programs were viewed as forms of personal development and empowerment for access to social, political and civic participation, changes would be needed in programs of study, curricular materials, pedagogy, educational policies and teacher education. As it is now, unrealistic expectations lead to disappointment and frustration. Therefore, the status quo reigns and there can be no increase in social, economic, political and civic participation, and possibly less, as adolescents and adults alike learn that they have little control over their lives in schools, at work and in the Canadian environment.

REFERENCES

Baker, C. (1996). *Foundations of bilingual education and bilingualism* (2nd ed.). Clevedon Avon, UK: Multilingual Matters.

Chambers, C., & Walker, L. (1991). Introduction. In L. Walker and C. Chambers (Eds.), *The literacy curriculum in Canada in the 1990s* (pp. 1–7). Proceedings of the Tenth Invitational Conference of the Canadian Association for Curriculum Studies, held at the University of Lethbridge, June 7–8, 1990. Lethbridge, AB: The University of Lethbridge.

Chamot, A.U., & O'Malley, J.M. (1994). *The CALLA handbook: Implementing the cognitive academic language learning approach.* Reading, MA: Addison-Wesley.

Chang, G.L., & Wells, G. (1990). Concepts of literacy and their consequences for children's potential as learners. In S.P. Norris & L.M. Phillips (Eds.), *Foundations of literacy policy in Canada* (pp. 207–226). Calgary, AB: Deselig Enterprises Ltd.

Coady, J. (1993). Research on ESL/EFL vocabulary acquisition: Putting it in context. In T. Huckin, M. Haynes, & J. Coady (Eds.), *Second language reading and vocabulary learning* (pp. 3–23). Norwood, NJ: Ablex.

Coady, J. (1997). L2 vocabulary acquisition: A synthesis of the research. In J. Coady & T. Huckin (Eds.), *Second language vocabulary acquisition* (pp. 273–290). Cambridge, MA: Cambridge University Press.

Collins, J. (1986). Differential instruction in reading groups. In J. Cook-Gumperz (Ed.), *The social construction of literacy* (pp. 117–137). Cambridge, MA: Cambridge University Press.

Cummins, J. (1988). From multicultural to anti-racist education. In T. Skutnabb-Kangas & J. Cummins (Eds.), *Minority education: From shame to struggle.* Clevedon Avon, UK: Multilingual Matters.

Derwing, T., Gibson, M., Borisenko, L., & San Sy, S. (1998). *Legal information and service barriers facing immmigrants and refugees in Edmonton.* Manuscript submitted for publicationp

Dixon-Krauss, L. (1996). Vygotsky's sociohistorical perspective on learning and its application to Western literacy instruction. In L. Dixon-Krauss (Ed.), *Vygotsky in the classroom: Mediated literacy instruction and assessment* (pp. 7–24). White Plains, NY: Longman.

Donmall, B.G. (Ed.). (1985). *Language awareness.* NCLE Papers and Reports, 6. London, UK: Centre for Information on Language Teaching and Research.

Farr, R., & Carey, R.F. (1986). *Reading: What can be measured?* Newark, DE: International Reading Association.

Freire, P., & Macedo, D. (1987). *Literacy: Reading the word and the world.* Westport, CT: Bergin and Garvey.

Gambell, T.J. (1989). Cognition, literacy and curriculum. In C.K. Leong & B.S. Randhawa (Eds.), *Understanding literacy and cognition: Theory, research and application* (pp. 269–285). New York: Plenum Press.

Hawkins, E. (1984). *Awareness of language: An introduction.* Cambridge, MA: Cambridge University Press.

Haynes, M. (1993). Patterns and perils of guessing in second language reading. In T. Huckin, M. Haynes, & J. Coady (Eds.), *Second language reading and vocabulary learning* (pp. 46–64). Norwood, NJ: Ablex.

Hébert, Y.M. (1997, November). *On the importance of language to identity and citizenship: Educators' perceptions of the integration of immigrant youth.* Paper presented at the 14th Biennial Conference of the Canadian Ethnic Studies Association, Montreal, PQ.

Hébert, Y.M. (1998). *A research-based focus on literacy and citizenship education issues.* Paper presented at the Netherlands-Canada Panel, sesson 1 on early interventions and policies, at the Third International Metropolis Conference, held November 30–December 3 in Israel and posted in the Metropolis virtual library: http://www.international.metropolis.net/

Hedley, C., Houtz, J., & Baratta, A. (Eds.). (1990). "Introduction" to *Cognition, curriculum, and literacy* (pp. 1–7). Norwood, NJ: Ablex.

Isajiw, Wsevold. (1999). *Understanding diversity: Race and ethnicity in the Canadian context.* Toronto, ON: Thompson Educational Publishing.

Kasbarian, M. (1997). Quelques reprères pour décrire les "langages des banlieues." Actes du colloque: *Touche pas à ma langue! [?] Les langages des banlieues.* Marseille, 26–28 septembre 1996. *Cahiers de la recherche et du developpement.* Numéro hors serie: 23–42.

MacKay, S.L., & Wong, S.-L.C. (1996). Multiple discourses, multiple identities: Investment and agency in second-language learning among Chinese adolescent immigrant students. *Harvard Educational Review*, 66(3), 577–608.

Olson, D.R. (1989). Literate thought. In C.K. Leong & B.S. Randhawa (Eds.), *Understanding literacy and cognition: Theory, research, and application* (pp. 3–15). New York: Plenum Press.

O'Malley, J.M., Russo, R.P., Chamot, A.U., Stewner-Manzanares, G., & Kupper, G. (1983). *A study of learning strategies for acquiring skills in speaking and understanding English as a Second Language: Use of learning strategies for different language activities by students at different langauge proficiency levels.* Rosslyn, VA: InterAmerica Research.

Parel, R. (1999). *Lexical inferencing strategies of low proficiency L2 readers.* Unpublished doctoral dissertation, Dept. of Linguistics and Modern English Language, University of Lancaster, Great Britain.

Rubin, J. (1987). Learner strategies: Theoretical assumptions, research history and typology. In A. Wenden & J. Rubin (Eds.), *Learner strategies in language learning* (pp. 15–30). London, UK: Prentice Hall International.

Simons, H.D., & Murphy, S. (1986). Spoken language strategies and reading acquisition. In J. Cook-Gumperz (Ed.), *The social construction of literacy* (pp. 185–206). Cambridge, MA: Cambridge University Press.

Stoller, F.L., & Grave, W. (1993). Implications for L2 vocabulary acquisition and instruction from L1 vocabulary research. In T. Huckin, M. Haynes, & J. Coady (Eds.), *Second language reading and vocabulary learning* (pp. 24–45). Norwood, NJ: Ablex.

Street, B. (1989). Literacy — 'Autonomous' v. 'ideological' model. In M.C. Taylor & J.A. Draper (Eds.), *Adult literacy perspectives* (pp. 57–69). Toronto, ON: Culture Concepts Inc.

Watt, D.L.E., & Roessingh, H. (1994). Some you win, most you lose: Tracking ESL student drop out in high school (1988–1993). *English Quarterly*, 26(3), 5–7.

Winne, P.H. (1989). A framework for developing theories about instructional effectiveness. In C.K. Leong & B.S. Randhawa (Eds.), *Understanding literacy and cognition: Theory, research, and application* (pp. 85–125). New York: Plenum Press.

Wotherspoon, Terry. (1998). *The sociology of education in Canada: Critical perspectives.* Toronto, ON: Oxford University Press.

Wray, D., & Medwell, J. (1999, March). Effective teachers of literacy: Knowledge, beliefs, and practices [38 paragraphs]. *International Electronic Journal for Leadership in Learning* 3(9) [on-line journal]. Available: http://www.ucalgary.ca/~iejllvolume3/wray.html

Moving "Beyond Balance" Towards a Multidimensional View of School Literacy

Marilyn Chapman

Fall, 1999. The telephone rings.

> *Dr. Chapman, I got your name from a friend who says you might be able to help me. Our principal is going to spend $25,000 on [Program X], one of those Direct Instruction programs where the teacher follows a script. He showed me something from the web that says inner-city children need a structured reading program like this one. The publisher gave us some materials that claim this program is proven effective by research. I worry because many of our kids are ESL and First Nations and this kind of approach doesn't allow them to make connections with their own experience and language. It will use up all our school funds so we can't afford anything else. Can you send me some articles I could give my principal and staff to read so that we can make a better decision? Please help!*

As a literacy educator and researcher in Canada over the last 30 years, I have learned and used many different approaches to literacy instruction. Never before, however, have I been so disconcerted with the direction some schools are taking in their efforts to improve literacy achievement. Most disturbing is that in many instances, research is being used, or rather, misused, as a rationale for misguided decisions that divert limited funds from more appropriate literacy resources.

With today's call for accountability, schools are increasingly turning to research to find "the best solution" for school literacy, especially for groups of children who experience difficulty. Much of the discussion has been centred around notions of balanced literacy. While the term seems to have originated in response to the phonics-versus-whole-language debate, unfortunately, balanced literacy is often anything but. Proponents of balanced literacy focus primarily on learning the written code and the skills of literacy. As Hébert and Racicot discuss in the framing chapter for this section, a focus on decoding ignores much of what we know about literacy as cognitive and cultural processes.

In this chapter, I argue that to improve school literacy achievement, (1) we need an instructional framework based on literacy as discourse, as communicating and making meaning, rather than focusing primarily on the written code, a set of symbols to be encoded or decoded; (2) we need to use research appropriately in informing school literacy programs; and (3) we need to go beyond "balance" in designing and implementing school literacy programs, to consider the multiple dimensions of literacy and learning. "A multidimensional program is the best option, rather than a balance created by synthesizing extreme positions or giving equal attention to them" (Joyce, 1999, p. 670).

A COMPREHENSIVE FRAMEWORK FOR SCHOOL LITERACY

In the framing chapter for this section, Hébert and Racicot discuss the false separation between reading as decoding, thinking, and integration. Although it involves symbolic encoding and decoding, above all, literacy is discourse: people read, write, and think about ideas and information in order to communicate with others, to understand, and be understood. Variable within different contexts, literacy is better defined as *literacies,* "socially constructed and embedded practices based upon cultural symbol systems and organized around beliefs about how reading and writing might be or should be used" (Hull, 1993, p. 36).

From a sociolinguistic perspective, "education for literacy is more naturally seen as a process of socialization, of induction into a community of literacy *practicers*" (Resnick, 1990, p. 171). Yet school literacy is not merely a preparation for "real literacy" outside of school, but a set of real literacy practices embedded within a learning community. As such, school literacy is intricately related to community-based literacy (the classroom and school are micro-communities), family literacy (teacher-student relationships have some family-like qualities and school literacy builds upon and is extended by home literacy experiences); and workplace literacy (the classroom is the children's workplace, and their work is learning).

In the search for "the best literacy program," the nature and purposes of literacy within and beyond school are sometimes forgotten. School literacy is not "balanced" unless it addresses both macro and micro levels of written language. Halliday's (1982) schema for an interrelated model of language and learning — learning language, learning about language, and learning through language — can provide a useful framework for thinking about the scope and dimensions of school literacy. A comprehensive approach (Figure 20.1) encompasses *learning literacy, learning about literacy, and learning through literacy*. In contrast to this comprehensive view of literacy, "balanced literacy" focuses primarily on learning literacy and learning about literacy and all but ignores learning through literacy.

FIGURE 20.1
A Comprehensive Model for School Literacy

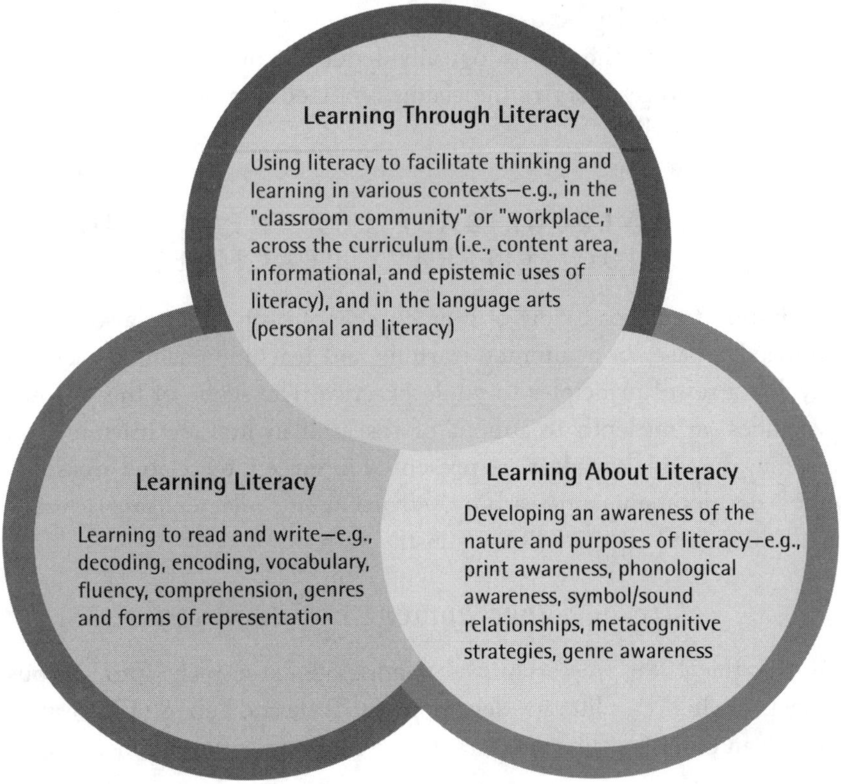

Learning Through Literacy

Using literacy to facilitate thinking and learning in various contexts—e.g., in the "classroom community" or "workplace," across the curriculum (i.e., content area, informational, and epistemic uses of literacy), and in the language arts (personal and literacy)

Learning Literacy

Learning to read and write—e.g., decoding, encoding, vocabulary, fluency, comprehension, genres and forms of representation

Learning About Literacy

Developing an awareness of the nature and purposes of literacy—e.g., print awareness, phonological awareness, symbol/sound relationships, metacognitive strategies, genre awareness

USING RESEARCH TO GUIDE SCHOOL LITERACY PROGRAMS

It is not sufficient simply to use "Research says ..." as a rationale for decision making. In using research to inform practice, it is important to take into account the scope and quality of research. The criteria suggested by Allington (1997) are helpful in using research to inform school literacy. These are outlined below:

- *convergence of evidence* — similar conclusions drawn by a number of research studies conducted in multiple sites and by multiple investigators
- *quality of evidence* — whether the research has met rigorous criteria, for example, in the blind, peer review process used in well-established journals
- *comparability* — when conclusions from research findings are appropriately generalized to similar contexts and populations
- *compellingness* (Allington's term for what I would call persuasiveness) — the degree to which the evidence is convincing, for example: Are the claims logically deduced from the research design and results? Are the claims reported honestly or are they exaggerated?

A KNOWLEDGE BASE FOR INFORMING SCHOOL LITERACY PRACTICES

In addition to a broad view of literacy, school professionals also need a knowledge base about literacy learning and teaching enabling them to develop a set of principles to guide practice. The scope of this chapter precludes an in-depth treatment of research in literacy learning and teaching. Instead, key ideas are presented in three interrelated areas: literacy development and learning, environments that enhance literacy acquisition, and effective literacy instruction.

Literacy development and learning

During the 1980s research was conducted extensively into various aspects of children's literacy development. Teale and Sulzby (1986) summarize an emergent literacy perspective on literacy development.

- Literacy development starts in early childhood long before children enter school.
- *Literacy development* is a more appropriate term than *reading readiness* because children develop as writers/readers, in an interrelated manner, rather than sequentially.
- Literacy develops in real-life activities in real-life situations for real purposes.
- Children learn written language through active engagement with their world through interactions with adults in reading and writing situations and exploring print on their own.
- Although children's literacy development can be described in terms of typical stages, children's progress occurs in a variety of ways and at different rates.

Research has provided a fuller understanding of how symbolic thinking emerges from the culture and community of the learner (National Research Council, 1999). Current understandings characterize literacy acquisition as complex and conditional, resulting from the interplay between cognitive and non-cognitive factors and the interaction of individuals within particular discourse communities. Rather than learning through direct instruction and practice, literacy rules are learned most effectively through meaningful engagement in literacy tasks and interactions with others. "Routines develop as learners internalize the principles of approaches that work — and they revise and refine their skills with repeated practice in functional settings" (Langer, 1991, pp. 17–18).

Literacy enhancing environments

Heath's (1983) investigation of uses of language and literacy in three different communities led to the understanding that varying ways of using language and literacy in the home and community differentially affect children's success in school. Understanding written language as a cultural phenomenon, as opposed to a natural one, compels us to become acquainted with children's actual ways of using writing in their discourse communities if we want to help all children to develop competence in using written language.

This understanding implies that schools not only build on students' existing experiences, but also that students need opportunities to develop abilities to compose and comprehend meaning in a variety of contexts, both academic and non-academic. Thus learning environments need also to be knowledge-based, focused on what students need to know to be successful, with an emphasis on sense-making and understanding the role of discipline-based knowledge (including literacy). Knowledge-centred environments are not at odds with learner-centred environments. If one conceives of teaching as "constructing a bridge between the subject matter and the student, learner-centered teachers keep a constant eye on both ends of the bridge" (National Research Council, 1999, p. 124).

Effective literacy instruction

While skills are important, ownership is the overarching goal of school literacy: motivation for learning to read and write comes from understanding why people read and write (Au, 1998). Rather than identifying a single best method to literacy instruction, there is a convergence of evidence from diverse perspectives about instructional practices that enhance literacy. These practices include integrating the language arts, integrating skills and meaning, engaging in focused discussion, making literacy functional and purposeful, and developing positive self-perceptions and expectations (Braunger & Lewis, 1997).

In a large-scale study in the United States, researchers at the Center for English Learning and Achievement (CELA, 1998) found these common factors in exemplary first-grade teachers' practices:

- high academic engagement and competence, with 90 percent of the children actually *doing* reading and writing 90 percent of the time
- excellent classroom management
- a positive, reinforcing, cooperative environment
- fostering of children's self-regulation
- holistic approaches that integrate explicit skills instruction
- a literature emphasis (fiction and non-fiction)
- a lot of real reading and writing
- a match of accelerating demands to students' competence and a great deal of scaffolding (support or guidance from an adult or more capable peers, enabling children to achieve greater success than they would do independently)
- strong connections in the language arts and across the curriculum

These findings exemplify comprehensive, multidimensional literacy programs. It is evident that effective literacy teachers have a broad view of literacy and deep understandings of how literacy is learned. They create learning environments that are both learner- and knowledge-centred and use a repertoire of instructional techniques. Rather than proceeding step-by-step through a school curriculum, adhering to a scope-and-sequenced guide to a commercial reading program or following a set of teacher-proof scripted lessons, effective teachers realize there is no substitute for the ongoing documentation and monitoring of learning to plan instruction for the children they teach (Au, 1998).

A CRITICAL REFLECTION OF GENRE WITHIN A COMPREHENSIVE LITERACY FRAMEWORK

With the current focus on decoding and the balanced-literacy debate in school literacy, discussions of literacy as communication have been virtually ignored. A comprehensive approach to school literacy reminds us to focus also on the macro, or discourse, level of literacy.

Genres are categories of oral or written discourse. For the most part, they have been viewed primarily as literary forms, definable by regularities in text structure (for example, the typical opening and closing phrases "once upon a time" and "lived happily ever after" in fairy tales). Recent explorations of genre have been influenced considerably by Mikhail Bakhtin's work (1979/1986). Bakhtin viewed genres as ways of using language that are embedded in and develop out of the various spheres of human activity, such as a mathematics lesson, religious service, or staff meeting. According to Bakhtin, "each sphere of activity contains an entire repertoire of ... genres [oral and written] that differentiate and grow as the particular sphere develops and becomes more complex" (p. 60). Bakhtin expanded the concept of genre from a literary construct to include a wide array of forms, differentiating between two major categories:

- *Primary genres* are types of discourse used in daily communicative activities. These genres are context-embedded, localized and intrinsically tied to time and place.
- *Secondary genres* are types of discourse situated within particular cultural or disciplinary contexts. They are more complex, not because of their structural characteristics, but because the contexts in which they have arisen — for example, artistic, scientific, sociopolitical situations — are more complex and highly developed and organized.

Traditional approaches to instruction have emphasized a genre's structure rather than its purpose. Instead, I suggest, we need to go beyond the teaching of generic forms that writers can slot ideas into, such as the five-paragraph theme, to an understanding of genres as flexible models reflecting an integration of

- *content* (what we want to express)
- *form* (ways of organizing our words and ideas)
- *function* (purposes for writing), and
- *context of situation* (the multidimensional setting including a range of factors, from global to specific)

We also need to help our students understand how genres assist communication by providing a set of signals or cues enabling a speaker/writer and listener/reader to interpret the particulars of a specific communicative interaction.

Rather than thinking of them as merely models or forms, we need to view genres as *situated, social actions*. For example, the genre research paper or expository report is not merely a text type that students need to learn. It is

- *situated,* in that it has arisen out of and is embedded in a particular context and sphere of activity (e.g., situations in which scientists or other researchers report results from their observations, experiments and so on),
- *social,* in that it is most effectively learned through and used in interaction with others (e.g., through a process of apprenticeship with others engaged in scientific inquiry and discussion, guided by a mentor/teacher who is knowledgeable in the field), and
- *active,* in that it is dynamic, flexible, purposeful, and useful, and learned through engagement — by doing (e.g., through participation in scientific activities, including researching, writing, and discussing one's work) (Chapman, 1999b).

Learning genres, learning about genres, learning through genres

Reconceived, "learning genres" means learning how to participate in the actions of a community. It was thought that genres were learned through encountering many instances of a particular form, being told or discovering its rules, internalizing this abstract definition, and then using this knowledge as an algorithm to generate new examples. New insights into genre learning, however, suggest a contrasting view: "a genre is invoked or invented (reinvented) as a response to a social situation, a response made by someone who wants to ... participate in a dialogue" (Hunt, 1994, p. 247). My own research has demonstrated that learning genres is an emergent process, as are other aspects of writing (Chapman, 1995).

Literacy learning also involves learning to use genres as cultural resources or cognitive tools (Berkenkotter & Huckin, 1993). Like other aspects of writing, learning genres is most effective in contexts that support engagement with writing, not simply following rules or applying formulas (Freedman, 1993). Genre is cultivated through engagement, exploration and inquiry, personal connections and meaning making, participation in a discourse community, apprenticeship and mentoring, collaboration, and talk about text (Chapman, 1999b).

The framework for a comprehensive literacy curriculum introduced earlier in this chapter can be applied to genre learning. Within the context of a classroom learning community, genre learning has three interrelated purposes: *learning genres* — widening students' genre repertoires; *learning about genres* — fostering genre awareness; and *learning through genres* — using genres as tools for thinking and learning in particular situations.

Situating genres in the elementary classroom

"Genre knowledge is a form of *situated cognition*" (Berkenkotter and Huckin, 1993, p. 485). Writing is situated when it is an integral and purposeful part of the various spheres of activity in the classroom. While curricular activities provide obvious opportunities for situating writing, daily routines can also provide contexts for writing. The classroom is a child's community (of learning) or "workplace," and routine activities can be thought of as situations for "community literacy" or "classroom workplace literacy" (Chapman, 1999b).

CLASSROOM "COMMUNITY" OR "WORKPLACE" GENRES

Workplace writing arises out of situations where it is necessary, relevant, gets things done, and is part of general and genuine communication (Bearne, et al., 1990, cited in Greenwood, 1994, p. 239). Because classroom workplace writing encompasses many primary genres, it is a logical starting place for very young children. Genres are usually tied to specific routines; as such, their purposes are immediate and "real" to young children. In elementary classrooms, children can learn through use the genres involved in organizational and administrative tasks such as recording book exchanges, keeping track of project work, and recording important events.

In classroom workplace situations, the emphasis is on learning genres and learning through genres rather than learning about genres. However, teachers can foster children's genre awareness when appropriate. For example, when a situation provides an authentic opportunity for writing letters, we can help young students understand that as well as containing a message, a letter must supply a reader with information about who a letter is addressed to, who it was written by and when, and where to send a reply. In this instance, we might teach students the textual features of letters inductively, to encourage them to "reinvent" the genre (Chapman, 1999b).

GENRES ACROSS THE CURRICULUM

Disciplines are communities of practice that construct knowledge and representations of reality in particular ways (Freedman & Medway, 1994). Berkenkotter and Huckin (1993) see genres as intellectual scaffolds "transmitted through enculturation, as apprentices become socialized to the ways of speaking [and writing] in particular disciplinary communities" (p. 482). Curriculum subjects are derived from and related to particular disciplines. As such, the curriculum areas can be vehicles for teaching both content knowledge and ways of thinking and communicating within a discipline.

Each curriculum area encompasses discipline-related content knowledge and skills and language, including genres. While the notion of having students write in particular genres in specific subject areas is a common occurrence, new notions of genre and genre learning can provide an expanded view of curriculum-based writing. It is an over-simplification, for instance, to associate expository writing with science and social studies, and narration and description with the language arts. Description, for example, is an important aspect of writing in science (e.g., recording observations); narrative can be a powerful tool in social studies (e.g., biographical and autobiographical accounts).

School genres "are characterized by quite different textual features and conventions [than those in related disciplines], given their classroom-based contexts and rhetorical functions" (Berkenkotter & Huckin, 1993, p. 488). From an emergent literacy perspective, school genres can be considered as developmental approximations because children in school are far removed from professional disciplinary communities. As students progress through secondary, post-secondary and graduate levels, they become increasingly closer to actual disciplinary practices; this is reflected in their genres. As Berkenkotter and Huckin (1993) suggest, becoming a member of a disciplinary community is "similar to second language acquisition, requiring immersion into the culture, and a lengthy period of apprenticeship and enculturation" (p. 487), whereas in schools students learn many "institutional or curriculum genres." Schools need to provide for a gradual transition or progression from provisional varieties that are more comfortable for younger and less experienced students (Freedman & Medway, 1994).

Focusing on the *epistemic* (knowledge-constructing) potential of genres — learning through genres — can allow teachers to create situations in which students can experience ways of discipline-based thinking and communicating. For example, we can engage students in hands-on science and cultivate scientific ways of thinking and using language. Teachers can use scientific language to talk about scientific concepts and help children learn to use genres to communicate scientific ideas, including many visual representations such as charts, maps, graphs, and diagrams.

The greatest potential for situating genres within the school subjects is to enable students to use them as cultural tools, as resources for supporting and extending thinking (Hanks, 1991, cited in Freedman, 1997). Our concern should not be so much with the similarity of a particular genre to those in related disciplines, but on the epistemic possibilities of the genre. Nor should we see widening students' repertoires as the ultimate goal, since a wider repertoire in itself will not necessarily guarantee that deep learning takes place.

Curriculum integration can also enable students to see connections among genres. To best serve literacy learning, integrated instruction needs to focus on "genres as cultural ways of communicating, and on being able to translate information from one form to another" (Shanahan, 1997, p. 17). Through classroom conversations about their own and others' writing, students can become more aware of a reader's or audience's expectations, coming to understand that textual features, rather than arbitrary rules to be followed, are conventions that enable writers and readers to communicate: they help frame a text so that readers can make sense of it (Bakhtin, 1986). Thus, genre awareness becomes useful rather than inert knowledge and form becomes functional.

GENRES IN THE LANGUAGE ARTS

Although traditional conceptions of genre focused almost exclusively on literary genres, these forms are, from a Bakhtinian perspective, the most remote from the immediate kinds of contexts in which other genres are embedded. We can create scientific contexts in the classroom with hands-on science activities and make the genres embedded in them socially situated, immediate, and real for students. The challenge comes in fostering this kind of connection with literary genres. Students in composition classes "have particular difficulty seeing the connection between their writing and other social practices" (Russell, 1997, p. 541). Perhaps the traditional approach to teaching literary genres, with its focus on textual features rather than the integration of function, form, situation, and purpose, has created this sense of "disconnection" and contributed to the idea that narrative is more decorative than useful.

In *The Culture of Education* (1996), Bruner proposes that there are two major ways in which people structure experience: *logical-scientific thinking* "for treating of physical things," and *narrative thinking* "for treating people and their plights" (p. 39). Bruner highlights narrative as "the mode of thinking and feeling that helps children (indeed, people generally) create a version of the world in which, psychologically, they can envisage a place for themselves — a personal world" (p. 39). On an immediate level, narratives — personal stories — are an integral part of thinking and communicating in our daily lives; in the broadest sense, narrative is a cultural thread that unites people.

In reflecting on how to "create narrative sensibility," Bruner (1996) suggests that "if narrative is to be made an instrument of the mind on behalf of meaning-making, it requires work on our part — reading it, making it, analyzing it, understanding its craft, seeing its uses, discussing it" (p. 41). The epistemic potential of narrative genres is realized more fully by shifting from learning about narrative (e.g., "story elements") to learning through narrative — narrative as a tool for creating personal identity and for connecting with others, one's culture, and one's world.

THE IMPORTANCE OF TEACHER KNOWLEDGE, CRITICAL THINKING, AND REFLECTION

Like most Canadian teachers, those in my province of British Columbia increasingly want to know what the research says about best practices in literacy instruction. Unfortunately, there is currently a movement towards an extreme polarization and politicization of literacy research and instruction. There is also the factor of big money to be made in the publishing industry. In marketing their programs, some publishers are citing questionable research as proof of their program's effectiveness. In other cases, there appear to be possible ethical issues in research that may have been deliberately misinterpreted (Allington & Woodside-Jiron, 1997; Taylor, 1998).

Many of the individuals making costly decisions such as purchasing reading materials and programs are uninformed about literacy learning and teaching — and sometimes, misinformed by unreliable sources or individuals who have a narrow, skills-based view of literacy learning that focuses almost exclusively on the micro level. Even more worrisome is that many educators fail to take a critical stance in reading promotional materials and articles on the Web (unaware that some Websites are ideologically and politically motivated or are fronts for commercial publishing companies).

Classroom teachers, especially in the primary grades, and school district language arts consultants are, for the most part, more informed about literacy learning and teaching than those who make key decisions about school literacy programs and resources. Never before has the role of informed and reflective teachers, knowledgeable about literacy and learning, been so critical. Such teachers are important not only in fostering literacy learning in their own classrooms, but also as a collective voice for a comprehensive and multidimensional approach to school literacy based on the appropriate use of a solid research base.

The "best literacy program" is a thoughtful, knowledgeable teacher. Effective literacy teachers use a variety of approaches to enhance children's literacy development and learning, from the micro-level (words) through the discourse level (genres). Rather than a narrow focus on balance, they provide comprehensive, multidimensional literacy programs to foster learning literacy, learning about literacy, and learning through literacy. Effective teachers make instructional decisions based on knowledge of the nature and purposes of literacy and how it is learned, on research on effective literacy instruction, and knowledge of the children they teach. In other words, their approach is one of "principled eclecticism" (Stahl, 1997). Rather than following educational pendulum swings, effective teachers are learners who construct new understandings based on what they already know. They continue to learn and to reflect on their practices.

As well as engaging in self-reflection, it is also important to seek support from a professional community — colleagues who are co-learners. Engaging in conversations about literacy teaching and learning provides us with opportunities to articulate our thinking and shed new insights into issues and challenges. Keeping active in professional development through in-service and workshops, belonging to professional organizations, taking courses, and reading professional books and journals are all ways teachers become active members of their professional community of teacher-learners. Teacher knowledge, critical thinking, and reflection — individually and collectively — are essential for continued improvement in school literacy.

REFERENCES

Allington, R.L. (1997). Whose claims are valid? *The School Administrator, 54*(8), 32–34.

Allington, R.L., & Woodside-Jiron, H. (1997). *Adequacy of a program of research and a "research synthesis" in shaping educational policy.* Albany, NY: National Research Center on English Learning and Achievement (CELA).

Au, K. (1998). Constructivist approaches, phonics, and the literacy learning of students of diverse backgrounds. In T. Shanahan & F. Rodriguez-Brown (Eds.), *47th Yearbook of the National Reading Conference* (pp. 1–21). Chicago, IL: National Reading Conference.

Bakhtin, M.M. (1986). *Speech genres and other late essays.* (V. W. McGee, Trans., C. Emerson & M. Holquist, Eds.). Austin, TX: University of Texas Press. (Original work published 1979)

Berkenkotter, C., & Huckin, T. (1993). Rethinking genre from a sociocognitive perspective. *Written Communication, 10*(4), 475–509.

Braunger, J., & Lewis, J. (1997). *Building a knowledge base in reading.* Portland, OR: Northwest Regional Educational Laboratory; Urbana, IL: National Council of Teachers of English; Newark, DE: International Reading Association.

Bruner, J. (1996). *The culture of education.* Cambridge, MA: Harvard University Press.

Center on English Learning & Achievement (CELA). (1998, Spring). Effective literacy instruction: Complex and dynamic. *English Update*, 1–8.

Chapman, M.L. (1995). The sociocognitive construction of written genres in first grade. *Research in the Teaching of English, 29*(2), 164–192.

Chapman, M.L. (1999a). *"Beyond balance" in literacy learning and teaching.* Keynote Address, Vancouver School District Early Literacy Conference, Vancouver, BC, October 1, 1999.

Chapman, M.L. (1999b). Situated, social, active: Rewriting genre in the elementary classroom. *Written Communication, 16*(4), 469–490.

Freedman, A. (1997). Situating "genre" and situated genres: Understanding student writing from a genre perspective. In W. Bishop & H. Ostrom (Eds.), *Genres and writing: Issues, arguments, alternatives* (pp. 179–189). Portsmouth, NH: Heinemann.

Freedman, A. (1993). Show and tell? The role of explicit teaching in the learning of new genres. *Research in the Teaching of English, 27*(3), 222–251.

Freedman, A., & Medway, P. (1994). Introduction: New views of genre and their implications for education. In A. Freedman & P. Medway (Eds.), *Learning and teaching genre* (pp. 1–22). Portsmouth, NH: Heinemann.

Greenwood, S. (1994). Purposes, not text types: Learning genres through experience of work. In A. Freedman & P. Medway (Eds.), *Learning and teaching genre* (pp. 237–242). Portsmouth, NH: Heinemann.

Halliday, M. (1982). Three aspects of children's language development: Learning language, learning through language, learning about language. In Y. Goodman, M. Haussler, & D. Strickland (Eds.), *Oral and written language development research: Impact on the schools* (pp. 7–19). Urbana, IL: National Council of Teachers of English.

Heath, S.B. (1983). *Ways with words: Language, life, and work in communities and classrooms.* Cambridge, MA: Cambridge University Press.

Hull, G. (1993). Hearing other voices: A critical assessment of popular views on literacy and work. *Harvard Educational Review, 63*(1), 21–49.

Hunt, R. (1994). Speech genres, writing genres, school genres, and computer genres. In A. Freedman & P. Medway (Eds.), *Learning and teaching genre* (pp. 243–262). Portsmouth, NH: Heinemann.

Joyce, B. (1999). Reading about reading: Notes from a consumer to the scholars of literacy. *The Reading Teacher, 52*(7), 662–671.

Langer, J. (1991). Literacy and schooling: A sociocognitive perspective. In E.H. Hiebert (Ed.), *Literacy for a diverse society: Perspectives, practices, and policies* (pp. 9–27). New York: Teachers College Press.

National Research Council. (1999). *How people learn: Brain, mind, experience, and school.* Washington, DC: National Academy Press.

Resnick, L. (1990). Literacy in school and out. *Daedalus, 119*(2), pp. 169–185.

Russell, D. (1997). Rethinking genre in school and society. *Written Communication, 14*(4), 504–554.

Shanahan, T. (1997). Reading-writing relationships, thematic units, inquiry learning ... In pursuit of effective integrated literacy instruction. *The Reading Teacher, 51*(1), 12–19.

Stahl, S. (1997). Instructional models in reading: An introduction. In S. Stahl & D.A. Hayes (Eds.), *Instructional models in reading* (pp. 1–29). Mahwah, NH: Erlbaum.

Taylor, D. (1998). *Beginning to read and the spin doctors of science: The political campaign to change America's mind about how children learn to read.* Urbana, IL: National Council of Teachers of English.

Teale, W., & Sulzby, E. (1986). Emergent literacy as a perspective for examining how young children become writers and readers. In W. Teale & E. Sulzby (Eds.), *Emergent literacy: Writing and reading* (pp. vii–xxv). Norwood, NJ: Ablex.

A Critical Reflection on the Rights of Passage
From Student to Teacher

Isa Helfield

> " *The moment I walked into the room I knew the rules of the game would be very different. I was immediately made witness to the children's rage and later to their torment.* "
>
> *(Helfield, 1997, p. 13)*

This chapter takes the personal position that we have lost all sense of human agency and of the unified human subject at the centre of intellectual study, challenging the fragmentation of the human being into a mind-heart dichotomy and suggesting that unlike Humpty Dumpty, the human being can be put together again. Pedagogy is seen as the instrument that finds that lost sense of humanity; therefore, when discussing pedagogy, my point of departure is always the ontological needs of the student. I pose the argument that true education reaches far beyond the popular consideration of economic utility and instead is metaphysical in nature — an attempt to satisfy the human need for self-knowledge and meaning. Children, as well as adolescent and adult students, need to know what it means to be human.

I begin my discourse by describing my experience with inner-city school children. This experience first prompted me to critically reflect on my role as a teacher and awakened my sensitivity to the emotional factors that affect learning. I comment on the ubiquity of fear that interferes with the lives of my adolescent and adult students today and describe the poisonous effect that fear has on learning by giving a thumbnail sketch of my own experience. I distinguish between the teleology (purpose) and the technology (mechanics) of education and comment on how we too often concentrate on the educational process instead of focusing on the human needs of the students, such as their search for meaning and self-knowledge. A link here is made to the earlier chapter by Hébert and Racicot that discusses factors affecting ESL students' ability to acquire literacy. The powerful connection between reason and emotion is illuminated in Goleman's (1995) theory of emotional intelligence, bringing into sharper relief our duty to bring mind and heart into the classroom. Finally, because students must have a reason for learning and feel that life has meaning, I discuss Postman's (1996) narratives and review his stance on the role of public schools in society.

BLACKBOARD JUNGLE

The year was 1970. I had just been reassigned to an inner-city school. I was to replace a Grade Seven teacher who had quit; her class was uncontrollable, some of its members violent. I wasn't worried. I felt confident that I could cope; after all, I had a reputation as a formidable disciplinarian. I didn't doubt for a minute that I would have those children firmly under my control within three days.

I could not have been more mistaken. Despite my repertoire of classroom management techniques, and my aggressive attempts to apply them, I could not establish any semblance of order out of the chaos that was all pervasive. Not only did the students not grant me any authority, but they also steadfastly refused to recognize my existence. They completely disregarded my being, and as time passed, I felt myself to be a mere apparition wandering unseen and unheard among the screaming, crying, raging adolescents. For the very first time in my teaching career I was at a complete loss, and I struggled with feelings of panic, failure and depression.

Desperation forced me to look inward, to reflect upon the utter lack of resonance in that classroom. I had to retreat within myself to struggle with my identity as a teacher. During the process I abandoned many shibboleths of pedagogy and, in their stead, I placed the recognition of the students at the forefront. I came to realize that it was urgent for me to acknowledge their humanity: I had to find a way to connect with them on a human level. They were not just objects to be taught, but rather living, feeling, human beings who were struggling to come to terms with their tumultuous lives.

MY EXPERIENCE SERVED AS A RITE OF PASSAGE

The concept of my role as teacher underwent a radical transformation, to wit, my mind was "radically cut away from the attitudes, attachments, and life patterns of the stage being left behind" (Campbell, 1968, p. 10). I began to focus my attention on the children themselves rather than on my role as teacher. I dropped the authoritarian stance and became a humanitarian leader instead. For the first time, I was conscious of the students' right and need for a proper experience of education. These children were entitled to a safe learning environment that would satisfy their emotional needs and stimulate their cognitive ones. Instead of supporting principles of dominance and status, I created a learning environment based on the principles of coordination and function. Trust, cooperation and mutual support provided the foundation for learning and growth. There was a lot of room for spontaneity and creativity. Each person functioned at his own level but at the same time was an important part of the whole. There was no competition. As Laborit (1997, p. 104) states in his discussion of hierarchies, "Each higher level embraces the level of complexity that precedes it; it does not give orders to this preceding level but informs it." Hierarchy of status was non-existent. It was two for the seesaw": human to human reciprocity and symmetry.

I also came to realize that teachers have the complementary right to a safe teaching environment, one that treats them with respect. In such an environment, teachers are regarded as valuable frontline workers whose daily experience is a primary source of data that helps determine educational policy. Critical thinking and reflective practice are both encouraged and supported. Instead of adhering to set objectives handed down by government bureaucrats, teachers are granted the autonomy to adjust a curriculum to meet the needs of their particular students.

> " *I started at the only place I could ... with them. I took them back to kindergarten, so to speak, and read to them. At first, this activity comprised the entire curriculum. I chose suspense stories whose characters*

experienced strong emotions. They immediately identified with the char-
acters and gathered up close to listen. We began to talk. Within a few days
they began to write their own stories and plays on the subjects that most
concerned them. Since justice was one of their common themes we visited
the courthouse and dramatized trials based on the stories of their lives.

Things often didn't develop as planned. A science experiment
examining the effect of light on plant growth turned out to be a scientific fiasco but an extraordinary triumph of life over death. Some
of the toughest boys insisted on taking their plants home and were
candid about the joy they felt on seeing them first thing in the morning. Others talked to and petted their sprouting creations. It was as if
this nurturing was a completely overwhelming experience, an act of
love so fantastic that the little plants served as the link they needed
back to humanity. (Helfield, 1997, p.14)

The ubiquity of fear

I have been involved in the field of education for almost 50 years, first
as a student and later as a teacher, working with bewildered children,
rebellious adolescents and discouraged adults. Fear was ubiquitous in
each group of learners. I have earned my "rights of passage: from student
to teacher" in that I, too, was a frightened, bewildered child who, over
the years, developed into a humanitarian teacher.

Fear was never far from the surface of my existence. Learning was impossible. Like most young children I desperately tried to please the teacher no
matter how insensitive or cruel she was. At first it was difficult for me
to give any semblance of what was considered normal functioning.
Unknowingly, I broke one of the most sacred tenets of a school system
dominated by male ideology: I showed emotion.

As time progressed I gradually learned that the expression of negative emotion was forbidden. I learned to hide any "unacceptable feelings" under a mask of indifference. I eventually stopped crying. I
began to function on two different levels at the same time. Outwardly,
I behaved like an automaton, but on the inside I was tied up in such
a frenzy of fear that I could not focus my attention on any structured
lesson. Terrified to displease the teacher, terrified to make mistakes
and be made to feel stupid publicly, my outward behaviour in school
sometimes made little sense to anyone.

> *Fear has no logic. It destroys confidence and common sense: my actions and my words were sometimes completely inappropriate to the situation at hand. Interestingly enough I was aware of this at the time but was helpless to control what I said or what I did. The teachers responded with impatience, hostility and dislike. Inside, I felt terrible shame and guilt. (Helfield, 1997, pp. 11–12)*

The greatest challenge that I face as a teacher is to get to know each of my students and to develop an understanding of what he or she needs from me. Despite my own early experiences in school, I must constantly remind myself that an individual's outward behaviour often belies an inner turmoil. Respect is the sine qua non of successful human relationships.

TELEOLOGY VERSUS TECHNOLOGY

The teleology (purpose) of education must not be confused with the technology (mechanics) of education. Schools must not be perceived as mere distributors of information. Instead they should be recognized as institutions of learning that have the responsibility to satisfy both the human needs of their individual students and the social needs of the communities they serve. A safe environment for teachers and students is where teachers teach students what they need to know. Children, adolescents, and adults have an overriding need to understand themselves and where they fit in their changing world. Like Socrates who said that the unexamined life is not worth living, Rubinoff (1969, pp.16–17) states that the most important question we ask ourselves is, "Who am I?" It has priority over all others because how we respond to it shapes our humanity. Self-image is one of the most important variables affecting our behaviour and world perception. Since it is acquired, teachers and parents play a crucial role in its development. In other words, a healthy educational environment provides students and teachers with opportunities for self-understanding and reflective thought. It recognizes that dignity and freedom are functions of self-knowledge. Healthy learning environments also emphasize the need for collaboration, sensitivity and responsibility towards others.

The success of both adult and juvenile students in school depends largely on our unwavering respect for them as individuals, our sensitivity to their needs, and our acknowledgement of their humanity. I place great importance on the teacher-student relationship — the critical factor in the dynamics of the educational process.

In the past, much time and financial resources have been directed towards the engineering of learning rather than on the students. Instead of focusing on phenomena that can be measured, manipulated and counted, educators must focus on phenomena that are lived through, experienced and shared. As Yvonne Hébert and Christine Racicot conclude in their exploration of the tensions between the dominant views of literacy (literacy as decoding, literacy as thinking, and literacy as integration), school success for ESL students may have more to do with social factors rather than the underlying approaches to literacy.

A safe learning environment places student emotional and cognitive needs front row centre. It concentrates on supplying students with reasons for learning and the enabling tools. Research that promotes one methodology over another does not touch the heart of educational matters. Take, for example, the ongoing debate over the best method to teach reading. Proponents of the whole language approach and the phonics approach continue to wage such a virulent battle that some teachers are forbidden to use the methodology they deem appropriate for a particular individual. The needs of their students are subordinated to the dominant philosophies of the "experts." When this happens, when any one style of teaching becomes pervasive, all pedagogical factors that cannot be standardized and programmed are considered useless; and as a consequence, human beings tend to be more easily discarded (Rubinoff, 1969).

"The single most important contribution education can make to the development of children is to help them recognize where their talents lie and encourage them to choose a field of endeavour that best suits them, where they will feel satisfied and competent" (Goleman, 1995). Too often, children are subjected to an education system where success is measured by the number of university degrees obtained and where failure is perceived if none are acquired. This definition of success is extremely narrow. There are so many other ways to succeed along with so many different abilities that help individuals reach their potential. Therefore, I believe that we should spend less time testing and ranking children, and more time helping them identify their natural competencies and gifts.

Educators must be aware that the ability of their students to learn is intimately connected to how they feel about themselves and the world around them.

EMOTIONAL INTELLIGENCE

Our humanity is most evident in our feelings, yet it is this affective aspect of our nature that is so often ignored. Humans are emotional beings and for that reason the term *Homo sapiens*, the thinking species, is a misnomer. We really have two minds — one thinks, one feels — and these two ways of knowing operate in close harmony, interacting to create our mental life. Even though culture has concentrated on rational thought alone, it is emotion that is central to our existence. For example, in making a decision or taking action, feelings count as much as intellect. Feelings are essential to thought, and thought to feeling; but when passions surge, the emotional brain takes over. "For better or worse, intelligence can come to nothing when the emotions hold sway" (Goleman, 1995, p. 4).

The relationship between the rational brain and the emotional brain has immense significance in that the latter strongly influences the way information is processed. Educators need to be sensitive to the emotional fabric of their students' lives and to understand that learning and feeling are not discrete activities. As Goleman (1995) points out, students who feel nervous, angry, or depressed don't learn; they neither process information nor do they deal with it well. A safe learning environment, then, is one in which teachers recognize the role that feeling plays in cognition. In such an environment it is understood that learning can be very difficult for those who are experiencing turmoil. A look of apathy on an adolescent's face or a rebellious act by another serves as a foil masking a chaotic life. In a similar vein, many adult literacy students returning to school are awash in emotion as they walk back into a classroom they left years before. Knowing that the emotional brain remembers, empathetic teachers can create a warm, nurturing classroom environment where personal connections are made before addressing the cognitive issues. Empathetic teachers bring mind and heart together in the classroom.

Despite the fact that cognitive intelligence offers virtually no preparation for the turmoil or the opportunities that life has to offer, despite the fact that a high IQ does not come with a guarantee of happiness and prosperity, schools and society continue to focus on academic abilities and ignore what Goleman (1995) has coined "emotional intelligence." This new concept, with self-knowledge as its basis, refers to a unique set of competencies including self-awareness, self-control, cooperation, zeal, persistence and self-motivation. How capable you are in handling these skills is crucial to how well you do in life. People who manage their own feelings well, and who read and deal properly with other people's feelings are at an advantage in life whether it be that of romance or the workplace. Both child and adult students with well-developed emotional skills are more likely to be effective in their lives because they can master their own emotions and plot their own life course. Those who cannot control their emotional life are imprisoned. They are constantly fighting inner battles that sabotage their ability for focused work and clear thought.

According to Goleman (1995), family life is our first school of emotional learning where we learn how to feel about ourselves. Our parents are our first teachers. They help us become emotionally intelligent by teaching us how to recognize and manage our own feelings, how to recognize and respond to the feelings of others (empathy), and how to handle feelings that arise in relationships. A child's success in school depends greatly on his emotional health before entering kindergarten. School success is not predicted by a child's fund of facts or a precocious ability to read, so much as by emotional and social measures including self-assurance and the ability to control impulse (p. 193).

In other words, an emotionally intelligent child is more socially skilled, has fewer behavioural problems and is generally a more effective learner. Schools must actively foster emotional intelligence in children especially in the early school years, for the skills they learn at this time form the foundation for all learning. Most importantly, emotional intelligence adds far more of the qualities that make us decent human beings.

MYTHS AND NARRATIVES: A SEARCH FOR MEANING AND VISIONS FOR THE FUTURE

To Robert Fulghum, the examined life is "no picnic"; however, he is fortunate in that he knows most of what is necessary to live a meaningful life. Fulghum (1986) acknowledges that wisdom has nothing to do with academic learning associated with universities or graduate schools, and everything to do with the social values taught in kindergarten. Sharing everything, playing fair, cleaning up after your own mess are but a few of the lessons he mentions that can be extrapolated into adult terms and applied to all aspects of our lives. However, the dawn of the 21st century is sometimes characterized by skepticism, disillusionment, alienation:

words that describe loss of meaning. Fernandez-Armesto (1998) explains that when people stop believing in something, they believe in anything as opposed to nothing. Consequently, chaos and evil thrive in the form of cults and sects.

Our human genius lies in our ability to make meaning through the creation of narratives, stories that have sufficient complexity and symbolic power to enable us to organize our life around them. Now, more than ever, we are desperately searching for myth, for narratives consisting of ideals and prescribed rules of conduct, that will give purpose to our existence. Such narratives are transcendental in nature, providing us with an explanation of the past, an understanding of the present and a vision of the future (Postman, 1996). Narratives are not scientific in nature. Rather, their validity is found in the conditions they achieve: a sense of personal identity, a sense of community, and a basis of moral conduct.

Because we live in times that decry past narratives, where so many of our citizens are angry, confused or indifferent, it is important that schools now assume more responsibility for building a public imbued with a feeling of confidence, a sense of purpose, a respect for learning, and an appreciation of differences. Instead of "broadcasting from their pulpits through mass media megaphones" that teacher accountability, standardized curriculum, standardized testing and computers will miraculously "fix us," government officials and school administrators must pay attention to matters that are really meaningful.

For example, officials and administrators must ensure that schools focus on the fundamental simplicity of teaching and learning where both teacher and student share a reason for the enterprise. "Free human dialogue, wandering wherever the agility of the mind allows, lies at the heart of education" (Postman, 1996, p. 27). If teachers are unable to provide the proper learning conditions, and if students are too demoralized to attend to the learning, then that is the educational problem that has to be solved, from within the experience of teachers and students.

People need narratives as much as they need food: they must have a reason for going to school. But today that purpose seems to be one of economic utility — preparation for entry into the world of work. This purpose promotes a troublesome conception of human nature: you are what you do for a living. Young people today are too knowledgeable to accept a definition that reduces them to a single dimension and that describes their society as an economy rather than as a culture. Economic utility is a by-product of a good education. However, any education system that is mainly about economic utility does little to enhance one's humanity. Subjects such as art, drama, music and philosophy are considered frills rather than the heart of the curriculum as I believe they should be, for they contribute towards the making of a civilized human being.

Postman (1996) asks us to be wary of statements suggesting that we change the nature of schools to make room for the new technologies. He advises us to consider the nature of children, and to take their human needs into account before redesigning our educational institutions. Schools are not just convenient places for the distribution of information; they are institutions that must deal with the teaching of social values.

In a similar vein, Goleman (1995) suggests that we must concentrate on finding solutions to human problems, for the present generation of children tend to be more lonely, more depressed, more angry and unruly than those of previous generations. In other words, it is a good time to place children in settings that emphasize collaboration, sensitivity to and responsibility for others. Computers cannot solve human issues or any other problems with schools. Critical reflection is imperative. New technologies may be a solution to the learning of subject material, but they work against the learning of what we really need to know. Like all the important technologies of the past, computers can enhance or diminish the quality of our lives. We must handle them with care.

The narratives underlying our present-day conception of schooling do not serve us well and it is time to replace them with new ones. Postman (1996) offers us five narratives that give us sufficient reasons for schooling: moral guidance, a sense of continuity, explanations of the past, clarity to the present, and hope for the future. They have a sense of transcendence; they constitute an ideal that we must struggle to reach. Together, they provide a model that is capable of overcoming contradiction.

Narrative 1. Planet Earth as a spaceship

The first narrative asks us to see planet Earth as a spaceship, and to consider all humans as its crew. It encourages us to feel responsible for our global home because we can no longer take its well-being for granted. It binds people together. If any part of our spaceship is sick, the rest of it is affected. The depletion of the ozone layer, for example, is not just Australia's problem, it is everybody's problem.

We must give students a feeling of pride about being human. We must encourage them to become more meaningfully involved in their own communities in order to develop a sense of responsibility towards the whole planet. What better way is there to nurture such a sense of awareness than to teach them such subjects as archeology, anthropology and astronomy? By studying civilizations we are studying people and providing a sense of meaning. Archeology, for instance, gives us an earthly perspective, a sense of the past, a feeling of continuity. The study of anthropology makes us aware of the vastness of humanity's range of difference and of our common points. Astronomy gives us a sense of awe.

Narrative 2. To err is human

Man is full of imperfection. It is in our nature to make mistakes. This second narrative refers to the fundamental uncertainty of all human knowledge and warns that anyone who claims to have absolute knowledge is both arrogant and dangerous. Schools must promote these ideas and caution that absolute knowledge does not exist. In speaking about textbooks, Postman (1996) believes that they mistakenly encourage a predisposition towards the notion of absolute truth. "Knowledge is presented as a commodity to be acquired, never as a human struggle to understand, to overcome falsity, to stumble towards the truth" (p. 116). Human beings learn by making mistakes and correcting them. School subjects should be taught from a historical perspective so that students can listen to stories of how we have made errors in the past, how we have attempted to correct them, and how errors continue to be made. The current classroom environment needs a high degree of tolerance for error. Historically, it hasn't. Making errors is a very human activity.

Narrative 3. The art of questioning

Our ways of life and living are based on argument. Each argument is based on a theme. What is the meaning of life? What is a human being? What are the limits of freedom? What constitutes good citizenship? In this third narrative, Postman suggests that schools should teach the importance of questioning the laws and principles that govern our lives. Students need to know how to argue and how to know which questions to argue about. They need to know that all points of view are admissible. We must teach them that the search for truth involves continuous argument and continuous questioning, for truth is constantly changing. More importantly, schools must make students aware of the inherent danger when arguments stop — the possibility of conflict, the possibility of bloodshed.

Narrative 4. 'E pluribus unum' (From many – one)

Schools must provide a narrative that makes a constructive and unifying use of diversity. Human nature is multifaceted. Great art, superior writing, outstanding music exist in all different cultures. All must be recognized, not because they are examples of great English poetry or of German music, but because they are wonderful examples of human creativity. In this fourth narrative, Postman (1996) says that diversity is the story that tells us that our interactions with people of different cultures make us into who we are. Using the English language as a metaphor, he explains that human survival depends on our ability to adapt to change and to adopt knowledge and customs from different cultures. Since all social problems show up in school, public schools need to find and promote important narratives for all students to believe in. Students must study all cultures rather than just their own and be made to feel that they are part of a greater whole.

Narrative 5. Our way with words

Our ability to speak, our use of language, is what makes us human. It's what we use to create the world. Words are not only used to express thought, but are also used to define and create meaning. We go where our words lead us. In this fifth narrative, Postman (1996) says that each time we create a sentence, we create a world. "We are organizing it, making it pliable, understandable, useful" (p. 84). He warns that words are powerful weapons. They can be used to lie and blur distinctions. They can turn humans into non-persons. Schools must make students aware of how we use language to transform the world and of how we, in turn, are transformed by our own invention. Should we not tell this narrative to the young, Postman asks, so they can investigate how we can advance our humanity by controlling our words? Should they not learn what happens when control is indeed lost?

Finally, Postman (1996) says that we must give prominence to the study of the arts because its subject matter is the best proof we have of the unity and continuity of human experience. He suggests, moreover, that we introduce the study of museums as a subject in school because they answer the most fundamental of all questions: "What does it mean to be a human being?" Each museum offers its own explanation about the nature of humanity in a specific time in history. But each one is extremely important because when they are all combined, they tell our story, the human one.

DENOUEMENT

September 6, 1990, the first day of school for my adult literacy students. I slowly work through the lonely crowd of strangers offering them a warm smile and a hearty handshake, hoping to ease the terrible fear that I know consumes them. A pair of angry blue eyes stare menacingly at me from the back of the crowd and draws my attention like a magnet. The rage and hatred emanating from his being startles and unnerves me; seldom before have I encountered an individual who radiates such a threat of violence.

He was a forty-five year-old "soldier" forced to enter enemy territory, defenseless, vulnerable, ashamed. He lacked the most important weapon of all: self-esteem. How could he feel as a man not knowing how to read, not knowing how to write? In my mind he epitomized the tragedy that results from a society that denies individuality and demands uniformity and obedience. A school system that barely gave lip service to innovation, creativity and spontaneity helped to destroy him and countless others by denying them any feelings of self-worth. Prevented from searching inward, they were robbed of the knowledge of themselves as valuable and worthy human beings.

His threatening physical presence, the only tool he had to exist in his world, masked the wonderful human being he really was. And we all suffer for it, for the world that created him prevented him from sharing his love and understanding, his poetry, and his vast experiential knowledge of the world and threw him out into life with only violence as a means of interacting. Had he been raised in a society that valued human life, that treasured human experience, that encouraged cooperation rather than competition, his life and many other lives would have been a more peaceful, less frightening place. (Helfield, 1997, p.14)

At the dawn of the millennium, it is natural for humankind to examine its existence; more precisely to study its roots, to look at its present and to anticipate its future. The 20th century will go down in history as the embodiment of man's inhumanity to man. As we move forward into the 21st century, we can only hope that it will also mark the dawn of a more humane society. It is therefore incumbent upon us all to actively work towards the attainment of that goal.

REFERENCES

Campbell, J. (1968). *The hero with a thousand faces.* Princeton, MA: Princeton University Press.

Fernandez-Armesto, F. (1998). *Truth: A history.* London, UK: Transworld Publishers.

Fulghum, R. (1986). *All I really need to know I learned in kindergarten.* New York: Ballantine Books.

Goleman, D. (1995). *Emotional intelligence.* New York: Bantam Books.

Helfield, I. (1996/97, Winter). Rights of passage: From student to teacher. *Women's EDUCATION des femmes.* Vol. 12, 11–14.

Laborit, H. (1997). *Decoding the human message.* New York: St. Martin's Press.

Postman, N. (1996). *The end of education: Redefining the value of the school.* New York: Random House.

Rubinoff, L. (1969). *The pornography of power.* New York: Ballantine Books.

CHAPTER 22

Literacy, Schooling, and Citizenship

David Dillon

Yvonne Hébert and Christine Racicot's framing chapter for this section on school-based literacy raises the intriguing question of a link between literacy and citizenship, intriguing not because it is a new question, but because educators tend not to consider it in much depth or from a critical perspective. Too often the simple and apparently obvious answer settled for is that citizens must be able to read and write in order to play their role in a democracy, without considering the nature or possibilities for the kind of participation that is assumed or implied. The role of citizens in a democracy and the kind of literacy that supports and accompanies it, as well as the role of schooling in that relationship, are the issues that I would like to explore by critically analyzing the kind of literacy and learning that schools tend to foster, often disempowering students, as both current learners and future citizens.

FREIRE — A MEMORABLE EXPERIENCE

I heard Paulo Freire, the noted adult literacy educator, speak at a panel discussion at the University of Alberta in the summer of 1984. The following anecdotes are reconstructed from my memory and notes. Not surprisingly, almost all questions were directed to Freire, who answered thoughtfully and respectfully as always. After a number of questions had been posed, someone from South America asked Freire, now that he was back in Brazil after the end of the military dictatorship that had deported him, if he still believed that literacy was so important in South

America. What about housing, health, jobs? Weren't these all so much more important than literacy and needed to receive first attention? Very uncharacteristically, Freire exploded angrily, asking the questioner if she thought that he had been arrested, tortured, deported, and exiled for 16 years from the sights, smells, and sounds of his country, of his home, because he had been teaching people to sound out words? All that happened to him, he pointed out, was exactly because he had been teaching people to read and write in such a way as to enable them to get better housing, to achieve better health, to find better jobs, and ultimately to change the unjust society they were living in. He had not treated literacy as something separate and different from how people live together in a society, he concluded, and that was why he had been deported.

Freire's approach to literacy education reflects two important starting points. The first is the essential difference in citizenship education that exists between representative democracy and participatory democracy (Westheimer & Kahne, 1998). Too often, they claim, school teaches representative democracy to students by teaching about government structures, the ways laws are enacted, the importance of voting for legislators, and so on. While this kind of information is certainly important for young people to know, it tends to imply that the job of running a democracy and making decisions is turned over to the people's representatives. In this light, voting delegates the people's power to elected officials. Participatory democracy, on the other hand, stresses the role of citizens to be informed and to vote, and especially to think critically, to pose questions, to identify issues, and above all to act collectively for the common good. In other words, *it is the responsibility of citizens themselves to ensure the creation of a more just society.*

Freire's second central point is to acknowledge that society is oppressively stratified. The distinction here is that differences in access to resources and chances for success in life are not due to inherent lacks or deficiencies of certain groups, but rather to a systemic discrimination in society and its institutions that reward those who are already more powerful (men, whites, the wealthier, the abled, heterosexuals, adults, etc.) and restrict those who are less so (women, people of colour, the poorer, the disabled, homosexuals, youth and the aged, etc.). In such a society, notes Freire, it is not a matter of some winning and others losing, but rather a situation in which all lose by having their humanity diminished. Participatory democracy seeks to name these oppressions and to struggle to transform society into a more just one.

What was Freire's approach to literacy education that got him into trouble with the powerful, repressive forces in his society? He summarized his approach and philosophy through an anecdote from his own practice. He was conducting a literacy class with a group of peasants in Brazil, and typical of much of the class time, the class was creating texts, with help where necessary, about their daily life. These texts became the texts they read as their course material. In many of the texts that they created, the learners referred to Freire and called him "Professor." So he asked them why they persisted in referring to him as "Professor" and not as "Paulo," as he had requested that they do. They answered that it was because he was above them in life and thus had to be addressed differently to show that distinction. He asked why he was above them in life and they answered that it was fate, God's will. Freire then asked if God loved them. "Of course," they answered. "God loves us all; he's our father." Freire asked further if, as parents themselves who loved their own children, they treated their children differently, especially in regard to material goods and status. "No, of course not," they quickly answered. "That would not be love." Freire continued by asking them if God, their loving father, would say, "I'll give Paulo an education, a comfortable life materially, and status as a professor and then I'll make these other children of mine peasants who are poor — and often hungry — and who have to work very hard all their lives for very little." "No," they answered right away. "A loving father would never treat his children so capriciously and unfairly." So Freire continued by asking them why he and they were in such different circumstances in life, why they didn't have the kinds of things he had. They answered excitedly, the light of new insight dawning on their faces, that it was because of the powerful in society, the "bosses."

There followed, related Freire, an exciting and moving discussion as they articulated their awakening — and exploding — insight about the effect that powerful forces in society had on their lives. They then generated different, more critical texts about their work situations, about their literacy class, and especially about practical steps they could begin taking together to alleviate some of the systemic injustices in their lives, the origins of which they now saw so much more clearly.

This short anecdote may seem distant from our context and concerns here in Canada, yet it contains, I believe, most of the key principles of Freire's approach to literacy — and citizenship — and thus is full of lessons for us in our society that is still suffering from oppression in its own way.

The oppression in Canadian society is not as dramatic as that in Brazil, but it seems more subtle and, thus, perhaps even more difficult to deal with. First, it is about creating a new and more accurate awareness, "consciousness raising." Yet, this new awareness cannot be simply added to what we already know. It is born only by dismantling our old familiar understandings, and by peeling away myths we have been operating under for some time. Not surprisingly, those old myths usually were not created by individuals themselves, but rather were promulgated by society's institutions — school, church, media, government, family — to control those with less power. Further, this new awareness usually prompts us to action in order to actually live the new insight and to transform the world around us that we now see with new, more critical eyes.

Such an approach to education generally seeks to foster individuals who feel they are agents in the making of history rather than victims of it, who shape and influence their own futures rather than waiting for the future to happen to them. Freire summarizes his approach poetically by saying that learners can learn to really read the word only by critically "reading" the world. By so doing, they can eventually learn to "rewrite" the world by acting upon it.

This anecdote is remarkable for its striking contrast with what usually passes for school-based literacy. What could the field of adult literacy learn from what I see as the pervasive and systemic role of typical schooling — and school-based literacy — as an oppressive and disempowering tool of a stratified society?

CRITICAL REFLECTION ON SOCIAL BIASES OF SCHOOL PRACTICE

Applying critical theory to education, many educators posit that, in our stratified society, schooling is one of society's main institutions used to maintain that stratification. Children from more advantaged social backgrounds tend to succeed in school while those from less advantaged backgrounds tend to fail, or at least do less well. This disparity has been acknowledged for several decades and schools have generally taken steps to address the issue of equity in school success through approaches such as multicultural education, inclusive education, and gender-sensitive initiatives. Yet despite several decades of such efforts, the differential levels of success in school — and life — have remained stubbornly ini-tractable. Thus, the rhetoric of equality of opportunity in school still remains a myth. However, recent research has begun to reveal how school practices are biased and thus maintain a social stratification by favouring childen from some backgrounds and disadvantaging others (Anyon, 1980; Heath, 1983; Ogbu, 1991).

Starting points

The attitudes that both teachers and children bring to the classroom on the first day of school can have very powerful effects on what transpires in the classroom. Research (Ogbu, 1991) has revealed that those who have been failed by school — as well as by the job market — over a long period of time are skeptical about the schooling system and suspect that it is still rigged unfairly against them. These distrustful attitudes are shared by many in these communities and certainly influence their children.

Teachers also bring their own attitudes and beliefs to the classroom. A recent large-scale study by Statistics Canada (in *Le Devoir*, 1999) reveals that many teachers working with children from disadvantaged backgrounds expect less from them. The study pointed out that teachers held this attitude because they believed that the children's parents helped them less with their schoolwork and encouraged them less to succeed in school than did the parents of children from more advantaged backgrounds. But the study tackled that very issue and found that the parents of disadvantaged children were equally as helpful and encouraging as other parents. The only difference was that they had less contact with and presence in the school than the other parents. This lack of contact could be a source of the teachers' misperceptions.

While there is no conclusive evidence of the effect of such attitudes on children's experience in school, it is difficult to imagine that such attitudes would not have a deleterious effect on children's school success in some way. For children it may feel like playing in a game that is rigged against you: after a while, continuing to try to do well could become increasingly difficult.

Language and culture biases in school practice

Intangible yet extremely powerful aspects of schooling are the cultural assumptions upon which teachers teach and manage students. Such interaction involves conceptual ways of seeing the world, organization of time, space, and materials, teaching roles, even body language. Because school is a cultural space, with its own rules and assumptions, some children find it familiar and others find it foreign, depending on their social backgrounds. Such feelings may make it easier or difficult for a child to adjust to school, and also seems to affect teachers' judgments about children, for better or for worse (Anyon, 1980; Heath, 1983).

Perhaps the best known study of this kind is Heath's *Ways with Words* (1983). Her examination of the language and cultural patterns of children from three different sociocultural backgrounds and their beginning experiences in school was telling. Her study included a detailed anthropological study of life, and especially child rearing, in the three communities. She found that in the lower-class black community there was little direct instruction of children by adults; they were given free rein to observe and listen to adults interacting and to find their own way into adult conversation as they were ready. This practice of taking their place in the adult world was highly valued by the community. In addition, boundaries of time and place were quite fluid. Children ate and slept when they were ready and usually stayed with tasks until they were finished. Toys were left where they were as children finished with them, to be found in the same spot the next time they wished to use them.

Such an anthropological picture of the practices in one community can become problematic as children from that community enter a different culture, that of the school. Heath discovered that teachers misread the cultural patterns of the children by judging their behaviour against the teachers' own middle-class background. Thus, when the children interrupted the teacher to contribute to the conversation, the teachers read that behaviour as a lack of manners. When children were confused by the tight schedule to follow in school, regardless of whether tasks were finished or not, or by the demands to put materials back in their proper place, the teachers assumed the children had no sense of order or self-discipline, implying for the teachers that something was deficient in the children's culture. Not surprisingly, children from this community began to have difficulties in school at an early age, often during kindergarten, difficulties categorized by the teachers as academic failure or disruptive behaviour.

In contrast to the experience of these children, Heath found that children whose cultural and linguistic patterns were closer to those of the school, because of being white or middle class, tended to experience less dissonance and to do better in school generally. In fact, it was the children of the more affluent managerial and professional families in her study that succeeded best in school.

These outcomes occurred despite the good intentions of teachers or the efforts of children, and they occurred because of a narrow cultural base in school, ignorance on the part of teachers of the cultural patterns of other communities, as well as a lack of awareness of the particular patterns characterizing their own sociocultural backgrounds. Teachers seemed to assume that their experience in the world was "universal" rather than a social construction and thus had trouble seeing from any other perspective. Furthermore, differences seemed to be viewed, not as mere differences, but as deficiencies. Thus, it seems that teachers may feel that children who are more similar to them are brighter and more capable, since they catch on more quickly to school ways. Conversely, they may perceive children who are different from them linguistically and culturally as lacking in some basic ways.

Teaching as self-fulfilling prophecy

The danger of unexamined cultural and linguistic assumptious in teachers' judgments about children is that teachers may be unknowingly adjusting their expectations and teaching practices with children from differing social backgrounds, thus helping to create different levels of success, and even different kinds of learning for different children.

Anyon's (1980) groundbreaking study of teachers' instructional interaction in schools serving different socioeconomic communities — working-class, middle-class, and upper-class — found basic differences in the nature of the tasks and schoolwork that teachers set for the children. Her findings revealed that teachers in the working-class and middle-class schools (representing the large majority of schools in society generally) tended to set tasks of rote memory, skill-and-drill exercises, and so on, with a strong emphasis on following directions, often mechanically, in order to find the right answer and be rewarded with grades. In other words, these were the kinds of tasks that educational psychologists would categorize as low-level cognitive activities or what critical educators would label as the "silencing of children." Anyon characterized them as tasks preparing children for life by teaching them to obey, follow directions, and accept "right" answers.

On the other hand, the teachers of children from upper-class backgrounds set high-level cognitive tasks for their students, essentially creative activity to be carried out independently and focusing on the development of children's analytic ability — as revealed in debates, explanations, opinion statements, decision making, and so on. In other words, they provided the kinds of tasks that empower children, helping them to find their own voices, and, as Anyon claims, preparing them for the more powerful and influential positions in society.

Further limiting patterns of teaching

The work of the Language Across the Curriculum movement of the 1970s and 1980s revealed the restrictive and limiting nature of much of the learning and literacy in typical classrooms. It established that (1) students typically had little chance in class to use their language, either orally or in writing and (2) interaction patterns between teachers and students, oral or written, were not only unique to school but also restrictive in scope.

Thus, the teacher often teaches by fishing for the right responses and leading students to the correct conclusions through a heavily directive teaching approach. Reading tasks are usually a matter of finding the right answers and then purveying them in writing back to the teacher to show that they had at least been found, if not completely understood. A large-scale study in the UK of the reading and writing habits of above-average secondary students (Lunzer and Gardner, 1979) found that students were willing and able to find answers to teacher-set questions or for report-back sessions, but largely unwilling — or unable? — to reflect more deeply on what was being read. "The reference book was treated more as a treasure trove of sentences and paragraphs which could be stolen and marketed again in another setting" (p. 305).

In such an approach right answers are actually capital which children earn through their efforts and then spend in order to purchase marks in school. The research also revealed that not only did children not write a great deal, but that much of their writing was either direct copying or paraphrasing of information. Only a small proportion of their limited work in writing was actually expressing themselves in their own words.

In short, the research revealed a heavy reliance on a particular approach to teaching; what Freire (1972) called a "banking approach" and Barnes (1976) called a "transmission approach." In this latter approach, teachers "transmit" the knowledge of school to students, through explanation, demonstration, and assigned readings and then ask from students demonstrations of their having learned the correct answers, through questioning, exams, and assignments. In Freire's banking metaphor, the teacher makes "deposits" of knowledge in the heads of the students and then later asks for "withdrawals" of that knowledge.

The most worrisome concern in this scenario is the kind of learner — and citizen — that is being fostered in such a classroom environment. Boomer (1988) speculates that the attitudes, or side effects, of a transmission approach on children may include learned helplessness — waiting for the teacher to structure the learning path, working because of fear or desire to please the teacher, and ultimately needing the teacher in order to learn because the learner cannot learn alone. Boomer notes that the possible long-term results of such attitudes may actually disarm children as independent learners outside of the context of school. He concludes by fearing, "Society may inherit a cautiously conforming citizen" (p. 122).

And there's the rub. Having learned to read, write, and think within a transmission or banking environment, the learner may well have been prepared to play his or her role within representative democracy, in a "cautiously conforming" way. The large majority of learners may be ill-prepared to engage in participatory democracy and the kind of critical literacy and engaged, proactive, collective action that it requires. Despite schooling's official rhetoric, its approach will have implicitly favoured a citizenship that tends not to question or challenge the status quo. It serves the powerful minority of students who already do well in society and whose interest is in maintaining the status quo from which they benefit so much.

School curriculum

School curriculum is often explained as the reflection of an ongoing debate in society about what is worthwhile for children to know. Thus, it is not surprising that the official curriculum of schooling — from history to literature and even to math — reflects the worldview, related knowledge, and interests of the dominant groups in society since their voices are generally more powerful. As a result, minority children tend not to see themselves reflected in school knowledge and can find school knowledge at least foreign if not alienating.

Granted, the increasing strength of various minority groups over recent decades — women, people of colour, the disabled, homosexuals more recently — has certainly had some effect on school curriculum. Witness Black History month, increased attention to women authors and scientists, even elective courses in some school boards on the homosexual experience. Yet change is slow and advances small and struggling. School curriculum still largely reflects the dominant aspects of society, but curriculum is a fairly tangible aspect of schooling that can be easily analyzed and targeted.

A deeper and more basic issue than the content of the curriculum, however, is the very nature of curriculum itself, the basic assumptions about its nature and purpose. Grundy (1987) offers a helpful framework for considering various notions and practices of curriculum. She bases her analysis on the work of Habermas whose concern is how groups work out the nature of knowledge and action depending on the human interest being served. Grundy categorizes three conceptions of curriculum as follows:

1. **Product** —This model is based on predetermined objectives and designed to control students' learning so that it conforms to the ideal concept/intention (reproduction); rests in teacher direction.
2. **Process** — Teacher and student interact in order to make meaning of the world; rests on teacher judgment.
3. **Praxis:** – Involving the application of skills and knowledge as distinguished from theorizing, praxis works towards freedom at two levels: (1) knowledge (consciousness) to become aware of perspectives that serve dominant interests, and (2) action in which the participants (teacher and students) act to change the structures in which learning occurs and which constrain freedom, often in unrecognized ways; rests on teacher and student problematizing.

Freire views these three approaches to curriculum through the metaphor of various manifestations of the Catholic Church that he experienced in Latin America. He refers to the "conservative church" (curriculum as product) as an oppressive, controlling force explicitly maintaining the status quo. The "liberal church" (curriculum as process) shows a more kind, human face, he contends, but accomplishes the same ends as the conservative church. Finally, what Freire calls the "prophetic church," or liberation theology (curriculum as praxis), is the only manifestation of the church that can change the status quo, that can free people. In a similar way, only a critical pedagogy is designed to question the dominant order and understanding to provide for personal and collective action in the world on the part of both students and teachers in order to transform our still-too-unjust society.

An inordinate proportion of the work in schools is curriculum as product or as process. In North America, even what educators consider to be progressive results in curriculum as process, such as the whole language movement. Very little work in schools would qualify as curriculum as praxis: curriculum attempting to unveil the biased and unjust practices in society and the dominant thinking that maintains it and that helps students learn to act on the basis of that knowledge to change awareness and structures limiting citizens' potential.

THE EMERGING PICTURE

This critical reflection reveals a schooling system that is a powerful force for maintaining an oppressively stratified society. It accomplishes this role, first, by dealing with a pluralistic population through "monocultural/monolingual" curriculum and instruction, an approach that represents only the perspective and the "ways with words" of the dominant aspects of society. Second, it fosters a disempowering learned helplessness (dependence, obedience, and uncritical thinking) in many students while preparing other students to continue their dominance in society. Such an analysis merely confirms in some detail Illich's (1971) claim that schools tend to school children into their places in our stratified society and, I might add, to school children into relatively passive roles as citizens, thus ensuring the continuity of the status quo.

Yet, as bleak as the picture may seem, these very insights of recent decades into how schooling plays its role as an acculturating and stratifying tool of the dominant forces in society have also provided the basis for some exciting alternative attempts at breaking this unjust and unhealthy cycle, and provide some strategic ways forward for educators and provide hope that change is possible. These alternatives generally exhibit two major characteristics, one that might be called a pluralistic approach based on the diversity of Canadian society, and the other that is usually referred to as critical pedagogy, designed to make our society more free and just.

The pluralistic alternative

There is no question that minority children eventually need to learn the culture and language of the dominant aspects of society to be able to function within the mainstream of society. However, recent school approaches validating and strengthening a child's home background and resources (often including a child's home language) are being included both as a strong starting point for school learning and as a way to strengthen the home and community identity of children. The goals are to avoid children's alienation, to enhance their chances for academic success, and to foster a healthy identity. To borrow a phrase from second language educators, this approach seeks to achieve an "additive" approach to learning and identity, rather than a "subtractive" approach. Note, above all, how these alternatives require the school, not only the children, to adjust and change. It seeks to make children's differences an asset rather than a liability. (Note: While this approach has thus far been implemented almost exclusively in minority education, it applies equally well for children from dominant backgrounds to help them see beyond their own singular perspective.)

The critical pedagogy alternative

As worthwhile as cultural sensitivity may seem, it is not sufficient in itself to foster participatory democracy or to create a more just society. So a second characteristic of these alternatives is reconceptualizing curriculum as praxis. Increasing efforts have been made in recent years by individual teachers, and occasionally by an entire school, to teach for social justice by engaging in a critical pedagogy with their students. This approach seeks first to question answers rather than to answer questions, then to inquire thoroughly into the question posed in order to arrive at a new awareness, and finally to act on the basis of this new awareness to address the identified bias. In short, these are the same principles that were contained in the anecdote from Freire's adult education class that I related earlier. A number of North American teachers have tried applying these principles in their teaching of children in school in order to teach against the grain. Their goal is to foster citizens with the ability to engage in critical thinking and collective action for the good of all in society, or in other words to foster those who can engage in participatory democracy (Shor, 1987; Ayers, Hunt, & Quinn, 1998).

EMERGING QUESTIONS AND ISSUES

Many literacy educators may feel that the notion of literacy has been lost or overshadowed in this chapter in favour of a focus on a particular approach to teaching or to citizenship. Perhaps. Or might a notion of literacy actually have been found or exposed? Are literacy and citizenship identical? Do we get, as a society, what we teach? Does our thinking about literacy need to start with notions of the kind of society we wish to have and the sort of citizens we need in order to create it?

Success in school tends to be an unquestioned goal of much of our effort as educators. What is the nature of typical school success for most students and what is the disempowering price often paid for it by future citizens? How can schooling be reconceptualized to help break the pattern of oppressive stratification in society?

It has long been assumed that adult literacy education shares much in common with school-based literacy, that it somehow builds and extends from school-based literacy. Should adult literacy education, however, use the flexibility and openness it usually enjoys, not to extend from the foundation of school-based literacy, but rather to break from it and work to counter and remediate it, if we Canadians are ever to have any hope for a truly participatory democracy and a more just society?

Clearly, our traditional approaches to school-based literacy have limited our potential as a society. Canada's promise as one of the most free and just nations in the world can still be achieved, but only if literacy education is reformed as a means of educating citizens for participatory democracy.

REFERENCES

Anyon, J. (1980). Social class and the hidden curriculum of work. *Journal of Education 162*(1), 67–92.

Ayers, W., Hunt, J.A., & Quinn, T. (Eds.). (1998). *Teaching for social justice*. New York: Teachers College Press.

Barnes, D. (1976). *From communication to curriculum*. Harmondsworth, UK: Penguin.

Boomer, G. (1988). Language, learning, and the hyperactive. In B. Green (Ed.), *Metaphors and meanings*. Australian Association for the Teaching of English.

Entre rêves et préjugés. (1999, August 16). *Le Devoir,* p. 1.

Freire, P. (1972). *Pedagogy of the oppressed*. New York: Seabury.

Grundy, S. (1987). *Curriculum: Product or praxis?* London, UK: Falmer Press.

Heath, S. (1983). *Ways with words*. Cambridge, MA: Cambridge University Press.

Illich, I. (1971). *Deschooling society*. New York: Harper & Row.

Lunzer, E., & Gardner, K. (Eds.). (1979). *The effective use of reading*. London, UK: Hutchison Educational.

Ogbu, J. (1991). Cultural diversity and school experience. In C. Walsh (Ed.), *Literacy as praxis*. Norwood, NJ: Ablex.

Shor, I. (Ed.). (1987). *Freire for the classroom*. Portsmouth, NH: Heinemann.

Westheimer, J., & Kahne, J. (1998). Education for action — Preparing youth for participatory democracy. In W. Ayers, J.A. Hunt, & T. Quinn (Eds.), *Teaching for social justice*. New York: Teachers College Press.

Literacy Diagnosis
Who Needs Help?

Victor Froese

In the earlier chapter by Hébert and Racicot two important questions were raised: What is meant by *literacy*? and What is sufficient? While these authors present a variety of views of literacy, my intention is to examine what is meant when we say that students are literate or illiterate, and how that is determined. When Statistics Canada (1989, p. 25) announced that "2.9-million Canadians are illiterate," what did they mean? Were that many Canadians really not able to read or write at all? Or were that many Canadians not able to meet some standard set by Statistics Canada? In other words, were Canadians somewhat literate but not literate enough for some purpose? Is it an either-or matter, a dichotomous variable; or is it a continuous variable? What are the standards and criteria that are useful in making such decisions?

QUESTIONING ASSUMPTIONS

The notion that one is either literate or illiterate is a tenuous assumption at best. Today we are more likely to speak about multiple literacies: computer literacy, cultural literacy, information literacy, functional literacy, school literacy, informational literacy, and so on. The assumption is that one may be literate in some areas but not necessarily in others. However, the progression to multiple literacies is not an easy one as noted by Brown (1991) "like any giant bureaucracy, the one-literacy school system will be slow to change, but not impossible" (p. 145). Clearly the concept of multiple literacies complicates decisions about who is literate and who is not.

Even if there was a unitary literacy measure, its very nature has changed over time, and that makes diachronic comparisons difficult if not meaningless. Kaestle, et al. (1991) documented the benchmarks of literacy over the past century and found that by the 1930s a level of literacy equivalent to Grade Three was acceptable, but by 1952 it had crept up to Grade Six equivalent, and by 1970 it was equivalent to high school graduation level, or Grade Twelve. A recent poll done for Southam News (Mofina, 2000, p. A7) indicates that 94 percent of the Canadians surveyed thought that having a post-secondary education would be critical to work success during the next decade. The dilemma then is that the literacy "crossbar" is being raised systematically and comparisons are relative to the dated height of the crossbar or the literacy criteria. Ironically, the public often interprets this phenomenon as declining standards!

A further complicating factor is that school literacy and other forms of functional literacy are not particularly congruent. School literacy often tends to focus on language forms rather than communication and is often not valued equally (Froese, 1997). School literacy may consist of exercises as curricular ends in themselves, whereas adult literacy serves adults' needs, activities, and careers. Therefore, it is necessary to consider the very nature of the criteria when comparing literacy levels in and out of school. Furthermore, levels of school literacy are often expressed in terms of grade level, a measure that is meaningless in the adult world.

Models of determining who is literate and who is not have changed over time. Traditionally, deficit or discrepancy models have been used to describe differences between ability and achievement, but more recently functional models have become more prominent. The latter simply states that achievement does not meet a specified standard and that a certain percentage of students have not reached the defining criteria (Gunning, 1998). For example, in Reading Recovery programs the students in the lowest 20 percent of achievement are provided with the specialized instruction. Shanker and Ekwall (1998) simply point out lists of skills compiled from a half-dozen basal reading series as the criteria for instruction, and even issue the warning:

Use this chart with caution. Not all students learn to read by acquiring the same set of reading skills in the same order. Some students learn to read quite well with the mastery of only a few of the various skills listed. (p. 217)

In this system or skills model, students' knowledge of a set of prescribed skills is determined, and the type of model used impacts the decision of who will receive assistance, and what they will be taught.

One important aspect not typically addressed in models of literacy diagnosis is the matter of gender differences. Historically, females have done better on many literacy measures in many countries around the world (Wagemaker, 1996), and large differences continue to be documented even in Canada. For example, according to the Council of Ministers of Education, Canada (1998, based on Charts 8 & 9), "Females show significantly higher percentage at all levels for both age groups." Such important differences will need to be taken into consideration when making judgments as to who requires special literacy instruction. The CMEC sponsors the School Achievement Indicators Program (SAIP) in Reading and Writing every four years, and involves all provinces and territories in this assessment process.

WHO NEEDS SPECIAL LITERACY INSTRUCTION? A CRITICAL REFLECTION

Students below average in achievement

Keillor (1985) describes a mythical population in which the men are all strong, the women are all handsome, and the children are all above average. It is this type of population that the lay public often appears to demand: a population in which everyone is above average. The difficulty is that the average achievement is relative to the group being considered, not an absolute value, and hence it is not useful as a criterion for providing special instruction. While it is possible to move up the average through instruction, approximately half the students would still be above and half below.

Another related notion is to consider those scoring below a particular grade level as requiring special instruction. However, grade level placements on tests are based on the group used to norm the test. That is usually a large group, with a nearly normal distribution, providing results where approximately half score above and half below a particular grade level achievement. The problem is that the public is blinded by statistical procedures obscuring common-sense observations: within any school grade there is a wide range of natural ability and achievement. School grade determined by age is not a particularly good predictor of achievement. To clarify this situation, Froese (1991) offers a simple but useful rule of thumb: "The range of ability will be approximately the same as the grade level, and spread approximately equally on both sides of the midpoint" (p. 55). For example, in a Grade Six class the range of literacy ability will normally be about six grade levels; that is, from Grade Three equivalent to Grade Nine equivalent. Therefore, selecting students below grade level as requiring special instruction is not recommended since it results in unrealistic expectations of a large portion of the population.

Students below potential in achievement

The deficit or difference model of diagnosis requires a measure of achievement to compare to some measure of learning ability or learning potential. When group intelligence tests were routinely administered to students, it was possible to compare a mental age (measure of ability) to a reading age (a measure of achievement), for example, and to obtain a discrepancy. The magnitude of the discrepancy determined whether a student might receive special instruction. The logic was that a higher mental age (i.e., ability) indicates that there is room for the student's achievement to grow (assuming that the mental age is higher than the reading age). For example, a student with a two-year difference between mental age and reading age would qualify for remedial instruction at the intermediate grade level. This was prorated for lower and higher grades. Such an approach is not practical today since intelligence tests, especially group tests, are rarely administered, and are in fact discouraged in many school jurisdictions.

A more feasible application of the difference model is to compare a student's ability to comprehend a passage when read independently with the ability to comprehend a similar passage when read orally by the teacher. The difference in these two approaches illuminates the difficulty of decoding. Usually, students comprehend the passage read to them better than when decoding is required as well. If there is a substantial difference in the two modes it is assumed that instruction in decoding, if successful, would result in better comprehension. Using the same logic it is possible to compare independent writing to dictated writing, reading comprehension with ability to dramatize comprehension. It is also possible to compare the comprehension of a film or video with the written text of the same story.

Functional models

Functional models define ability to deal with a literacy situation in a particular context. For example, can a student function adequately in a language arts class, or can the student read and write as well as the majority of other students in the same class? In functional models the comparison is a relative one; that is, the comparison is made between the language function of a single student and the other students in the class. The comparison is not to an absolute standard such as Grade Five level, but between these particular students who may be at a variety of levels even though all are in Grade Five.

Another application of the functional model is to identify a certain percentage of the target group for special literacy instruction. For example, the lowest 5 percent, 10 percent, 15 percent or perhaps 20 percent of students in reading or writing achievement are identified for special needs teaching. In Reading Recovery programs the lowest 20 percent are targeted for such instruction. Based on results of the National Assessment of Educational Progress (NAEP) in the United States, approximately 25 percent of the population has some difficulty in reading (Gunning, 1998, p. 6). In this case students in Grades Four, Eight and Twelve are tested. Similarly, the recently released results of the NAEP writing assessment (International Reading Association, 2000) indicated that 16 percent of Grade Four, 16 percent of Grade Eight, and 22 percent of Grade Twelve students did not reach the basic level, the level denoting partial mastery of the knowledge and skills fundamental for proficient work at a given grade.

In Canada, the Council of Ministers of Education (1998) report similar findings. Results are provided in terms of the percentage of students achieving at defined Levels One to Five, where Level One is the lowest and Level Five is the highest. Generally, achievement at Level One and Level Two is not considered adequate, but is at Level Three to Level Five. It was found that 3.2 percent of 13-year-olds and 2.3 percent of 16-year-olds did not reach Level One in reading; 22 percent of the former and 8.2 percent of the latter did not reach Level Two in reading. For writing, only 0.5 percent of both age groups were found not to reach Level One, and only 4.8 percent and 1.9 percent respectively were found not to reach Level Two in writing. The overall results in this assessment met the expectations of educators and non-educators according to judgment panel results presented in the document (CMEC, 1998, Charts 11–14).

Many provinces today have their own assessment programs and hence results at the provincial level may be juxtaposed with those from the School Achievement Indicators Program (SAIP). For the province of British Columbia, the SAIP (1998, based on Charts 36–39) found that in reading 3.5 percent of 13-year-olds and 1.4 percent of 16-year-olds did not achieve Level One, and 25.1 percent and 9.9 percent respectively did not reach Level Two. For writing 1.3 percent of 13-year-olds and 1.0 percent of 16-year-olds did not achieve at Level One, and 5.5 percent and 2.9 percent respectively did not reach Level Two.

In British Columbia all students are tested in Grades Four, Seven and Ten (approximately ages 10, 13, and 16). Three descriptive criteria are used: Not yet within expectations, Meets expectations, Exceeds expectations. The reading results indicated that for Grade Four, 14 percent of girls and 19.6 percent of boys do not yet meet expectations; for Grade Seven, 11.5 percent of girls and 16.9 percent of boys do not yet meet expectations; and for Grade 10, 12.4 percent of girls and 22.7 percent of boys do not meet expectations. For writing, in Grade Four, 9.7 percent of girls and 19.8 percent of boys do not meet expectations; in Grade Seven, it is 1.5 percent and 5.1 percent respectively; and at Grade Ten, it is 13 percent and 27.7 percent for girls and boys respectively (British Columbia Ministry of Education, 1998).

Based on a functional model, these data and examples illustrate that it is possible to identify a proportion of students for special instruction in literacy. However, the actual percentage is dependent on the instrument used and the judgment panel's conclusions. In terms of these literacy measures of reading and writing it is also necessary to consider gender differences as important since the achievement results are substantially different. In some cases, almost twice as many boys as girls did not meet expectations.

PRINCIPLES OF DIAGNOSIS FOR SPECIAL LITERACY INSTRUCTION

A process of becoming informed

Diagnosis is a process that requires people to make judgments based on constellations of observations and clusters of information. It is a complex process that must at first be tentative; only after a number of recursive cycles does it become more evident what best suits an individual learner. Even at early literacy stages Clay (1998) warns us that "numerical test scores or pass-fail data derived from group scores cannot guide teachers whose children show literacy awareness, but of different kinds" (p. 62). In a similar vein Glazer and Searfoss (1988) remind us that "we know of no standardized testing tool that assesses the strategies students use for learning" (pp. 7 and 9). They suggest using "multiple tools, multiple environments, multiple strategies, and multiple settings for collecting data ..." In short, diagnosis is a process of becoming informed, based on multiple sources of information.

Procedures are complex

From the very beginning, students achieve literacy in different ways. Clay (1998) points out that "Remarkable learning has already occurred before children pass through the school doors" (pp. 1–2). Students do not use the same learning strategies or follow the same sequences of skill acquisition. We are reminded of Schanker and Ekwall's (1998) warning that "Not all students learn to read by acquiring the same set of reading skills in the same order." Students read under different physical conditions and for different purposes as they participate in school and home activities.

However, teachers do not share the same beliefs about students, and they do not necessarily have the same standards, qualifications or experiences in dealing with literacy related matters. Interpreting student achievement is likely to have many variables that must be considered in order to arrive at a reasonable diagnosis.

Competencies and difficulties

It is becoming clearer that teachers must look for strengths on which to build further instruction. Clay (1998) suggests that "teachers who try to find out what children do not know (and much testing is directed to this) are looking for initial points of contact in the wrong places. What they need to do is find points of contact in children's prior learning, the things that children *can* do ..." (p. 3). Glazer and Searfoss (1988) state, "Students should be *observed* in activities where successful text comprehension occurs" (p. 8). (Italics are in the original text in both cases.) When looking for competencies, the diagnostic process becomes a positive rather than a negative one.

Even student difficulties may often be approached in positive ways, through one of the other language arts — reading, writing, speaking, listening, drama, viewing, representing and children's literature — in which the student has competencies. For example, reading comprehension may be built through dramatization or through oral discussion, either of which may be a strength for a particular student. Eeds (1988) suggests that a number of language concepts are "developed through *oral language* use, and children exhibit a growing awareness of how these systems operate differently under the constraints of *written language*" (p. 51). And Readance and Martin (1988) suggest that "Students can show they have *understood a text* [i.e. in reading] by producing miscues, retelling passages, or *dramatizing stories*" (p. 68). (Italics added by the author.)

Instructional change

Diagnosis should lead to a process of asking questions about an individual and doing something about them; this is a recursive process. It is necessary to observe students interacting with literacy materials under teaching conditions for best results. Most students requiring special teaching (those not meeting expected standards) have already been "taught" without positive result, and it is necessary to establish the cause rather than repeating the non-successful teaching practice. If a student has not learned some sound-symbol relationship under normal developmental instruction the first time around, it is necessary to ask whether basic phonemic awareness (pre-phonics) has been established rather than simply re-teaching the same skill or ability.

Informal procedures and instruments

Many literacy experts agree that the results of standardized tests do not provide much direction for instruction. This is because they are group tests designed for group accountability, and their psychometric qualities are not up to providing individual diagnosis. Typically for group prediction, tests with reliability coefficients of 0.7–0.8 are adequate, but for individual diagnostic purposes a reliability coefficient above 0.9 is desired. Provincial testing programs and the Canadian School Achievement Indicators Program are essentially forms of standardized tests. The tasks on these instruments are not much like classroom practice. For example, reading passages are short with questions following and do not require integration with other information, while writing tasks are prescribed and do not allow reflection, revision, or rewriting.

In contrast to the formal standardized tests, informal devices are able to approximate normal classroom activities more closely. Informal testing is not technically deficient or casual because the difference is in how the information is interpreted. Various standards are used but they are not norm referenced, which means compared to some group standard. Informal measures may include the results of observations over time of ways strategies are used, portfolio samples of completed work, lists of books read, reading protocols, surveys, and checklists. Since informal assessment is done by teachers or other professionals, it takes into account much more information than that of a standardized task. This provides rich data about individuals and is more often used by teachers to modify instruction than the results of standardized tests that often provide only a single score such as a grade equivalent, a standard score, or an achievement category to summarize what has been done. Not so long ago we were exhorted by the major professional organizations about this matter. According to a policy outlined by the Canadian Council of Teachers of English (1985) "evaluation, to be appropriate, must reflect in a balanced manner the many dimensions of proficiency." Similarly a joint statement by the International Reading Association and the National Council of Teachers of English (1989) read "in educational decision making it is dangerous to rely on any single score as a measure of learning" (p. 24).

Diagnostic teaching

A classic way of integrating assessment and instruction is through diagnostic teaching. Some time ago Strang (1975) observed that good teachers who "respond immediately to the strengths and difficulties they observe in children's reading may be as effective and far more practical than elaborate test batteries" (p. 92). Put crassly, time spent on testing is time not spent on practicing literacy, and observing a student under real learning conditions can provide the teacher with much more information for subsequent instruction than a score on an assessment instrument. The language arts provide much opportunity to assess similar skills and strategies under different conditions. For example, the teacher may observe a student's reading comprehension by studying a student's drawings or writings about the topic under study. Teaching and learning occur in a variety of settings — instructional, individual, interactive, recreational, testing — and each brings unique challenges for the teacher.

Self-diagnosis, self-assessment, and learning

An assessment framework developed by Froese (1996) postulates three dimensions: WHO does the assessing? HOW is the assessment done? and WHAT is assessed? Who includes the teacher, the student, peers such as other students, parents, learning assistance teachers and clinicians. Research has shown that in successful classrooms reading and writing activities occur every day. This means that the responsibility for some assessment must be delegated although overall responsibility lies with the teacher. Because of this, there are many positive spin-offs: students must learn to take some responsibility for self-diagnosis and self-assessment, and in order to do so must learn and internalize the criteria for evaluation. Through such a process, learning can be seen as a personal and as a shared responsibility. Students typically will work harder at things they have selected or goals they have set for themselves. Glazer and Searfoss (1988) put it this way: "Empowered students realize that the knowledge and purpose they bring to the text is as important as, or even more important than, the text information itself" (p. 4). Ultimately these realizations lead to more student-centred learning and instruction.

Language across the curriculum

The integration of literacy instruction (reading, writing) with orality (speaking, listening), viewing, representing, drama, the study of literature, and other subject areas is a necessity in today's crowded curriculum. There simply is not enough time in the school day to teach each of these language arts serially. Part of the solution lies in teaching aspects of language where they are required — report writing in social studies, critical reading in science, oral expression in film study — or any suitable permutation.

Further, the study of textbooks or informational books requires strategies different from those for narrative text. Typically, informational text presents illustrative materials, such as charts, graphs, diagrams, or photos that the reader can study after leaving the text, then returning to it and integrating the information garnered from the illustrations into the text content. Such interrupted reading is not typically required in narrative text. But in narrative texts, imagery, metaphor, and irony may abound, requiring a learned understanding of unique cultural information for complete comprehension. Therefore different teaching strategies are needed depending on the text both in reading and in writing. The former represents the deconstruction of meaning and the latter the construction of meaning. The principle behind language across the curriculum (Froese, 1994) is as follows:

> All learning involves discovery. Therefore learning literacy skills unique to particular content areas in the context of those content areas makes it optimally relevant and meaningful. Further, language has a heuristic function; we learn about social issues by reading and writing about social issues. The act of composing requires both factual information and language-related skills — specialized vocabulary and particular structures and formats for presenting it. And the best way to learn language-related competencies is to use them purposefully for practical communication purposes.

Complex problem or simple solution?

Some years ago a colleague of mine had a poster in his office stating in very bold letters: **To every complex problem there is a simple solution.** And in very fine print at the bottom it added: And it is wrong! The lesson to be learned is that complex problems tend to have complex solutions, if any at all. Who should receive special literacy instruction and what that instruction might be like qualify as complex questions, and hence the following suggestions should be considered as work-in-progress rather than definitive answers.

Ideally, we should agree to criteria for identifying those requiring special literacy instruction. Data presented earlier in this chapter indicate that it could be almost 25 percent of the population, but more commonly it is considerably lower — up to 5 percent when considering Canada-wide results (CMEC, 1998). When gender is factored into the equation, almost twice as many boys as girls will require special literacy instruction. However, literacy is a multidimensional, continuous variable. People cannot be classified as literate or illiterate — virtually all have some functional literacy skills; however, they may be different, and therefore cannot be compared directly. For example, some are information literate, some computer literate, some mathematically literate. It makes little sense to say that one is more literate than another, and today it is unlikely that someone will be literate in every field or area. There is simply too much information.

Furthermore, levels of functional literacy have steadily increased — doubled twice in the past 60 years — and are likely to continue in our technologically sophisticated society. In order to provide literacy instruction based on diagnosed needs, it will be necessary to observe individuals in authentic situations and to rely less on one-shot group test results. It will be necessary to empower students to engage in lifelong learning by allowing them to participate in the planning and assessment of instruction. It will also be necessary to allow them to build on areas of language competence whether in literacy, orality, drama, or hypertext in order to cope functionally in other areas. Emphasizing deficiencies such as "being illiterate" makes little sense and often marginalizes people who are extremely competent in collateral areas or even in another language.

A TIME FOR RECONCEPTUALIZING

Biblically speaking, young men have visions and old men dream dreams. From a look at the literature on literacy diagnosis one gets the odd feeling that not much of either is happening, and even the visions expressed in *Reexamining Reading Diagnosis* (Glazer, Searfoss & Gentile, 1988) seem not to have come to fruition. These authors presented a framework for "multiple tools, multiple environments, multiple strategies, and multiple settings for collecting data on which to base description of students performance." (p. 9). The political climate today demands single-score, one-shot testing.

The field of literacy is ripe for rethinking, updating, and reconceptualizing. Unfortunately, university clinics, where much of such work generally occurs, are also fading into the past (Froese, 1993). Literacy is fundamental to all subject areas and difficulties with language comprise a great deal of special instruction. For example, Lloyd (1991) cites that of the students referred for special instruction, 31 percent are referred for reading problems, 15 percent for writing problems, and 12 percent for other language problems; in short, 58 percent of referrals are for literacy difficulties! Clearly we must assure that those engaged in special instruction are well trained in literacy and related language arts processes and skills, but today's special education textbooks hardly reflect this reality.

Our expectations about what sort of literacy instruction school systems can provide must become more realistic. Regardless of how well planned and intentioned literacy instruction is, not everyone can be expected to reach a high level, or even be above average level. However, some degree of literacy can be expected of all, but at a functional level relevant to the learning ability of the individual. It may be necessary and more realistic to adjust expectations rather than instruction for a very small percentage of students. It seems that the typical provincial curricula are probably aimed at the average student but this does not adequately account for those who are not likely to reach that level, even given more time. If we take expectations of the public on the SAIP (CMEC, 1998, Charts 11–14) as examples, it clearly indicates that 5 percent of the student population is not expected to reach even Level One. For that group a different set of expectations should be developed.

We still have only a very general understanding of what literacy is and how its difficulty is assessed or evaluated, and how that is different for school-age students and for adults. Pegging reading ability to grade levels is somewhat meaningless since grade level is not a fixed or absolute standard. It may be more fruitful to develop benchmarks that are closely related to well-established sources of text such as newspapers, magazines, books, or hypertext. One could say, then, that a person is able to handle textual materials similar to what is found in *OWL, Maclean's, Sports Illustrated, Toronto Sun, Globe & Mail, Saturday Night*, the *CBC Home Page*, or other well-known sources of text or hypertext. The examples illustrate a range of difficulty in text and each has carefully targeted a particular audience. In this way it is possible to match literacy ability to difficulty of a text rather than a grade level.

As a young, soon-to-be-married man, I was determined to personally build our own house. It was a time-consuming but rewarding undertaking, and the house was under construction for several years with building material spread all around even while we lived in it. A friend commented that whenever he visited us, the house always smelled new! Metaphorically that is what diagnosing special literacy needs is all about — continually smelling out new textual construction.

REFERENCES

Barton, D. (1994). *Literacy: An introduction to the ecology of written language*. Oxford, UK: Blackwell.

British Columbia Ministry of Education. (1998). *1998 Provincial assessment of reading and writing: Highlights*. Victoria, BC: Author.

Brown, R. (1991). The one-literacy school house in the age of multiple literacies. *Educational Horizons, 69*(3), 141–145.

Canadian Council of Teachers of English. (1985). *Evaluation policy*. [Brochure prepared by P.J.A. Evans]. Ottawa, ON: Ottawa Valley Centre, Ontario Institute for Studies in Education.

Clay, M. (1998). *By different paths to common outcomes*. York, ME: Stenhouse Publishers.

Council of Ministers of Education, Canada. (1998). Results of the 1998 reading and writing assessment, *SAIP 1998 — Reading and writing*. Toronto, ON: Council of Ministers of Education, Canada. (http://www.cmec.ca/saip/rw98le/pages/ResultsE.stm)

Eeds, M. (1988). Holistic assessment of coding ability. In S. Glazer, L. Searfoss, & L. Gentile (Eds.), *Reexamining reading diagnosis: New trends and procedures*. Newark, DE: International Reading Association.

Froese, V. (1991). *A language approach to reading*. Scarborough, ON: Nelson.

Froese, V. (Ed.). (1993). *Reading clinics in western Canada*. Winnipeg, MB: University of Manitoba.

Froese, V. (1994). Language across the curriculum. In A. Purves (Ed.), *Encyclopedia of English studies and language arts*. New York: Scholastic/National Council of Teachers of English.

Froese, V. (1996). Assessment: Form and function. In V. Froese (Ed.), *Whole-language: Practice and theory*. Scarborough, ON: Allyn & Bacon Canada.

Froese, V. (1997). Basic issues of language instruction. In V. Froese (Ed.), *Whole-language: Practice and theory*. Toronto, ON: Harcourt Brace Canada.

Glazer, S., & Searfoss, L. (1988). Reexamining reading diagnosis. In S. Glazer, L. Searfoss, and L. Gentile (Eds.), (1988). *Reexamining reading diagnosis: New trends and procedures*. Newark, DE: International Reading Association.

Glazer, S., Searfoss, L., & Gentile, L. (Eds.). (1988). *Reexamining reading diagnosis: New trends and procedures*. Newark, DE: International Reading Association.

Gunning, T.G. (1998). *Assessing and correcting reading and writing difficulties.* Boston, MA: Allyn & Bacon.

International Reading Association. (December 1999/January 2000). *Reading Today,* 3–4.

International Reading Association and National Council of Teachers of English (1989). *Cases in literacy: An agenda for discussion.* Newark, DE: Authors.

Kaestle, C., Damon-Moore, H., Stedman, L., Tinsley, K., & Trollinger, Jr. W. (1991). *Literacy in the United States: Readers and reading since 1880.* New Haven, CT: Yale University Press.

Keillor, G. (1985). *Lake Wobegon Days.* New York: Viking.

Lloyd, J. (1991). Why do teachers refer pupils for special education. *Exceptionality: A Research Journal, 2*(3) 115–126.

Mofina, R. (2000, January 1). Post-secondary education viewed as future passport to employment. *Vancouver Sun.*

Readance, J., & Martin, M. (1988). Comprehension assessment: Alternatives to standardized tests. In S. Glazer, L. Searfoss, & L.M. Gentile (Eds.), *Reexamining reading diagnosis: New trends and procedures.* Newark, DE: International Reading Association.

Shanker, J., & Ekwall, E. (1998). *Locating and correcting reading difficulties (7th ed.).* Boston, MA: Allyn & Bacon.

Statistics Canada. (1989). *Survey of literacy skills used in daily activities.* Ottawa, ON: Author.

Strang, R. (1975). *Reading diagnosis and remediation.* Newark, DE: International Reading Association/ERIC/CRIER.

Wagemaker, H. (Ed.). (1996). *Are girls better readers? Gender differences in reading literacy in 32 countries.* Delft, Netherlands: International Association for the Evaluation of Educational Achievement.

SECTION SYNOPSIS

School-Based Literacy
From Decoding to Critical Consciousness

Anthony Paré

THE COMPLEX PORTRAYAL OF LITERACY

The chapters in this section on school-based literacy capture the remarkable gains we have made in our understanding of literacy over the past four decades. They provide convincing proof that we have moved well beyond the impoverished notions that shaped literacy theory, research, and instruction at mid-century — notions that have been challenged and gradually redefined between the 1960s and now. The picture of literacy emerging from the chapters is elaborate, dynamic, multi-dimensional, and plural. The authors speak of *literacies,* and describe human meaning-making as a complex social activity, one deeply embedded in the purposes and practices of individual cultures and communities. Most importantly, they acknowledge the deeply transformative power of literacy, and the subsequent need to help people develop a critical literacy consciousness.

Hébert and Racicot's opening chapter sets the stage for this complex portrayal of literacy. The three views they sketch describe what might be considered the three stages in our expanding definition of literacy: from product to process to social action. They offer an impressive list of the linguistic, cognitive, metacognitive, rhetorical, and social skills required for participation in literacy, and make a convincing argument in favour of a cohesive model of literacy. Such a model combines the three views and corresponding skills into an organic and dynamic whole. The authors trace the intricate relationship between lowly decoding skills and the lofty claims made for literacy's powerful role in cognition and culture.

All codes are symbolic; all represent the world to insiders in the specialized and socially shared signs that create and capture a collective reality. Proficiency at manipulating those symbols *is* literacy, and it leads to the ability to think in and through those symbols. Thinking in ways specific to social groups leads to group membership. Thus, decoding becomes thinking, and thinking becomes integration. Understanding these links is critical if we are to see why literacy is more than merely additive, that is, more than the simple accumulation of skills or strategies. Acknowledging the transformative power of literacy allows us to raise school literacy above the mundane transfer of prescriptions and conventions to something more substantial and significant.

This understanding of literacy is reflected in all of the chapters in this section, and it marks probably the most critical development in current approaches to human meaning-making. We have moved beyond literacy across the curriculum, which was an essential conceptual stage, to a more profound grasp of literacy's influence both in the world and on the person. No longer is literacy seen as a mere tool or external behaviour — a set of skills, strategies, or gestures to be picked up and abandoned at need. We now recognize literacy as the human activity through which we make meaning of our world and ourselves. When we participate in particular literacy practices, we are transformed; we literally make our world and ourselves through language and other symbol systems.

THE EXPANDED NOTIONS OF GENRE

Chapman draws on the rich theories and research now developing in genre studies, to help us see one of the critical ways in which literacy performs its transformative work. She demonstrates how contemporary studies of genre have gone beyond the textual regularities that usually characterized genre discussions to consider the full socio-rhetorical context in which a given text operates. Studies of academic and workplace genres (Dias, Freedman, Medway, & Paré, 1999) explain patterns in textual products and practices by locating those patterns in the routines and rituals of an encompassing social activity, and by demonstrating how the regularities in literacy practices help groups to achieve their goals. The

integration to which Hébert and Racicot refer is the ability to participate successfully in those regulated literacy practices.

This expanded notion of genre has allowed theorists and researchers
to fuse text and context, product and process, cognition and culture into
a single, dynamic concept. In addition, by enlarging the focus of attention in literacy studies to include the full social and symbolic action of
textual practice, the reconception of genre encourages us to consider
the interconnections among these once-separated aspects of literacy. A
genre approach in the classroom could exploit that interconnectedness
to help students understand that literacy rules, guidelines, and conventions are characteristic of particular human communities and that they
elicit the knowledge-making activities typical of those communities.
Such an approach would allow schools to go beyond the balance that
Chapman describes between learning literacy (decoding/encoding) and
learning through literacy (literacy across the curriculum) to what she
calls learning about literacy. However, to avoid instructional approaches
that could result in a narrow knowledge of literacy — a kind of genre
grammar — we need open and critical approaches to literacy. To do that
we need the teaching and learning environment that Helfield describes.

Helfield argues that schools must satisfy the human needs of individual students and the social needs of the communities they serve. She further suggests that schools should be developing the whole person, and
resisting the current pressure to train students for particular roles in the
workforce. To do that, says Helfield, we must make the school a safe
environment for students and teachers, a place where people can
explore the function of literacy beyond the merely instrumental. Such
an exploration not only extends each individual's literacy experiences,
but also subjects the literacy experience itself to a close and critical
look. What does it mean to be literate? How does literacy make us
human? How do different literacies shape us differently? What are the
positive and negative effects of literacy? How does literacy operate within societies to create advantage and disadvantage, power and oppression,
access and denial?

Dillon addresses some of these questions and forces us to consider
how literacy can maintain and challenge authority and power. His central question should be the first one answered in any discussion of
school-based literacy: Should our approach to literacy begin with
notions of the kind of society we wish to have and the sorts of citizens

we need in order to create it? Dillon's answer to that question is "Yes," and his discussion pushes our notions of literacy past decoding, cognition, and integration towards action, resistance, and liberation. He suggests that literacy is essential to true citizenship, and that a critical literacy means a critical populace — one not willing to support injustice or oppression. It seems a grand claim, but if we believe in the transformative effect of literacy, what other conclusion could we reach? We cannot continue to argue for the importance and power of literacy without acknowledging its ability to do both good and bad. If literacies make our world and ourselves, as Dillon and others argue, we must create a school-based literacy that is critical and self-conscious.

Finally, Froese underscores the complexity and multidimensionality of literacy by reflecting on evaluation — the educational practice that always seems to diminish the object of its attention to something minor and measurable. As he convincingly demonstrates, such a reduction is impossible with literacy, which breaks out of all attempts to restrain it. Moreover, by providing evidence that levels of functional literacy have risen steadily in Canada, Froese allows us to resist the persistent and misinformed calls for a return to the basics, and to turn our attention to a more complex, participatory view of literacy.

No discussion of school-based literacy would be complete without consideration of classroom practice. How do teachers encourage and enact the kind of complex, active, and critical literacy promoted in this section? Each chapter offers valuable suggestions, and in closing I would like to add my own recommendation. Nothing beats the lively, engaged classroom, of course, where teachers and students are involved in literacy practices that seek to have some impact on themselves and the world. In such an environment, students are playing with multiple symbol systems, seeing the many worlds and ways of thinking they create, and experimenting with membership in the communities that employ those systems. But to move beyond decoding, cognition, and integration to a critical literacy, students and teachers may wish to explore critical pedagogy, or the closely allied approaches to critical literacy and critical language awareness (e.g., Caldas-Coulthard & Coulthard, 1996; Clark & Ivanič, 1997; Muspratt, Luke, & Freebody, 1997). These and other critical literacy discussions share certain perspectives. *They see literacy in all of its specialized disciplinary and institutional manifestations as always local, always saturated with values and beliefs, and always shaped by and for particular social actions and ends.* Furthermore, they acknowledge the formative effects of literacy — that is, the cognitive, social, cultural, and ideological influence of literacies on those who participate in them. To attain the kind of critical and participatory school-based literacy called for in this section, we will need to develop approaches that reflect this multidimensional and formative nature of literacy.

REFERENCES

Caldas-Coulthard, C., & Coulthard, M. (Eds.). (1996). *Texts and practices: Readings in critical discourse analysis.* London, UK: Routledge.

Clark, R., & Ivanič, R. (1997). *The politics of writing.* London, UK: Routledge.

Dias, P., Freedman, A., Medway, P., & Paré, A. (1999). *Worlds apart: Writing and acting in academic and workplace contexts.* Mahwah, NJ: Erlbaum.

Muspratt, S., Luke, A., & Freebody, P. (Eds.). (1997). *Constructing critical literacies: Teaching and learning textual practice.* Cresskill, NJ: Hampton Press.

Adult Literacy –
A New Era of Responsibility

Maurice C. Taylor

When we say that a field of practice has come of age it means that it has passed through a number of years of formation, growth and widening relationships, with periods of uncertainty and critical review. A coming of age denotes a recognition of maturity and such is the case in the field of adult literacy. We have witnessed an unprecedented expansion of literacy activities with a myriad of programs delivered in the community, at the workplace, in the family and school systems. This growth has prompted the development of local, provincial and national infrastructures to guide and implement these literacy practices. Resource networks, databases, research granting schemes and training opportunities have emerged to support the work of the field. As a result of this collective enterprise, adult literacy has moved from a peripheral issue to one of national importance that signals a new era of responsibility not so much concerned about status or levels of activity but about quality.

Three interconnected themes are offered here as a closing discussion. These themes are like windows on the converging points in the four literacy domains — community-based, workplace, family and school-based — serving to demarcate the new responsibilities of the field as we search for ways to increase practice coherence. The first lies in deepening our understanding of what is meant by collaborative partnerships and their importance as quality indicators. The second theme challenges us to seriously think about an emerging concept in the adult literacy process — situated cognition, which means that adult learning can be understood only within the social world or context in which it occurs. The final theme examines action research as an integral part of providing quality literacy services.

DEVELOPING COLLABORATIVE PARTNERSHIPS

A distinguishing feature of partnerships is that the relationship among the partners is as important as the new knowledge or learning being sought. As Saltiel (1998) points out, at the core of collaborative partnerships lies an intense relationship centred on mutual goals. This psychological aspect of working together is critical in understanding the concepts related to partnerships. The uniqueness of each partner relationship is determined, not only by the people working together, but also through the shared wisdom of the partnership context.

Partnerships provide the power to transform ordinary learning experiences into dynamic relationships that can result in a synergistic process of accomplishment. In a collaborative partnership, participants build on each other's talents to do what they could not have done alone. According to Kerka (1997), these partnerships can be viewed as a strategy for accomplishing systematic change in an organization and the key to successful collaboration lies the personal commitment to work within a relationship that includes patience, trust and the awareness that the goals will take time to accomplish. In a similar vein, Baldwin and Austin (1995) report that collaboration happens when "members share a common mission, have clear goals, define operating guidelines, provide mutual support and work in an atmosphere of trust, respect and affection" (p. 55).

Concise portrayals of collaborative partnerships are difficult to define because of their uniqueness. However, there are certain commonalities of successful collaborative partnerships which Sgroi and Saltiel (1998) noted in different learning contexts. The first of these key elements consists of a deep trust and respect between participants as they work towards, their common goals in the belief that they can accomplish more together than they can alone. These qualities help solidify the team process. Katzenbach and Smith (1993) maintain that trust in teams develops as a result of working towards a common goal and is not necessarily present at the outset of the relationship. Real teams do not develop until they have surmounted the obstacles that stand in the way of performance. By overcoming these barriers together, "people on teams build trust and confidence in each other's capabilities" (p. 18).

A second key element of partnerships is the shared vision to which members can aspire. This mutual goal potentiates the new learning and acts as the glue cementing the partnership. It is often the strength of the shared goal that determines the success of a partnership: members supporting each other are not just invested in the outcome of the performance, which is typical for teams. Working together with a shared vision empowers the partners to achieve more than they set out to do as individuals.

Another distinguishing feature of collaborative partnerships is the different, but complementary personality traits and qualities, temperament and style, as well as skills and knowledge. This kind of relationship is like an elastic band that stretches and returns to its original goal, or charts the course for a better one (Sgroi & Saltiel, 1998). Sometimes partners bring their differences to the work and integrate these differences into a unique operating team, making the relationship worthwhile to all participants.

THE IMPORTANCE OF SITUATED LEARNING OR COGNITION

One promising approach to a deeper appreciation of adult literacy and learning lies in the situated cognition theory based on the role of the adult learners' real-life experience. Kirschner and Whitson (1997) suggest that knowledge and skills are learned in contexts that reflect how knowledge is obtained and applied in everyday situations. In situated cognition theory, learning is viewed as a sociocultural phenomenon rather than the action of an individual acquiring general information from a decontextualized body of knowledge. As Merriam and Brockett (1997) point out, what we know and the meanings we attach to what we know are socially constructed. Therefore, learning and knowing are intertwined with real-life situations.

By embedding the literacy content in the ongoing experiences of the learners and in the context of real-world challenges, knowledge is acquired and learning transfers from the classroom to the realm of practice. According to Lave (1997), to situate learning means to place thought and action in a specific place and time. It also means involving other learners, the environment and the activities to create meaning. Learners create their own knowledge out of the raw materials of experience — the relationships with other participants, the activities, the environmental cues and the social organization that the community develops.

The elements of situated cognition and learning

The elements of situated cognition — content, context, community and participation — offer dynamic opportunities for instructors to engage with learners in novel and meaningful ways. Content includes the facts and processes of the literacy task. Situated learning emphasizes higher order thinking processes rather than only the acquisition of facts independent of the real lives of the participants. Content situated in learners' daily experiences becomes the means to engage in reflective thinking. Application rather than retention becomes the mark of a successful instructional encounter. Shor (1996) maintains that, by placing content within the daily transactions of life, an instructor and learner can negotiate the meaning of the content and frame it in terms of the relevant issues and concerns, providing opportunities for learners to cooperate in investigating problem situations and making the content applicable to the ways that learners approach their environments.

A second element in situated learning is *context,* referring to the situations, values, beliefs and environmental cues through which the learner gains and masters the content. As Courtney, Speck, and Holtorf (1996) state, context also involves power relationships, politics, competing priorities and the learners' interaction with the norms of a community, organization or family. Context is not just bringing life events to the classroom, but re-experiencing events from multiple perspectives. It can be described as drawing out and using experiences as a means of intervening in the learner's social and psychological environment. Context can also be viewed as providing the setting for examining experience, while community provides the shaping of that learning.

Another aspect of situated learning is *community* — the group with which the learner will create and negotiate meaning. Through community, learners interpret, reflect and form meaning. Community provides the setting for the dialogue with others to see various and diverse perspectives on any issue. It joins practice with analysis and reflection, resulting in the creation of shared knowledge in the learning community (Stein, 1998). Community provides the opportunity for the interaction whereas participation provides the learner with the meaning of the experience.

Participation in situated cognition refers to the process of learners, working with instructors, solving problems related to everyday life circumstances. Participation describes the interchange of ideas, attempts at problem solving, and the active engagement of learners with each other and with the materials of the instruction. Lave (1997) points out that, from a situated cognition perspective, learning occurs in a social setting through dialogue with others in the community. It is through this process of inter-action with others that meaningful systems among learners are established.

SOLVING PROBLEMS THROUGH ACTION RESEARCH

There are many opportunities for literacy research. For example, the newly created initiative called Valuing Literacy in Canada, jointly fund-ed by the Social Sciences and Humanities Research Council and the National Literacy Secretariat, is designed to develop a literacy research community in Canada. This initiative examines literacy issues from a broad multidisciplinary perspective, enabling a fuller appreciation of the social, economic and cultural effects on the ability of adults to partici-pate in all facets of Canadian life. One of the objectives of the program is to encourage cooperation between academics and adult literacy prac-titioners to ensure that the research is meaningful.

Another avenue for practitioners is through the action research approach. Simply stated, this is a type of practical research that develops new approaches to solving problems in the classroom or in the working world context. Based on the early work of Dewey and Lewin, action research places the emphasis on reflective thinking. It is an approach to problem posing and solving that moves through four phases:

1. **Planning** — A problem in the realm of literacy practice is identified.

2. **Acting** — A plan is implemented.

3. **Observing** — Practitioners collect data on the plan in action.

4. **Reflecting** — Outcomes are analyzed, evaluated and plans may be revised. (Kuhne & Quigley, 1997)

Another method of action research is in the work of Altrichter, Posch and Somekh (1993). This model also offers many suggestions, examples and exercises as a way into action research.

1. **Finding a starting point** — The focus is on using a research diary to identify issues for a project or an investigation, followed by data collection and analysis.

2. **Action strategies** — These are developed and put into practice in response to a clarification and analysis of the situation.

3. **Analysis and theory generation** — The instructor-researcher shares knowledge and experience that evolves into theory arising from practice through the critical appraisal.

Merriam and Simpson (1995) describe how these approaches to action research are different from other forms of social science research. In action research approaches, the researcher serves as a facilitator for problem solving and, in some cases, acts as a catalyst between the findings and those individuals most likely to benefit. Second, the results are intended for immediate application by those engaged in the research project. Third, the design is formulated while the research is in progress and not predetermined at the outset.

Modelled on successful K–12 practitioner action research methods, this approach offers empowerment to both practitioner and learners as they take ownership of the results. Kuhne and Quigley (1997) point out that action research is a form of inductive research involving systematic procedures combining observation, data collection and analysis into a process. With the emphasis on reflective thinking, there is potential to achieve useful answers to practical problems. According to Kemmis and McTaggart (1990) it is action research only "when it is collaborative activity that is achieved through critically examined actions of individual group members" (p. 5).

Action research is hands-on research that every instructor and program developer can do. Empowering people to take common problems from different practice settings and developing a body of newly constructed knowledge from a grass-roots perspective, it also sheds new insights into the way we talk about common problems. These basic research tools offer the promise of professional development for long-term impact in the field of practice.

As the field of literacy comes of age, the combined themes of developing collaborative partnerships, "situating" the literacy learning, and engaging in action research provide the cornerstones for this new era of responsibility. If there is one simple message depicted throughout this book, it is an appreciation of the remarkable changes that have occurred in expanding the world of the learner beyond a culture of silence. As so aptly foreseen by James Draper, a Canadian pioneer in the field, bringing about such changes "involves a process of reflecting and exploring the realm of new possibilities so that literacy makes a difference to daily life of the individual" (1989, p. 449).

REFERENCES

Altrichter, H., Posch, P., & Somekh, B. (1993). *Teachers investigate their work.* London, UK: Routledge Press.

Baldwin, R., & Austin, A. (1995). Toward a greater understanding of faculty research collaboration. *Review of Higher Education, 19*(11), 45–70.

Courtney, S., Speck, S., & Holtorf, P. (1996). The impact of the motivation, volition and classroom context on adult learning. *Proceedings of the 15th annual midwest research-to-practice conference in adult, continuing and community education.* Lincoln, NB: University of Nebraska.

Draper, J. (1989). International communication and national development: The vital role of literacy. In M. Taylor & J. Draper (Eds.), *Adult literacy perspectives.* Toronto, ON: Culture Concepts Inc.

Katzenbach, J., & Smith, D. (1993). *The wisdom of teams; Creating the high performance organization.* Boston, MA: Harvard Business School Press.

Kemmis, S., & McTaggart, R. (1990). *The action research planner.* Geelong, Victoria: Deakin University Press.

Kerka, S. (1997). *Developing collaborative partnerships.* Columbus, OH: ERIC Clearinghouse on Adult, Career and Vocational Education, Center on Education and Training for Employment, Ohio State University.

Kirschner, D., & Whitson, J. (Eds.). (1997). *Situated cognition: Social, semistic and psychological perspectives.* Mahwak, NJ: Lawrence Erlbaum Associates.

Kuhne, G., & Quigley, A. (1997). Understanding and using action research in practice settings. In A. Quigley & G. Kuhne (Eds.), *Creating practical knowledge through action research: Posing problems, solving problems and improving daily practice.* San Francisco, CA: Jossey-Bass.

Lave, J. (1997). The culture of acquisition and the practice of understanding. In D. Kirschner & J. Whitson (Eds.), *Situated cognition: Social, semistic and psychological perspectives.* Mahwah, NJ: Laurence Erlbaum Associates.

Merriam, S., & Brockett, R. (1997). *The profession and practice of adult education.* San Francisco, CA: Jossey-Bass.

Merriam, S., & Simpson, E. (1995). *A guide to research for educators and trainers of adults*. Malabar, FL: Kreiger Publishing Co.

Saltiel, I. (1998). Adult students as partners in formal study. In I. Saltiel, A. Sgroi, & R. Brockett (Eds.), *The power and potential of collaborative learning partnerships*. San Francisco, CA: Jossey-Bass.

Sgroi, A., & Saltiel, I. (1998). Human connections. In I. Saltiel, A. Sgroi, & R. Brockett (Eds.), *The power and potential of collaborative learning partnerships*. San Francisco, CA: Jossey-Bass.

Shor, I. (1996). *When students have power: Negotiating authority in a critical pedagogy*. Chicago, IL: University of Chicago Press.

Stein, D. (1998). *Situated learning in adult education*. Columbus, OH: ERIC Clearinghouse on Adult, Career and Vocational Education, Center on Education and Training for Employment, Ohio State University.

MEMBER OF THE SCABRINI GROUP

Quebec, Canada
2000